Grey and White Hulls

Ian Bowers · Swee Lean Collin Koh
Editors

Grey and White Hulls

An International Analysis of the Navy-Coastguard Nexus

Editors
Ian Bowers
Royal Danish Defence College
Copenhagen, Denmark

Swee Lean Collin Koh
S. Rajaratnam School of International Studies
Nanyang Technological University
Singapore

ISBN 978-981-13-9244-3   ISBN 978-981-13-9242-9 (eBook)
https://doi.org/10.1007/978-981-13-9242-9

© The Editor(s) (if applicable) and The Author(s), under exclusive license to Springer Nature Singapore Pte Ltd. 2019
This work is subject to copyright. All rights are solely and exclusively licensed by the Publisher, whether the whole or part of the material is concerned, specifically the rights of translation, reprinting, reuse of illustrations, recitation, broadcasting, reproduction on microfilms or in any other physical way, and transmission or information storage and retrieval, electronic adaptation, computer software, or by similar or dissimilar methodology now known or hereafter developed.
The use of general descriptive names, registered names, trademarks, service marks, etc. in this publication does not imply, even in the absence of a specific statement, that such names are exempt from the relevant protective laws and regulations and therefore free for general use.
The publisher, the authors and the editors are safe to assume that the advice and information in this book are believed to be true and accurate at the date of publication. Neither the publisher nor the authors or the editors give a warranty, expressed or implied, with respect to the material contained herein or for any errors or omissions that may have been made. The publisher remains neutral with regard to jurisdictional claims in published maps and institutional affiliations.

Cover image: © PJF Military Collection/Alamy Stock Photo

This Palgrave Macmillan imprint is published by the registered company Springer Nature Singapore Pte Ltd.
The registered company address is: 152 Beach Road, #21-01/04 Gateway East, Singapore 189721, Singapore

Acknowledgements

The idea for this volume was born out of a two-day workshop held in Singapore in November 2016. The workshop, titled *Navies, Coast Guards, The Maritime Community and International Stability*, brought together academics and practitioners from Europe, Asia, and Australia. It revealed a substantial diversity in international approaches to the navy-coast guard nexus and highlighted the need for an in-depth examination of the subject. The editors would first like to thank the Norwegian Embassy in Beijing. Without their financial support, the workshop and this volume would not have been possible. We would also like to thank the participants and invited guests of this workshop for their input and ideas. Professor Geoffrey Till and Jo Inge Bekkevold deserve particular praise for their support and guidance. Equally, we would like to thank the event organisers at the S. Rajaratnam School of International Studies for their efforts in making the workshop possible. Finally, the editors would like to thank the team at Palgrave Macmillan for guiding this project through the publication process.

CONTENTS

1 Introduction 1
  Ian Bowers and Swee Lean Collin Koh

Part I Northeast Asia

2 Integrating the China Coast Guard
  with the PLA Navy 17
  Anguang Zheng

3 The JMSDF and JCG: Toward Cooperation
  and Contribution 37
  Takuya Shimodaira

4 Establishing a Maritime Security Joint-Force
  Partnership Between the Republic of Korea Navy
  and the Korea Coast Guard 55
  Sukjoon Yoon

Part II Southeast Asia

5 Navy-Coast Guard Emerging Nexus:
   The Case of Vietnam 73
   Truong-Minh Vu and The Phuong Nguyen

6 Singapore's Maritime Security Approach 95
   Swee Lean Collin Koh

7 The Navy-Coast Guard Nexus and the Nature
   of Indonesian Maritime Security Governance 109
   Muhamad Arif

Part III Europe

8 Arctic Coast Guards: Managing New Challenges? 135
   Andreas Østhagen

9 Ensuring Security in the Mediterranean Sea:
   The Italian Navy and Coast Guard 159
   Alessandra Giada Dibenedetto

10 Russia's Navy-Coastguard Nexus 181
   Ingvill Moe Elgsaas and Liv Karin Parnemo

Part IV North and South America

11 The United States 203
   Jonathan G. Odom

12 Ready to Secure: A Sea Control Perspective
   on Canadian Fisheries Enforcement 223
   Timothy Choi

13	The Navy-Coast Guard Nexus in Argentina: Lost in Democratization? Nicole Jenne and María Lourdes Puente Olivera	245
14	Conclusion Swee Lean Collin Koh and Ian Bowers	271

Index 281

Notes on Contributors

Muhamad Arif is a researcher at The Habibie Center's ASEAN Studies Program. He is also a lecturer at the Universitas Indonesia, co-teaching courses on the Revolution in Military Affairs, the Evolution of International Security Thoughts, and Indonesian Defence Strategy. Arif was a program officer for Defence and Security Studies at PACIVIS-Center for Global Civil Society Studies and graduate student research assistant at the RSIS' Malaysia Programme.

Ian Bowers is an associate professor at the Institute for Strategy, Royal Danish Defence College. His research focuses on sea power, coercion, Asian security and military technology. He is the author of *The Modernization of the Republic of Korea Navy: Seapower, Strategy and Politics* (Palgrave, 2019). He has published in international peer-reviewed journals including the *Naval War College Review*, *The Korean Journal of Defense Analysis*, and *The Journal of Strategic Studies*. He holds a Ph.D. in War Studies from King's College London.

Timothy Choi is a doctoral candidate at the University of Calgary's Centre for Military, Security and Strategic Studies, as well as a research fellow with the Centre for the Study of Security and Development at Dalhousie University. Funded by the Social Sciences and Humanities Research Council of Canada, his doctoral dissertation examines the nature and character of sea power as part of the modern maritime strategies of countries with small navies during peacetime; his case studies involve the maritime services of Denmark, Norway, and Sweden. In 2017–2018, he was the Smith Richardson predoctoral fellow in maritime, naval, and strategic studies at Yale University's International Security Studies unit.

Alessandra Giada Dibenedetto is currently an analyst at the Defence and Security desk of the Center of International Studies (Ce.S.I.) in Rome. Previously, she worked with the Research Division of the NATO Defense College where she was involved in many projects such as contributing to research papers and reports, organizing conferences and briefing the public. Ms. Dibenedetto graduated from King's College, London, where she completed a Master's program in Intelligence and International Security. Her dissertation analyzed the limitations of the EUNAVFOR Operation Sophia in the Southern-Central Mediterranean Sea. She holds a Bachelor's Degree in Political Science and a Master's Degree in International Relations both obtained from LUISS Guido Carli University, Rome. Her areas of interest, have been translated into a number of publications, include military affairs, maritime and border security, EU-NATO cooperation and European security.

Ingvill Moe Elgsaas is a senior fellow at the Norwegian Institute for Defence Studies (IFS) in Oslo. She holds a Ph.D. in political science from the Norwegian University of Science and Technology, an M.Phil. in Russian and East European Studies from the University of Oxford, and a B.A. in Russian studies from the University of Bergen. Her research combines her background in Russian studies with a keen interest in the Arctic/High North and security studies. Dr. Elgsaas previously worked for the Norwegian Defence Research Establishment and has been with the IFS since 2014. Her current research focuses on emergency preparedness in the Russian Arctic with particular attention paid to Arctic counterterrorism.

Nicole Jenne is an assistant professor at the Pontificia Universidad Católica de Chile, Institute of Political Science, and an associated researcher at the Center of International Studies (CEI). She holds a Ph.D. in International Relations from the European University Institute (EUI), Florence. Nicole's research and teaching interests are in the areas of International Relations and international security, especially regional security.

Swee Lean Collin Koh is a research fellow at the Institute of Defence and Strategic Studies, a constituent unit of the S. Rajaratnam School of International Studies (RSIS). He holds a Ph.D. from Nanyang Technological University. His research focuses on maritime security and naval affairs in the Indo-Pacific, focusing on Southeast Asia in particular.

The Phuong Nguyen is a Masters candidate at the Institute of East Asia Studies, University Duisburg-Essen, Germany where he focuses on Southeast Asian defense and regional security and strategy. He has published several commentaries on *The Asia Maritime Transparency Initiative* and *The Diplomat*.

Jonathan G. Odom is judge advocate (i.e., licensed attorney) in the U.S. Navy. Currently, he serves as a Military Professor of International Law at the George C. Marshall European Center for Security Studies (Germany), where his principal areas of research and teaching are public international law, international territorial-maritime disputes, and maritime security.

Andreas Østhagen is a research fellow at the Fridtjof Nansen Institute in Oslo, Norway (2017–). He is also a Ph.D. candidate at the University of British Columbia (UBC) in Vancouver (2015–), and a senior fellow and leadership Group member at The Arctic Institute in Washington, DC (2011–). Previously, Andreas worked for the Norwegian Institute for Defence Studies (IFS) in Oslo (2014–2017), and at the North Norway European Office in Brussels (2010–2014).

Liv Karin Parnemo has over 12 years of experience working as an advisor and senior advisor on security policy with the Norwegian Armed Forces and has also worked as a researcher at the Norwegian Institute for Defense Studies (IFS) in Oslo. Her area of expertise encompasses Russian foreign and security policy. She is currently a senior advisor at the Department of Long-term Planning and Defence Policy at the Norwegian Ministry of Defense.

María Lourdes Puente Olivera is the director of the School of Politics and Government, Pontifical Catholic University, Argentina. She holds a Master's degree in International Affairs from the Facultad de Ciencias Sociales (FLACSO) and is currently pursuing her Ph.D. in International Affairs at the University of Salvador. From 1989 until 2010, she was a senior analyst in the Department of International Affairs of the Argentine Navy. From 2011 to 2012, she was the National Director of Military Strategic Intelligence in Argentina's Ministry of Defense. From 2014 to 2018, she worked as an advisor on strategic affairs for a deputy of the Frente Renovador party. Since 1991, Lourdes has also taught several courses in political science at the Catholic University of Argentina and Austral University.

Takuya Shimodaira (Captain, JMSDF) is a senior research fellow of Security Studies Department and Policy Simulation Office at the National Institute for Defense Studies (NIDS). He joined NIDS in 2016. He was visiting military professor in Joint Military Operations Department, US Naval War College from 2014 to 2016. He is director of the Crisis & Risk Management Society of Japan, adjunct lecturer at Kokushikan University and lecturer (joint-appointment) at National Graduate Institute for Policy Studies (GRIPS).

Truong-Minh Vu is director of the Center for International Studies (SCIS) and vice dean of the Faculty of International Relations at the University of Social Sciences and Humanities in Ho Chi Minh City- Vietnam National University. His research interests encompass international and strategic relations of Southeast Asia. His scholarly articles and analyses have been published on *The National Interest*, *The Asan Forum*, *Revista Brasileira de Política Internacional*, Global Asia, East Asia Policy, ASIEN. *The German Journal on Contemporary Asia*, *The Asia Maritime Transparency Initiative* and *RSIS Commentaries*.

Sukjoon Yoon is currently a research fellow of the Korea Institute for Military Affairs (KIMA). Before joining KIMA, he served in the Republic of Korea Navy, reaching the rank of Captain. He holds a Ph.D. from Bristol University. He is a nonresident senior research fellow of the Korea Institute for Maritime Strategy (KIMS) as well as a member of the executive research committee of the SLOC Study Group-Korea, member of the CSCAP-Korea and a member of the advisory committee of the Korea National Diplomatic Academy (KNDA).

Anguang Zheng is an associate professor at the School of International Studies, Nanjing University and adjunct professor at Johns Hopkins- Nanjing Center. He received a doctoral degree in 2004 from Nanjing University. His academic interest and studying fields include:

international relations theory, American Diplomacy, global governance of public affairs. He has published two monographs and many articles in such journals as *American Studies, Contemporary International Relations*, and *International Political Studies*. He studied at the University of Illinois at Champaign-Urbana as Freeman Fellow between 2012 and 2013 and at the Korea Foundation for Advanced Studies of Korea from 2007 to 2008. He also worked with David Lampton at SAIS, Johns Hopkins University in 2015.

Abbreviations

ACGF	Arctic Coast Guard Forum
AIS	Automatic Identification System
AOPV	Arctic Offshore Patrol Vessel
AOR	Area of Responsibility
ARA	Armada Argentine [Argentina Navy]
ASB	Anti-Smuggling Bureau (China)
BAKAMLA	Badan Keamanan Laut Republik Indonesia—[Indonesian Maritime Security Agency]
BAKORKAMLA	Badan Koordinasi Keamanan Laut [Maritime Security Coordinating Agency]
C2	Command and Control
C3	Command, Control and Communications
C4ISR	Command, Control, Communications, Computers, Intelligence, Surveillance and Reconnaissance
CARP	Administration Commissions of the Río de la Plata
CC2C	Changi Command and Control Centre (Singapore)
CCG	Canadian Coast Guard
CCG	China Coast Guard
CGS	Canadian Government Ship
CIWS	Close-in Weapons System
CMAG	Comprehensive Maritime Awareness Group (Singapore)
CMPB	China Maritime Police Bureau
CMS	China Maritime Surveillance
CNO	Chief of Naval Operations
CONICET	The National Council for Scientific and Technical Research (Argentina)

COSCOM	Coastal Command (Singapore)
CPC	Communist Party of China
CSDP	Common Security and Defense Policy
CUES	Code for Unplanned Encounters at Sea
DFO	Department of Fisheries and Oceans (Canada)
DHS	Department of Homeland Security
DI/TII	Darul Islam/Tentara Islam Indonesia [Islamic Armed Forces of Indonesia]
DMD	Department of Militia and Defence (Canada)
DMF	Department of Marine and Fisheries (Canada)
DoD	Department of Defense (United States)
EDA	Excess Defense Articles
EEZ	Exclusive Economic Zone
EFZ	Exclusive Fisheries Zone
ERF	Emergency Response Forces (Singapore)
EUNAVFOR	European Union Naval Force
FAC	Fast Attack Craft
FBS	Federal Border Service (Russia)
FLEC	Fisheries Law Enforcement Command (China)
FPS	Fisheries Protection Service (Canada)
FPZ	Fisheries Protection Zone
FSB	Federal Security Service (Russia)
GAC	General Administration of Customs (China)
GDP	Gross Domestic Product
GMF	Global Maritime Fulcrum
HA/DR	Humanitarian Assistance/Disaster Relief
HACGAM	Heads of Asian Coast Guard Agencies Meeting
ICA	Immigration and Checkpoints Authority (Singapore)
ICG	Iceland Coast Guard
IFC	Information Fusion Centre (Singapore)
IMO	International Maritime Organization
IMSO	International Mobile Satellite Organization
IUU	Illegal, Unreported and Unregulated Fishing
JCG	Japanese Coast Guard
JDA	Japanese Defense Agency
JGSDF	Japanese Ground Self-Defense Force
JIATF	Joint Interagency Task Force
JIIM	Joint Interagency Intergovernmental and Multinational
JMOD	Japanese Ministry of Defense
JMSDF	Japanese Maritime Self-Defense Force
JO	Joint Operation
JRCC	Joint Rescue Coordination Centre
JSDF	Japanese Self-Defense Force

JTF	Joint Task Force
KCG	Korea Coast Guard
KMP	Korean Maritime Police
LEDET	Law Enforcement Detachment
LRAD	Long Range Acoustic Device
LRIT	Long Range Identification and Tracking
MENA	Middle East and North Africa
MERCOSUR	Common Market of the South
MGP	Maritime Great Power
MHA	Ministry of Home Affairs (Singapore)
MINDEF	Ministry of Defence (Singapore)
MIO	Maritime Interdiction Operations
MLE	Maritime Law Enforcement
MLEA	Maritime Law Enforcement Agency
MND	Ministry of National Defense (Vietnam)
MOA	Memoranda of Agreement
MOFA	Ministry of Ocean and Fishery Affairs (ROK)
MOTR	Maritime Operational Threat Response
MPA	Maritime and Port Authority of Singapore
MSA	Maritime Safety Administration (China)
MSA	Maritime Security Agency (Japan)
MSTF	Maritime Security Task Force (Singapore)
NAFO	Northwest Atlantic Fisheries Organisation
NATO	North Atlantic Treaty Organization
NLL	Northern Limit Line
NMCOP	National Maritime Common Operating Picture (Singapore)
NMOG	National Maritime Operations Group (Singapore)
NMSG	National Maritime Sense-making Group (Singapore)
NMSS	National Maritime Security Strategy
NOA	National Oceanic Administration (China)
NORDEFCO	Nordic Defence Cooperation
NPAFC	North Pacific Anadromous Fish Commission
NPCGF	North Pacific Coast Guard Forum
NSPD	National Security Presidential Directive
NWMP	North-West Mounted Police
OMSI	Oceanic Maritime Security Initiative
ONF	One National Fleet
OPCON	Operational Control
PAFMM	People's Armed Forces Maritime Militia
PAP	People's Armed Police (China)
PCG	Police Coast Guard (Singapore)
PLAN	People's Liberation Army Navy
PLH	Patrol Ship—Large Helicopter

PNA	Perfectura Naval Argentina [Naval Prefecture]
PPA	Offshore Multipurpose Patrol Ships
RCN	Royal Canadian Navy
RHCC	Regional Humanitarian Assistance and Disaster Relief Coordination Centre (Singapore)
RN	Royal Navy
ROCRAM	Operative Network of regional Cooperation among Maritime Authorities of the Americas
ROKN	Republic of Korea Navy
RPG	Rocket Propelled Grenade
RSAF	Republic of Singapore Air Force
RSN	Republic of Singapore Navy
SAF	Singapore Armed Forces
SAR	Search and Rescue
SatCen	European Satellite Centre
SC	Singapore Customs
SCDF	Singapore Civil Defence Force
SCGI	Sea and Coast Guard Indonesia
SICAP	Integrated Information System (Argentina)
SLOC	Sea Lines of Communication
SMCC	Singapore Maritime Crisis Centre
SOA	State Oceanic Administration (China)
SOLAS	Safety of Life at Sea
SOMS	Straits of Malacca and Singapore
TAC	Total Allowable Catch
TACON	Tactical Control
TNI	Tentara Nasional Indonesia [Indonesian Military]
TNI-AL	Tentara Nasional Indonesia-Angkatan Laut [Indonesian Navy]
UNC	United Nations Command
UNCLOS	United Nations Convention on the Law of the Sea
UNSC	United Nations Security Council
USCG	United States Coast Guard
USN	United States Navy
VCG	Vietnam Coastguard
VPA	Vietnam People's Army
VPN	Vietnam People's Navy
WGCGF	Western Pacific Coast Guard Forum
WoG	Whole-of-Government
WPNS	Western Pacific Naval Symposium

List of Figures

Fig. 6.1   Singapore's Maritime Security Architecture
           (*Source* By author based on available official information)   100

Fig. 12.1 A two-dimensional spectrum for sea control, with the ideal
           forms "Command of the Seas" and "Null Command"
           on opposite corners. Any sea control phenomenon
           can have varying degrees of contestation and exercise,
           falling somewhere within this spectrum. The numbers
           are ordinal reference points for resource requirements.
           The spectrum should only be used with one of the four
           ways of making use of the seas for a given series
           of phenomena to avoid qualitatively different resources
           requirements   226

List of Figures

LIST OF TABLES

Table 1.1	Deriving the determinants of the navy-coastguard nexus	8
Table 2.1	Former and current Chinese maritime law enforcement structure	22
Table 2.2	The provincial flotillas of the CCG	27
Table 2.3	The build-up of Chinese MLE forces	28
Table 3.1	JCG patrol vessels and patrol craft	42
Table 3.2	Total coast guard tonnage increases for Japan and China, 2010–2016	43
Table 3.3	Future JMSDF force structure outlined in the National Defense Program Guidelines for FY2019 and beyond	44
Table 8.1	Characteristics of Denmark, Iceland, and Norway	139
Table 8.2	The different types of maritime tasks/challenges becoming more prevalent in the Arctic areas in question	142
Table 8.3	The various coast guards and their roles, mandates, and organisational affiliation	147

CHAPTER 1

Introduction

Ian Bowers and Swee Lean Collin Koh

There are multiple sources of instability on the world's oceans. On a state level, geostrategic ambition and competition at sea have become almost inseparable from disputes over maritime territory and sovereignty creating littoral environments rife with geopolitical tension. At the same time, lawlessness, including illegal, unreported and unregulated (IUU) fishing, people smuggling and other transnational, transboundary maritime security threats, is growing in prominence and poses a significant challenge to good order at sea. The ramifications of this new reality at sea directly impinge upon security and stability on land and are driving significant changes in the operationalisation of maritime security and defence.

This evolving geostrategic environment at sea challenges traditionally held concepts of naval operations, mission delineation and the use and utility of civilian or paramilitary maritime law enforcement agencies (MLEA). For naval forces, the return of great power competition in both

I. Bowers (✉)
Royal Danish Defence College, Copenhagen, Denmark
e-mail: iabo@fak.dk

S. L. C. Koh
S. Rajaratnam School of International Studies,
Nanyang Technological University, Singapore
e-mail: iscollinkoh@ntu.edu.sg

© The Author(s) 2019
I. Bowers and S. L. C. Koh (eds.), *Grey and White Hulls*,
https://doi.org/10.1007/978-981-13-9242-9_1

Asia and Europe has heralded a renewed emphasis on deterrence and warfighting. However, maritime security and good order at sea, concepts that gained substantial traction during the post-Cold War years, have simultaneously risen in prominence and are now central tenants of the national security thinking in maritime states across the world.[1]

National security and naval strategy are thus increasingly conceived across a continuum where warfighting and broader notions of maritime security are closely connected in both operations and strategic goals. Consequently, maritime law enforcement missions and the military and civilian agencies that carry them out have growing strategic relevance as the maintenance of maritime sovereignty, economic rights and the enforcement of good order at sea become hot-button strategic issues in capitals across the world.[2] This is evident in the maritime doctrines of states and international organisations which seek to provide a "comprehensive or holistic account of the challenges to be faced at sea".[3]

Traditionally, navies and MLEA have maintained a degree of operational distance. National defence and security are the primary determinants of any navy's operations. Therefore, first and foremost navies must equip and prepare for wartime contingencies.[4] However, most navies maintain a secondary emphasis on maritime security operations or what Booth describes as a policing function role.[5]

---

[1] However, of course it is necessary to take into account the region-specific contexts and nuances. In East Asia, for instance, government authorities have long been grappling with such transboundary and transnational challenges at sea such as IUU fishing, human trafficking, arms and drugs smuggling, as well as illicit trade. As such, enforcement actions carried out against such lawlessness have long become a part of a traditional set of missions performed by maritime agencies in this region.

[2] The increasing emphasis by major so-called Western powers on the free and open use of the seas particularly in East and South Asia, but also in Europe and the Arctic is a demonstration of the importance of this issue. See Alex N. Wong, Briefing on the Indo-Pacific Strategy, US Department of State, April 2, 2018, https://www.state.gov/r/pa/prs/ps/2018/04/280134.htm; Japan Ministry of Foreign Affairs, Priority Policy for Development Cooperation FY 2017, April 2017, 9–10, https://www.mofa.go.jp/files/000259285.pdf.

[3] Christian Bueger and Timothy Edmunds, "Beyond Seablindness: A New Agenda for Maritime Security Studies," *International Affairs* 93, no. 6 (2017): 1297–1298.

[4] Lyle J. Morris, "Crossing Interagency Lines: Enhancing Navy-Coast Guard Cooperation in Gray Zone Conflicts of East Asia," *Asia-Pacific Journal of Ocean Law and Policy* 3 (2018): 278–279.

[5] Ian Speller, *Understanding Naval Warfare* (Oxon: Routledge, 2014), 154.

In contrast, MLEA, which may include but are not limited to coastguards, maritime police and maritime militia, carry out law enforcement and maritime security duties as their primary function.[6] MLEA have traditionally been tasked with a wide variety of missions including protecting maritime sovereign rights, enforcing national maritime laws as well as providing other public goods such as search and rescue (SAR) and environmental protection.[7] This does not mean that national defence does not fall under their operational orbit, but rather it is a lower priority when compared with their military counterparts.

The contemporary maritime environment is blurring the lines between the operations of navies and MLEA as they now frequently perform similar roles despite their different operational approaches and priorities. MLEA are now key instruments in a state's maritime policies and by extension security strategies. States which previously have not possessed such agencies or have hitherto accorded them low priority are now developing or bolstering them to manage the multitudes of maritime challenges they face. The MLEA of some states have found themselves on the frontline of interstate tensions, not just protecting maritime sovereignty and economic rights, but also contesting rival claims. This is resulting in the proliferation of larger and more heavily armed MLEA vessels particularly, but not exclusively, in the contested waters of East Asia. For those states that solely possess a navy which simultaneously performs traditional warfighting and maritime law enforcement missions, there has been an ongoing reprioritisation of roles directed towards the capacity to address low-intensity threats at sea while also maintaining warfighting capabilities. Vitally, states with more than one actor at sea are reconceptualising the way their maritime agencies work together. For instance, states are bringing their navies and MLEA closer together, promoting synergy between them and when feasible developing joint operational concepts and encouraging joint operations.

It is important to acknowledge the geographic scope of this shift in maritime operations. The near global promulgation of the United Nations Convention on the Law of the Sea (UNCLOS) has codified international laws regarding the delineation of maritime territory and

---

[6] Prabhakaran Paleri, *Coast Guards of the World and Emerging Maritime Threats*, Ocean Policy Studies, Special ed. (Tokyo: Ocean Policy Research Foundation and The Nippon Foundation, 2009), 51.
[7] Ian Speller, *Understanding Naval Warfare*, 154–155.

economic rights. Although this has provided a degree of certainty when boundaries are agreed, the gaps within the provisions enshrined in the convention, especially with respect to the interpretations of the exclusive economic zone (EEZ) regime, have, in the words of Geoffrey Till, "triggered as many disputes as it has resolved".[8] Essentially, UNCLOS has extended and magnified maritime sovereignty and economic disputes, turning them into issues of national pride and strategic importance.[9] Equally, the unregulated nature of the ocean as a global commons allows for the exploitation of the sea both as a medium of transport and as an easy, if over-exploited, resource trove. Crucially, lawlessness and human deprivation which originates from weak or unstable forms of governance on land are often transferred across borders via the sea.[10]

For example, in the East Asian geostrategic maritime environment, multiple and diverse military and civilian actors now operate at sea, contesting maritime territory, exploiting weaknesses and forwarding national strategic agendas in a coordinated manner that falls considerably short of traditionally understood war at sea. In maritime flashpoints such as the East and South China Seas, MLEA vessels or "white hulls" are interacting with naval "grey hulls" with significant implications for the maintenance of maritime crisis stability.[11] In the Mediterranean, a humanitarian crisis with substantial political and strategic ramifications for Europe continues to unfold. Military and civilian maritime agencies have deployed to meet the challenge of refugees crossing the Mediterranean to reach the shores of Europe while also managing the consequences of a renewed Russian presence and continued instability in the Middle East.[12]

---

[8] Geoffrey Till, *Seapower: A Guide for the Twenty-First Century*, 2nd ed. (Oxon: Routledge, 2009), 311.

[9] Bernard Cole, *Asian Maritime Strategies: Navigating Troubled Waters* (Annapolis: Naval Institute Press, 2013), 33.

[10] Examples of this include the mass movement of refugees across the Mediterranean since 2015 or the use of the sea as a means of transport for terrorist and other criminal activities. For an overview of these issues, see United Nations Office on Drugs and Crime, *Combatting Transnational Organised Crime Committed at Sea, Issue Paper* (New York: United Nations, 2013).

[11] See Lyle Morris, "Blunt Defenders of Sovereignty: The Rise of Coast Guards in East and Southeast Asia," *Naval War College Review* 70, no. 2 (2017): 75–112.

[12] See United Nations High Commissioner for Refugees, *The Sea Route to Europe: The Mediterranean Passage in the Age of Refugees* (New York: UNHCR, 2015).

Meanwhile, in the Arctic, warming waters are altering the strategic picture, potentially creating a new environment for competition at sea.[13] In all of these theatres, the maritime security structures of multiple nation-states are adjusting to this new set of strategic challenges.

UNDERSTANDING THE NAVY-COASTGUARD NEXUS

Using case studies, this volume seeks to explore these new maritime strategic dynamics. It examines how states have created or are transforming their maritime security architectures to meet the realities of today's security challenges in the maritime domain. We call this organisational and strategic approach the navy-coastguard nexus. This term does not imply a dual agency approach to maritime security, as is seen for example in the United States; rather, it is an expression which encompasses how a nation-state's strategic and organisational structures respond to a blurred maritime landscape. In doing so, the volume seeks to answer the following questions.

- What are the internal and external drivers of the navy-coastguard nexus?
- What are the operational, cultural and organisational barriers to altering the navy-coastguard nexus?
- What implications does a shifting navy-coastguard nexus have for stability at sea?

NAVY-COASTGUARD NEXUS ORGANISATIONAL TYPOLOGIES

There is a wide array of national organisational structures designed to manage the navy-coastguard nexus. There is no one optimal approach as each organisational structure and consequent delineation and prioritisation of missions and areas of operation is determined by a wide array of internal and external factors. However, we have identified three broad organisational models which can help define how states approach the navy-coastguard nexus:

---

[13] See Rolf Tamnes and Kristine Offerdal, "Introduction," in *Geopolitics and Security in the Arctic: Regional Dynamics in a Global World*, ed. Rolf Tamnes and Kristine Offerdal (Oxon: Routledge, 2014), 1–11.

- The **sole agency** structure has one primary actor which meets most if not all a state's maritime security requirements. That actor could be either a navy which also has total responsibility for maritime law enforcement and the provision of public goods or a MLEA that has a limited or no military function. While this sole agency approach is more commonly associated with smaller, resource-limited states such as Ireland, Iceland or New Zealand, larger states including the United Kingdom have also adopted this organisational structure. This is a commonly observed structure, with many of the world's navies taking responsibility for the entire spectrum of peace- and/or wartime operations. In this structure, the sole maritime agency will work alongside other relevant agencies such as police, customs and immigration and SAR services but may also possess limited or full constabulary powers.
- The **dual agency structure** is the most commonly understood, but by no means the most commonly seen, maritime security architecture. In this case, there are a single defined civilian or paramilitary MLEA which operate separately from the navy. The United States, Japan, South Korea, Sweden and others have adopted this approach. Traditionally, this has resulted in a clear delineation of labour between both forces, with each having its own procedures, equipment, operational priorities and areas of operation.[14] Coordination between both agencies may occur, dependent on bureaucratic, strategic and geographic approaches and priorities. Further, in some cases, a state will have a navy and a coastguard, but both are operated under one single parent agency. This is true in the case of Norway, where naval officers are "dual-hatted" sometimes serving on naval vessels and other times on coastguard ships.
- The **multiple agency structure** has several MLEA operating alongside a military naval force. In this case, often there can be overlapping responsibilities and jurisdictions between the diverse MLEA. China for instance operates a coastguard and a maritime safety administration alongside a navy. Similarly, Italy has a number of civil

---

[14] It is important to note that this clear delineation may for some countries exist more in theory than in practice, especially when the navy, for example, has to step in to intervene on behalf of its MLEA counterpart simply because the latter lacks the requisite capability to perform certain tasks.

and paramilitary forces operating at various distances and locations around the Italian coast. This multiple agency structure may also take the form of a navy and a single civilian or paramilitary organisation having certain jurisdiction or control over diverse, multiple MLEA. This is the case for Indonesia which has a navy and a maritime security agency that has several MLEA under its umbrella with varying degrees of control over each.

DETERMINANTS OF STRUCTURE AND TRANSFORMATION

How a state understands and operationalises the navy-coastguard nexus is driven by several factors. Geoffrey Till argues that such a nexus usually develops in one of two distinct ways. The first is an organic process, where a state's needs evolve over time and organisational shifts occur gradually in response to internal and external circumstances.[15] The second is a "conscious decision" to develop a specific maritime security architecture.[16]

While true, this division of determinant processes does not provide an adequate framework for the central questions this volume poses. Instead, this volume draws upon the literature on military transformation and innovation. This literature has limitations including, a US-centric bias, an overt emphasis on technological drivers and a lack of analysis on innovation at times between war and peace.[17] However, it does lend a guiding hand in determining both why and how security organisations innovate.

Table 1.1 draws upon a framework developed by Theo Farrell to explain British military innovation. Adjusted and adopted for the navy-coastguard nexus, this framework identifies three major factors to determine why a nation-state both creates and adjusts its maritime security architecture, and four significant factors that shape, both positively and negatively, how this process occurs.

The state's perception of its external maritime security environment constitutes the primary driver of the navy-coastguard nexus. This security environment determines how states prioritise and respond to threats

[15] Till (2009), 315.
[16] Ibid.
[17] Per M. Norheim-Martinsen, "New Sources of Military Change—Armed Forces as Normal Organisations," *Defence Studies* 16, no. 3 (2016), 312–326, 319–320.

Table 1.1 Deriving the determinants of the navy-coastguard nexus

Determinants of military innovation		Determinants of the navy-coastguard nexus	
Drivers	External threat Emulation	Drivers	National maritime interests Maritime operations Emulation
Shaping factors	Resources Domestic politics Military culture	Shaping factors	Resources Maritime geography Strategic culture Bureaucratic/domestic politics

Source Adapted from Theo Farrell, "The Dynamics of British Military Transformation," *International Affairs* 84, no. 4 (2008): 777–807, 708–783

to their national maritime interests. The use of the term "national maritime interests" is deliberately chosen over the often used "maritime security". Maritime security is an imprecise term, with its meaning often dependent on the needs of the user.[18] National maritime interests better encapsulate the linkage between security at sea and national security and are preferred in this context due to the increasing breadth of security interests and threats at sea.[19] As described above, interests may transcend direct military threats and could include civil and non-state actors. Further, such interests may not emanate from sovereign or jurisdictional maritime zones but from further afield.

The United States provides a good example of the potential diversity of maritime interests and their impact on the navy-coastguard nexus. The US Navy, being the primary power projection instrument of the United States is largely engaged in military blue-water operations. Thus, traditionally, there has been a clear separation between it and the US Coast Guard which is primarily designated with protecting the continental US coastlines from both national security and law enforcement threats. However, as Jonathan G. Odum highlights in his chapter in this volume, direct challenges to national sovereignty and security or shifts in international legal structures can alter this delineation. This has resulted in reprioritised naval and coastguard operations and the

[18] See Christian Bueger, "What Is Maritime Security?" *Marine Policy* 53 (2015), 159–164.

[19] Paleri, *Coast Guards of the World and Emerging Maritime Threats*, 189.

creation of new integrated structures designed to cope with these new challenges.

Closely connected with the security environment are the changing nature of maritime operations and the requirement to respond to such changes. As has been described, operations at sea have become increasingly blurred between naval and civilian actors. There is evidence that states are using civilian or paramilitary actors to enforce or contest sovereignty and advance their strategic interests. One reason is that assigning a warship equipped for high-intensity warfighting to fisheries/EEZ patrol not only wastes capabilities but may create a militaristic impression when none is needed and give observers a misleading impression of force disproportionate to what is required.[20] Moreover, responding to such actions is made more difficult by the ambiguous nature of the threat presented. China, Vietnam and Iran have all developed models of the navy-coastguard nexus which allows them to use paramilitary actors at sea in a more offensive or assertive role.

Emulation is also a determining factor in deciding the nature of the navy-coastguard nexus. The US Navy and Coast Guard model has been replicated by several countries, particularly those with close relationships with the United States. South Korea and Japan both have maritime security architectures which closely mirror that of the United States in terms of structure, if not priorities. It can be argued that Vietnam, having witnessed the success of the Chinese approach where naval, MLEA and maritime militia operate in concert, is emulating this structure to counter Beijing's actions in the South China Sea. Hanoi has described its coastguard as the "core force in protecting national security, and maritime order and safety",[21] and is allocating more resources to bolster its strength.

Of course, while the three above factors act as drivers for establishing or altering a navy-coastguard nexus, a number of other elements also have crucial roles to play. Resources, including available finances and personnel, have a substantial role in determining the size and shape of a state's maritime security architecture. In a maritime environment with multiple potential missions, resource limitations may restrict

[20] Harold J. Kearsley, *Maritime Power and the Twenty-First Century* (Aldershot, UK: Dartmouth, 1992), 46.

[21] "Vietnam Coast Guard—Core Force in National Security Protection," *The Voice of Vietnam*, August 28, 2018.

the number and type of roles both navies and MLEA can carry out. Often, resource constraints constitute a core factor in determining the type of organisational structure a state will pursue to meet its maritime interests, and this is indicated in the large number of maritime security structures which utilise a single agency approach as this tends to be more cost-effective. However, such a choice under conditions of limited platform availability reduces the type of missions a navy or MLEA can perform.

Maritime geography also plays a substantial role in determining the navy-coastguard nexus. The size and security of a state's EEZ, the state's proximity to threatening maritime powers, sea lanes of communication and strategic chokepoints and the ratio of relative strategic importance between the land and the sea all influence the size and shape of a state's maritime security architecture.

Strategic culture often shapes how a maritime security architecture transforms itself and can act as a brake on innovation within the navy-coastguard nexus. Strategic culture consists of the "identity, norms and values" that have developed within both military and civilian security organisations.[22] These are often difficult to change and can require substantial external shocks to surmount. In the case of the navy-coastguard nexus, often navies and MLEA have very different cultural and operational beliefs which can be difficult to overcome. Additionally, in an environment where closer cooperation can often result in overlapping jurisdictions, internal prejudices and jealousies may reduce the effectiveness of the navy-coastguard nexus.

Finally, and relatedly, domestic politics—which are often overshadowed by external factors such as threat perceptions and international or regional geopolitical dynamics—also play a substantial role in determining the nature and transformation of the navy-coastguard nexus. Christian Bueger highlights that the provision of maritime security is a major inter-agency challenge even on a national level.[23] Like strategic culture, domestic political preferences and constituencies may act to hinder transformation if it is perceived as damaging to special interests. Inter-agency divergences over how national maritime interests are defined could result in varying forms of the navy-coastguard nexus.

[22] Theo Farrell, "The Dynamics of British Military Transformation," *International Affairs* 84, no. 4 (2008), 783.
[23] Bueger, 163.

However, it should be noted that strong civilian leadership can result in significant institutional change, particularly if they have the support of the institutions themselves.

STRUCTURE OF THE VOLUME

Taking a cross-regional approach in examining the navy-coastguard nexus, this volume includes large, medium and small states in Asia, Europe and the Americas. This broad range of case studies, including China, the United States and Russia, highlights the diversity in approach to the navy-coastguard nexus and reveals that there is no one optimal, "one size fits all" organisational structure. Instead, there is a wide array of drivers that influence a nation-state's maritime security architecture and its organisational approach to managing security at sea, or broadly speaking, securing its national maritime interests.

Part I examines the navy-coastguard nexus in Northeast Asia. This is a region that sees substantial and sustained tensions in the maritime domain. There are a number of potent naval and maritime law enforcement actors, working together and competing with one another. In Chapter 2 Zheng Anguang analyses how China has consolidated its MLEA and how they are used alongside the People's Liberation Army Navy (PLAN) to promote China's maritime interests across East Asia and beyond. The central part of this chapter examines the China Coast Guard (CCG), its development out of a diverse pool of MLEA and the consequences of its recent placement under, what is effectively, military administration.

In Chapter 3 Shimodaira Takuya highlights how Japan's perception of its external maritime security environment and its emphasis on the primacy of international norms at sea is transforming its approach to maritime security. He argues that while both the Japan Maritime Self-Defense Force (JMSDF) and the Japan Coast Guard (JCG) are operating in an increasingly close manner, further integration is required if Japan is to meet its strategic goals in East Asia. Further, he argues that this close cooperation could lead to the value-added benefit of Japan contributing to maritime security in waters beyond its immediate vicinity. In Chapter 4 Sukjoon Yoon examines the case of the Republic of Korea. In this chapter, Yoon argues that better cooperation between the coastguard and the navy is an optimal outcome to meet the challenges the ROK faces. However, he also highlights how structural, bureaucratic and operational differences and competition have and continue to hinder closer inter-agency cooperation.

Part II addresses the navy-coastguard nexus in Southeast Asia, a region rife with interstate tensions (in particular, over the South China Sea) and unconventional maritime security threats such as kidnap-for-ransom attacks against ships in the Sulu and Celebes Seas. Chapter 5, written by Vu Truong-Minh and Nguyen The Phuong, examines the Vietnamese Coast Guard (VCG), its rapid expansion and how it is now an integral part of Vietnam's broader maritime security strategy. The chapter describes the close operational relationship between the VCG and the Vietnamese Navy. The external environment and particularly China's challenge to Vietnamese maritime interests are a significant driver of this growth and integration. However, hurdles remain in ensuring that the structures being built are sustainable and effective over the long term. In Chapter 6 Collin Koh examines Singapore's approach to its maritime security. In this case, the Republic of Singapore Navy is the dominant agency within a whole-of-government maritime security architecture, centred on the multi-agency Maritime Security Task Force. In Chapter 7 Muhammad Arif looks at Indonesia. This archipelagic nation has a large number of maritime security interests and continues to advance the policy of becoming a Global Maritime Fulcrum. Yet Arif argues that despite efforts to bolster the Maritime Security Agency (BAKAMLA), significant problems exist in creating a coordinated approach with the Indonesian Navy. This latter organisation continues to dominate Indonesia's maritime security apparatus and plays a leading role in countering threats to Indonesia's maritime security.

Part III examines the navy-coastguard nexus in Europe. By focusing on both the Northern and Southern waters of the region, the chapters show how geography plays a large role in determining the nature of a government's approach to its maritime security architecture. Human security challenges in the Mediterranean and shifting geography in the Arctic present unique problems to which long-established agencies and divisions of labour are being forced to adapt. In Chapter 8 Andreas Østhagen takes up the challenge of exploring three small maritime states in the North Atlantic: Denmark, Norway and Iceland. He argues that each is being increasingly challenged by their maritime security responsibilities and strategic situation, yet, despite their proximity, each has a different approach. Østhagen examines why this has occurred and what operational challenges arise from three different organisational structures interacting on the high-seas. Chapter 9, written by Alessandra Dibenedetto, examines the case of Italy. Focusing on the refugee crisis in the Mediterranean, Dibenedetto traces the origins of the different Italian MLEA and their interaction with the Italian Navy. She argues that the current pressures imposed by the refugee crisis have not only challenged the separation of powers between the various branches but have also exposed some operational inefficiencies in Italy's maritime security architecture. Uniquely, the need to fit within international frameworks, and specifically the EU response to the refugee crisis, has forced a change in Italy's navy-coastguard nexus. In Chapter 10 Ingvill Elgsaas and Liv Parnemo explore the nexus between the Russian Navy and the Federal Security Service (FSB) Coastguard in the Arctic theatre of operations. They argue that the division of responsibilities is diffuse, largely owing to the wide scope of the FSB's mandate. There are unclear lines of responsibility which in reality allow for flexibility in terms of operational mandates and the authors show that there is increasing evidence of cooperation between the two services.

Part IV explores the navy-coastguard nexus in North and South America. Chapter 11, written by Jonathan G. Odom, examines the case of the United States. He argues that the United States has successfully managed its navy-coastguard nexus since the foundation of the nation. Further, he describes the responsiveness of both the US Navy and Coast Guard to new challenges and their willingness to alter the navy-coastguard nexus to meet new and future threats. In Chapter 12 Timothy Choi looks at the case of Canada. Basing his argument in the concept of peacetime sea control, Choi uses historical and contemporary examples to show how Canada's navy-coastguard nexus continuously shifts in response to changes in the maritime strategic environment. In Chapter 13 Nicole Jenne and María Lourdes Puente Olivera examine the navy-coastguard nexus in Argentina. They demonstrate that democratisation has had a significant impact on Argentina's navy-coastguard nexus, with governments more willing to fund the prefecture (Argentine coastguard) at the expense of the navy. And while inefficiencies do exist, the existing structure largely meets Argentina's maritime security needs. Finally, the volume concludes with Chapter 14 where the editors draw some conclusions from the presented case studies and seek to underline policy-relevant ramifications.

PART I

Northeast Asia

CHAPTER 2

Integrating the China Coast Guard with the PLA Navy

Anguang Zheng

"Four Dragons" Unified into One: Maritime Great Power Strategy and the Formation and Restructuring of the China Coast Guard

China has an 18,000 km coastline, 370,000 square km of territorial sea, and 3,000,000 square km of exclusive economic zone (EEZ). But for a very long time, China has had weak maritime law enforcement capacities, caused by the absence of an integrated coast guard. An American scholar argued in 2010 that[1] China was relatively weak in the crucially important middle domain of maritime power—the one between commercial prowess and hard military power, which is concerned with maritime governance and enforcing a nation's own laws and ensuring "good order" off its coasts.

Despite major improvements over the last decade, China's maritime enforcement authorities remain balkanized and relatively weak. They are

---

[1] Lyle J. Goldstein, "Five Dragons Stirring Up the Sea: Challenge and Opportunity in China's Improving Maritime Enforcement Capabilities," *CMSI Red Books* 5 (2010), http://digital-commons.usnwc.edu/cmsi-red-books/5.

A. Zheng (✉)
School of International Studies, Nanjing University, Nanjing, China

© The Author(s) 2019
I. Bowers and S. L. C. Koh (eds.), *Grey and White Hulls*,
https://doi.org/10.1007/978-981-13-9242-9_2

described in a derogatory fashion by many Chinese experts as "five or nine dragons stirring up the sea (五龙闹海 or 九龙闹海)."[2] In Northeast Asia, China's weak maritime enforcement capability in terms of net operational capacity is the exception, especially when compared to the coast guard capacities of Japan (or, outside the region, of the United States). Indeed, Japan's Coast Guard was once described as almost, if not quite, a second navy for Tokyo.[3]

Prior to 2013, China relied on at least five major maritime administrative agencies to enforce maritime law. Bureaucratic competition and political infighting between these "Five Dragons" inhibited China from pursuing a comprehensive maritime law enforcement strategy.[4] They were the Anti-Smuggling Bureau (ASB), the China Maritime Police Bureau (CMPB), China Maritime Surveillance (CMS), the Fisheries Law Enforcement Command (FLEC), and the Maritime Safety Administration (MSA). These five entities were subordinate to different higher authorities. The ASB was subordinated to the General Administration of Customs and Ministry of Public Security. This armed entity was responsible for criminal investigations and smuggling cases along China's inland border posts and rivers. The CMPB, also known as the China Coast Guard (CCG), subordinated to the Ministry of Public Security, was an active-duty maritime police force responsible for combating maritime crime. CMS was subordinated to the State Oceanic Administration (SOA) and Ministry of Land and Resources. It was responsible for asserting China's marine rights and sovereignty claims in disputed maritime regions. The FLEC was subordinated to the Ministry of Agriculture. It enforced PRC fisheries laws and handled fishery disputes with foreign entities across China's EEZ. The MSA remains active and is subordinated to the Ministry of Transport, which is responsible

---

[2] Liu Yulong, 中国海警的历史沿革和发展前景探析 [An analysis on the history of CCG and its Prospects for Developments], 法制与社会 [*Legal System and Society*], no. 5 (2017); Wang Jie and Chen Zhuo, 我国海上执法力量资源整合研究 [Research on the Integration of Maritime Law Enforcement Resources in China], 中国软科学 [*Chinese Soft Science*], no. 6 (2014); and lv Jing, Zhu Lequn and Li Jing, Analysis on the Safety of China's Near-Sea Line of Communication in the Context of Institutional Reform [新机构改革背景下的我国近洋通道安全保障探析], 中国软科学 [*Chinese Soft Science*], no. 12 (2013).

[3] Richard J. Samuelson, "New Fighting Power: Japan's Growing Maritime Capabilities and East Asian Security," *International Security* 32, no. 3 (Winter 2007/2008): 99–102.

[4] "Are Maritime Law Enforcement Forces Destabilizing Asia?" *ChinaPower*, https://chinapower.csis.org/maritime-forces-destabilizing-asia/.

for safety of life at sea (SOLAS), maritime pollution control and cleanup, port inspection, and maritime investigation.

For a long time, China planned to reform its maritime law enforcement regime. As early as 2005, then Chinese Premier, Wen Jiabao, proposed a reform of the maritime law enforcement system, including a pilot scheme that integrated the maritime law enforcement agencies in the Beibu Gulf and in the South China Sea.[5] But this proposal was never realized.

Another significant reform attempt was made in 2012, when the Communist Party of China (CPC) held the 18th National Congress and Xi Jinping was elected as the General Secretary of CPC.[6] During this Party Congress, China vowed to implement a Maritime Great Power (MGP) strategy with far-reaching influence.[7]

While Chinese government documents from as early as 2003 listed "building China into an MGP" (or simply "building MGP") as a strategic imperative, the term surged in political significance on November 8, 2012,[8] when then President Hu Jintao mentioned in his report to the 18th Congress of CPC, "We should enhance our capacity for exploiting marine resources, develop the marine economy, protect the marine ecological environment, resolutely safeguard China's maritime rights and interests, and build China into a maritime power."[9]

On the afternoon of July 30, 2013, the eighth group study session on the development of a maritime power was held by the Political Bureau of the CPC Central Committee. CPC General Secretary Xi Jinping, who presided over the study session, stressed that to develop the maritime

---

[5] Liu Yulong, 中国海警的历史沿革和发展前景探析 [An Analysis on the History of CCG and Its Prospects for Developments], 法制与社会 [*Legal System and Society*], no. 5 (2017): 170.

[6] Actually Xi was linked very well with China's maritime strategy policy making. In 2012, Xi Jinping, then Vice President, was appointed as leader of office of Central Maritime Right and Interest Leading Group (中央海洋权益领导小组办公室), the top maritime policing body in China.

[7] About the comprehensive studies on China's MGP thinking and strategy, please see Liza Tobin, "Underway: Beijing's Strategy to Build China into a Maritime Great Power," *Naval War College Review* 71, no. 2 (2018): 17–48.

[8] Liza Tobin, "Underway: Beijing's Strategy to Build China into a Maritime Great Power," 24.

[9] Hu Jintao, Report at 18th Party Congress, http://language.chinadaily.com.cn/news/2012-11/19/content_15941774.htm.

sector is an important part in China's efforts to construct a socialist country with Chinese characteristics. In his speech during this session, he maintained that

> to protect our nation's maritime rights and interests, we should take a more balanced approach. We love peace and will adhere to the path of peaceful development, but that doesn't mean that the country will abandon its legitimate rights and interests, in particular with regard to the nation's core interests. Safeguarding state sovereignty and security is consistent with the interests of development, and enforcement should be enhanced to match the improvement of comprehensive national strength.

He also said,

> We should settle dispute [sic] peacefully through negotiations and strive to maintain peace and stability. Meanwhile, we should be prepared to cope with complicated issues, and improve our capabilities to resolutely maintain the nation's maritime rights and interests. China will continue to follow the principle of 'sovereignty residing with us, shelving disputes and seeking joint development' for areas over which China owns sovereign rights, promote friendly cooperation for mutual benefits, while pursuing and expanding common converging interests with other countries.[10]

Gradually building maritime power became a new national goal and strategy. For China, a MGP is one that both develops the seas and its resources to benefit the country and safeguard its maritime territories and rights, and develops its marine resources and maritime economy, protects its marine ecology, and boosts its coastal defenses.

By becoming a great maritime power, China can improve the development pattern of its marine resources—making it more reasonable and orderly—coordinate the distribution of land and sea resources, and make its maritime economy sustainable. It will also help China develop innovative marine technology by promoting deeper research into significant

---

[10] 习近平在中共中央政治局第八次集体学习时强调进一步关心海洋认识海洋经略海洋推动海洋强国建设不断取得新成就 [Xi Jinping at the 8th Politburo Study Session Emphasizes Continuing Being Concerned with the Ocean, Knowing the Ocean, and Planning and Controlling the Ocean, to Unceasingly Make New Achievements in Promoting the Building of Maritime Great Power], *Xinhua*, July 31, 2013, http://www.xinhuanet.com/politics/2013-07/31/c_116762285.htm.

marine issues, and it will help China protect its marine ecology and biodiversity. On the military front, it will help China strengthen its maritime forces and coastal security, and protect its overseas interests.[11]

It was against this background that China, for the first time in its history, began a major reform and restructuring of its maritime administration system. In March 2013, China announced it would form a unified coast guard commanded by the SOA. The new coast guard has been in operation since July 2013. Meng Hongwei, the vice minister of Public Security, was named as the head of the Maritime Police Bureau and deputy director of the SOA. The agency held a press conference on March 19, 2013, to announce the appointment after the restructuring plan was unveiled on March 10, 2013, to integrate the country's maritime law enforcement forces.

Under the plan, the newly built Maritime Police Bureau, which was the same as CCG, would unify multiple marine forces, including the CMS, the coast guard forces of the Ministry of Public Security, the FLEC of the Ministry of Agriculture, and the maritime anti-smuggling authorities of the General Administration of Customs. The restructured body integrates the functions and roles of China Marine Surveillance, the coast guard forces under the Ministry of Public Security, the FLEC with the Ministry of Agriculture, and maritime anti-smuggling police of the General Administration of Customs. SOA is also rendered as the "National Oceanic Administration" (NOA), while the terms "China Coast Guard" and "China Maritime Police Bureau (CMPB)" are used interchangeably. Finally, four of the "five dragons" are unified into a powerful one (Table 2.1).

The move was made as part of the Chinese government's efforts to restructure its cabinet to enhance maritime law enforcement and strengthen protection and use of its oceanic resources. The new SOA is supervised by the Ministry of Land and Resources, while the CCG implements maritime law enforcement and safeguards the country's sovereignty over territorial waters within the jurisdiction of the CCG under the "operational direction" (业务指导) of the Ministry of Public Security.[12]

[11] Ibid.
[12] 国务院办公厅关于印发国家海洋局主要职责内设机构和人员编制规定的通知 [State Council General Office's Notion on Publishing the Rules on the Internal Institutes and Personnel of SOA], http://www.gov.cn/zwgk/2013-07/09/content_2443023.htm.

Table 2.1 Former and current Chinese maritime law enforcement structure

Former agency	Subordinate to	New agency	Subordinate to
The Coast Guard Forces	Ministry of Public security	China Coast Guard (China Maritime Police Bureau)	National Oceanic Administration
China Maritime Surveillance	State Oceanic Administration		
Fisheries Law Enforcement Command	Ministry of Agriculture		
Maritime Anti-Smuggling Authorities	General Administration of Customs		

Xinhua reported on July 9, 2013, that the maritime police command, a department under the SOA, was tasked with commanding and deploying marine police officers. The maritime police had three branches, namely the North Sea Branch, the East Sea Branch, and the South Sea Branch, with a total of 11 corps across China's coastal provinces, autonomous regions, and municipalities. China Daily reported on July 10, 2013, that China's maritime authority was to boost its law enforcement capability with the allocation of some 16,300 marine police officers to safeguard maritime rights and interests. The Maritime Police Command Center, a department under the SOA, would give orders to the Maritime Police Bureau, draw up law enforcement regulations, and organize daily training.

The new administration's duties regarding integrated marine management and maritime law enforcement were strengthened. Three maritime police branches, 11 police corps, and its detachments across China's coastal provincial-level regions were set to perform law enforcement.[13] The integration of the four maritime divisions is conducive to unity of command and can help avoid jurisdictional and operational overlaps. In addition, the new agency also made law enforcement more powerful. Except for China Marine Surveillance, those four administrative divisions that were previously not allowed to be equipped with weapons can now be armed.[14]

---

[13] Ibid.
[14] "Restructured China Coast Guard Takes to the High Seas," *Global Times*, July 23, 2013, http://www.globaltimes.cn/content/798257.shtml.

China's Maritime Law Enforcement Challenges

The coast guard is now at the sharp end in defending what China sees as its sovereign territory.[15] Although the move was aimed at solving the problems of low efficiency in maritime law enforcement, improving protection and use of oceanic resources, and better safeguarding the country's maritime rights and interests, this task has proven very challenging.

According to some publicly available reports, even by March 2018, the integration was not yet completed. For example, on the official Web site of Ocean and Fishery Department of Fujian Province, there is news mentioning the Ocean and Fishery Law Enforcement Corps of Fujian Province, which is the same name as that before 2013.[16] There are many reasons to account for this situation.

One of the most important things is the huge diversity among the "four dragons." The four entities brought together to form the CCG resided in different departments; they all functioned on completely different organizational structures, and their personnel steeped in different cultures and trained for different missions. China Marine Surveillance and the China Fisheries Administration were administrative organizations, largely made up of civil servants supported by other full time and contract personnel. Their legal powers were limited to imposing civil penalties. For its part, the Border Defense Coast Guard—that is, the "old" CCG—comprised the maritime units of the Border Defense Forces, a branch of the People's Armed Police (PAP). They looked and operated like military—indeed had military ranks and were called "active duty" [现役]—and yet, they had police powers. The fourth force comprised specialized police officers within the General Administration of Customs anti-smuggling division.[17]

The second reason is probably sectional interest. The personnel of the four entities, because of the different subordinating higher authorities,

---

[15] Megha Rajagopalan and Greg Torode, "China's Civilian Fleet a Potent Force in Asia's Disputed Seas," *Reuters*, March 5, 2014, https://www.reuters.com/article/china-asia-maritime/chinas-civilian-fleet-a-potent-force-in-asias-disputed-seas-idUSL3N0L-W55T20140305.

[16] http://www.fjof.gov.cn/xxgk/hydt/stdt/201803/t20180322_1483156.htm.

[17] Ryan D. Martinson, "The Militarization of China's Coast Guard," *The Diplomat*, November 21, 2014, https://thediplomat.com/2014/11/the-militarization-of-chinas-coast-guard/.

have different wages. The personnel of the anti-smuggling police of GAC have the highest salaries among the four agencies. But this agency is also the smallest, so they are very reluctant to be integrated into the CCG, whose main body obviously is the Border Defense Coast Guard and the China Fisheries Administration. Some police officers from ASB even publicly urged the government not to integrate them into CCG by writing an open letter to the leaders of GAC and SOA.[18] Such an occurrence is very unusual in Chinese politics.

The not-so-successful reform of 2013 resulted in further restructuring in 2018, although it also is part of a much greater institutional reform and restructuring initiative, including the party, administration, military, and police. On March 2018, it was announced that the coast guard shall be placed under the administration of the PAP (PAP), which since January 1, 2018, is under the unified control of the Central Military Commission (CMC). The decision stipulated that under the new command chain, the PAP units will take orders directly from the force's headquarters, which, likewise, will follow directives from the CMC.[19] On July 1, 2018, CCG was transferred to the command of PAP. A coast guard contingent (*dadui* 大队) was founded in the PAP, also known as China Coast Guard Bureau, according to the news release of China Ministry of Defense.[20]

The return of CCG to the PAP means it will be incorporated into the CMC system and will no longer take orders from the State Council (China's cabinet). One of the principles of the Institutional Reform of Party and Administration in 2017 is "military is military, police is police, and civilian is civilian."[21] Under this principle, the PAP transformed from

---

[18] 拱北海缉处民警集体致海关总署于广洲署长 (国家海洋局刘赐贵局长) 的公开信 [An Open Letter to Yu Guangzhou, director of GAC, and Liu Cigui, director of SOA, by the polices of Anti-Smuggling Division of Gongbei Custom], http://club.kdnet.net/dispbbs.asp?id=10577657&boardid=25.

[19] "Command of Armed Police Force to Be Unified," *China Daily*, December 28, 2017, http://en.people.cn/n3/2017/1228/c90000-9309202.html.

[20] "Chinese Coast Guard to Be Under the Command of Armed Police from July 1," *Xinhua*, June 28, 2018, http://www.xinhuanet.com/english/2018-06/28/c_137287 657.htm.

[21] 王满传 张 克: 牢牢把握深化党和国家机构改革的目标 [Wang Manchuan, Zhang Ke, Focusing Firmly the Aims of the Institutional Reform of Party and Administration], 求是 [*Qiu Shi*], no. 9 (May 2018).

"armed police" into a military force and is no longer a police agency. Because the CCG has been returned to PAP, it has become part of the Chinese military system. This reform is a significant pivot in the CCG's position.

THE BIGGEST COAST GUARD IN THE WORLD: DUTY, STRUCTURE AND CAPACITIES OF CCG

Given that the CCG was returned to the PAP and is therefore under the control of CMC, those exact roles the CMC assigns to it after the restructuring become unclear. However, the basic roles the CCG plays will not change too much. It is known to perform mostly coastal and oceanic search and rescue or patrols, including anti-smuggling operations. During wartime, it may be placed under the operational control of the PLA Navy.

On June 9, 2013, the State Council General Office published the "Rules on the Internal Institutes and Personnel of SOA," which indicates that the principal duty of CCG is to "promote the ability of MLE and safeguard the maritime order as well as right and interest." Specifically, it includes as follows[22]:

- Patrol of territorial waters and disputed territories, like Diaoyu Island[23] and Huangyan Island[24];
- Comprehensive MLE, like anti-smuggling, anti-piracy, anti-stowing away, etc.;
- Maritime policing and ship inspections;
- Harbor and coastal security, safeguard the Boao Forum, CPC Central Bureau Beidaihe Summer Vacation, and Ocean Oil and Gas Rig Platforms, Ocean Scientific Research and Survey;
- Research and survey;

[22] 国务院办公厅关于印发国家海洋局主要职责内设机构和人员编制规定的通知 [State Council General Office's Notion on Publishing the Rules on the Internal Institutes and Personnel of SOA], http://www.gov.cn/zwgk/2013-07/09/content_2443023.htm; 杨洋、李培志: 中国海警海军融合式发展问题研究 [Yang Yang, Li Peizhi, On Integration Development of China Coast Guard and Navy], 公安海警学院学报 [*Journal of China Maritime Police Academy*] 16, no. 1 (2007): 11.

[23] Also known as Senkaku Islands to Japan.

[24] Also known as Scarborough Shoal, or Panatag Shoal to the Philippines.

- Search and Rescue, maritime emergency aids;
- Fisheries protection;
- Cooperate with the PLA in military operations.

On June 22, 2018, the Standing Committee of the National People's Congress, China's top legislature, adopted a decision to define the newly reformed coast guard powers.[25] It was decided that the coast guard will be responsible for fighting criminal maritime activity, safety, and enforcing laws in areas including maritime resource exploitation, environmental protection, fishery management, and smuggling. In fighting maritime crimes, the coast guard will exercise police powers granted by relevant laws. The coast guard also will exercise the powers of relevant administrative organs in performing its other duties. The coast guard will develop a legal cooperation mechanism for enforcement with public security and other administrative authorities.

According to these documents and a scholarly paper published by the *Journal of China Maritime Police Academy*, it is known that the CCG is assigned to support the PLAN to safeguard China's maritime right and interests. Both are the important forces for China's maritime defense.[26]

Structure and Capabilities

Some scholars argue that the CCG is the biggest coast guard in the world.[27] There are 3 branches (*fenju*, 分局) in the CCG, including North China Sea (Beihai, 北海) Branch, East China Sea (Donghai, 东海) Branch, and South China Sea (Nanhai, 南海) Branch. Each branch is in charge of the maritime activities in accordance with sea and coastal provinces. There is a CCG Corp (*Zongdui*, 总队) in each coastal province. The largest operational unit of the CCG is a CCG flotilla, which is a regimental-level unit in China's military administrative hierarchy. Every

---

[25] Decision by the Standing Committee of the National People's Congress on the Duties and Powers of China Coast Guard on Maritime Rights Maintain and Law Enforcement [全国人民代表大会常务委员会关于中国海警局行使海上维权执法职权的决定], http://www.npc.gov.cn/npc/xinwen/2018-06/22/content_2056585.htm.

[26] 杨洋、李培志：中国海警海军融合式发展问题研究 [Yang Yang, Li Peizhi, On Integration Development of China Coast Guard and Navy], 公安海警学院学报 [*Journal of China Maritime Police Academy*] 16, no. 1 (2007): 11.

[27] Andrew Ericson, "China's Three 'Navies' Each Have the World's Most Ships," https://warisboring.com/chinas-three-navies-each-have-the-worlds-most-ships/.

Table 2.2 The provincial flotillas of the CCG

Coastal province (from North to South)	Flotillas	Location
Liaoning	1st flotilla	Dalian
	2nd flotilla	Dandong
Tianjin	1st flotilla	Tianjin
Hebei	1st flotilla	Qinhuangdao
Shandong	1st flotilla	Weihai
	2nd flotilla	Qingdao
Jiangsu	1st flotilla	Taicang
Shanghai	1st flotilla	Shanghai
Zhejiang	1st flotilla	Taizhou
	2nd flotilla	Ningbo
Fujian	1st flotilla	Fuzhou
	2nd flotilla	Quanzhou
	3rd flotilla	Xiamen
Guangdong	1st flotilla	Guangzhou
	2nd flotilla	Shantou
	3rd flotilla	Zhanjiang
Guangxi	1st flotilla	Beihai
	2nd flotilla	Fangchenggang
Hainan	1st flotilla	Haikou
	2nd flotilla	Sanya

coastal province has 1 to 3 Coast Guard flotillas. Currently, there are twenty CCG flotillas across the country (Table 2.2).

The equipment of the CCG has developed very much in recent years. Although there is no exact number of the vessels in CCG, the quantity and quality are developing rapidly. It was reported that China has commissioned more than 100 ships into the coast guard force since 2012.[28]

Buildup of Chinese MLE Forces

Chinese Coast Guard ships are painted white with blue stripes and have the wording CCG in English and Chinese on their hulls. Typical Coast Guard ships include the 130-ton Type 218 patrol craft (100 crafts),

---

[28] Charissa Echavez, "China Deploys World's Biggest Coast Guard Cutter CCG 3901 to Patrol South China Sea," *China Topix*, May 12, 2017, http://www.chinatopix.com/articles/114102/20170512/china-coast-guard-peoples-liberation-army-ccg-3901-cutter-south-china-sea.htm#ixzz5Dxk8oiRm.

Table 2.3 The build-up of Chinese MLE forces

2013	2018
– 78 offshore-capable patrol and surveillance vessels – Over 366 patrol boats for inshore duties	– 118 offshore-capable patrol and surveillance vessels – 130 coastal patrol craft – About 200 patrol boats for inshore duties – 2 former PLA Navy landing ship tanks serving as hospital vessels and in island supply roles – 21 auxiliaries including 9 research and survey vessels, some of which were formerly PLA Navy

Source International Institute for Strategic Studies (IISS), *The Military Balance 2013* (Oxford: Oxford University Press, 2013), 295; IISS, *The Military Balance 2018* (Oxford: Oxford University Press, 2018), 258

armed with twin 14.5 mm machine guns, assorted speedboats, and few larger patrol ships (Table 2.3).

The CCG has received quite a few large patrol ships that would significantly enhance their operations. CCG operates hundreds of small patrol craft for maritime patrol services. These craft are usually quite well armed with machine guns and 37 mm anti-aircraft guns. In addition, these services operate their own small aviation units to assist their maritime patrol capabilities. CCG operates a handful of Harbin Z-9 helicopters, a maritime patrol aircraft based on the Harbin Y-12 short takeoff and landing (STOL) transport, and a larger maritime surveillance aircraft based on the MA60 transport, which is the largest one in the CCG.[29]

In 2012, China began to build 2 cutters for CCG whose displacement is over 10,000 tons.[30] In March 2016, the first cutter CCG 2901 was deployed in the East China Sea Branch CCG, because the initial number is "2." Therefore, one of its duties is to patrol around Diaoyu Island.[31]

---

[29] 中国海监西飞新舟 60 飞机在我国南海巡航执法作 [MA60 Plane of China Maritime Surveillance Petrol on South China Sea for Law Enforcement], 中国民用航空网 [*China Civilian Aviation Online* (website)], http://www.ccaonline.cn/news/item/374289.html.

[30] 中国万吨海警船下水涂装完成 排水量世界第一 (China's 10,000-ton CCG Vessel Is the First in the World), http://news.ifeng.com/a/20141215/42719412_0.shtml.

[31] 中国 2901 船为全球第一大执法船 配最致命武器 [CCG Vessel 2901 Equipped Most Fatal Weapon Is the Biggest Law Enforcement Ship in the World], 搜狐网 [*Sohu* (Website)], http://mil.sohu.com/20160328/n442559095.shtml.

In May 2017, it was reported that China had deployed the 12,000 ton CCG 3901 cutter to patrol the South China Sea. The CCG 2901 and 3901 cutters are the world's biggest coast guard cutters and are larger than the Japan Coast Guard's *Shikishima* class which, at a 6500 ton full-load displacement, was hitherto the largest maritime law enforcement vessel in service. These ships are armed with 76 mm H/PJ-26 rapid-fire naval guns, two auxiliary guns, and two anti-aircraft guns.

Comparing to its American and Japanese counterparts, the CCG possesses much fewer aircraft. But in the future the number of CCG aircraft will rise. In June 2015, a Z-18 maritime patrol helicopter was said to be deployed on each of the 12,000 ton cutters.[32] In the same month, a MA-60H maritime patrol aircraft with CCG painting was revealed in the Chinese media.[33]

Operations

The use of civilian maritime security agency vessels has consistently been a successful tactic by China in staking claims to maritime territories. During the 2012 Huangyan Island and Diaoyu Island tensions, the CMS and FLEC ships were responsible for directly managing the disputes on a daily basis, while the PLA Navy maintained a more distant presence away from the immediate vicinity of the contested waters. China prefers to use its civilian maritime agencies in these disputes and use the PLA Navy further ashore from disputed areas or as an escalatory measure. According to Chinese statistics, there were about 40,000 people in maritime law enforcement jobs.

Chinese vessels maintained regular patrols in 2013 in the territorial waters surrounding the Diaoyu Islands to safeguard the country's maritime rights, said Liu Cigui, director of the SOA, on January 16, 2014.[34]

---

[32] 中国海监版直18直升机曝光 或装备万吨海警船 [Helicopter Zhi-18 of China Marine Surveillance Version Unveiled Could be Deployed on 10,000-ton CCG Vessel], 新浪网 [*Sina*(website)], http://mil.news.sina.com.cn/2015-06-26/1107833913.html.

[33] 中国海监西飞新舟 60 飞机在我国南海巡航执法作 [MA60 Plane of China Maritime Surveillance Petrol on South China Sea for Law Enforcement], 中国民用航空网 [*China Civilian Aviation Online* (website)], http://www.ccaonline.cn/news/item/374289.html.

[34] "Maritime Official Details China's 2013 Patrols," *Xinhua*, January 17, 2014, http://en.people.cn/90786/8515363.html.

Liu also stated at a national maritime work conference that China had also achieved effective management and control over Huangyan Island last year, and Chinese ships have carried out patrols in the territorial waters around Beikang Ansha and Nankang Ansha since August. CCG vessels conducted 36 regular patrols on 262 days in 2013, covering all the sea areas under China's jurisdiction. The vessels sailed close to 18 sites that have been encroached upon by other nations, operated around the Nansha Islands for observation and patrolled the territorial waters surrounding the Diaoyu Islands 50 times, said Liu.

"In 2014, the SOA will safeguard the country's legal rights and stability, and resolutely maintain China's maritime rights," he vowed. According to Liu, the SOA will reinforce patrols in territorial waters surrounding the Diaoyu Islands, Huangyan Island, Ren'ai Jiao, Beikang Ansha, and Nankang Ansha. It will likewise secure the base points of the country's territorial sea, he said, adding that China will also deepen maritime cooperation to create a win–win situation and stipulate strategies for a "maritime Silk Road" to promote sea-based economic collaboration.

The CCG also conducts periodic joint training sessions with foreign counterparts, including the US Coast Guard. It also participates in the annual North Pacific Coast Guard Agencies Forum in Alaska, along with United States, Canadian, Japanese, South Korean, and Russian coast guards. As part of an exchange program, CCG members have been assigned to serve on US Coast Guard Cutters.

Fused Development: China Coast Guard and PLA Navy

The CCG's predecessor was part of the Chinese People's Public Security Central Column (中国人民公安中央纵队), which was part of the PLA to maintain the domestic public order in September 1949 just before the foundation of PRC. In 1982, the PAP was established which included the Maritime Police Corp (海警部队). The PAP was under the dual leadership of the CMC and the State Council. Between 1982 and 2018, China's MLE forces underwent a process of civilization and professionalization highlighted by the establishment of the CCG in 2013. But the 2018 reform strengthens the militarized control again.

However, even before the 2018 restructuring, the CCG had a very close connection with the PLAN. Some Chinese scholars have proposed the fused development of the CCG and PLAN.³⁵ Strategically, the CCG and PLAN are the two most important forces safeguarding China's maritime rights and interests. A governmental white paper named *The Diversified Employment of China's Armed Forces* published in 2013 detailed the cooperation in safeguarding maritime rights and interests between the CCG, other civilian authorities, and the PLAN:

> In combination with its routine combat readiness activities, the PLAN provides security support for China's maritime law enforcement, fisheries, and oil and gas exploitation. It has established mechanisms to coordinate and cooperate with law-enforcement organs of marine surveillance and fishery administration, as well as a joint military-police-civilian defense mechanism.³⁶

The white paper mentioned above maintains that the PLAN has worked in coordination with relevant local departments to conduct maritime survey and scientific investigation; build systems of maritime meteorological observation, satellite navigation, radio navigation, and navigation aids; release timely weather and sea traffic information; and ensure the safe flow of traffic in sea areas of responsibility.

Together with the marine surveillance and fishery administration departments, the PLAN has conducted joint maritime exercises and drills for protecting rights and enforcing laws. It has also enhanced its capabilities to coordinate command and respond to emergencies in joint military–civilian operations to safeguard maritime rights. The "Donghai Collaboration-2012" joint exercise was held in the East China Sea in October 2012 and involved 11 ships and eight planes.³⁷

At his 2013 study session on maritime issues, President Xi Jinping laid out the "four transformations" (四个转变) to guide the country's

---

³⁵ 杨洋、李培志: 中国海警海军融合式发展问题研究 [Yang Yang, Li Peizhi, On Integration Development of China Coast Guard and Navy], 公安海警学院学报 [*Journal of China Maritime Police Academy*] 16, no. 1 (2007): 11–15.

³⁶ Information Office of the State Council of the People's Republic of China, *The Diversified Employment of China's Armed Forces* (Governmental White Paper), April 2013, Beijing, http://www.scio.gov.cn/zfbps/ndhf/2013/Document/1312843/1312843.htm.

³⁷ Information Office of the State Council of the People's Republic of China, *The Diversified Employment of China's Armed Forces*, April 2013, Beijing, http://www.scio.gov.cn/zfbps/ndhf/2013/Document/1312843/1312843.htm.

maritime work. Paraphrased, these were as follows: (1) transforming the maritime economy toward quality and efficiency, (2) transforming marine-development methods toward sustainable use, (3) transforming marine science and technology so that innovation would play the leading role, and (4) transforming the protection of national maritime rights and interests so that planning would be unified.[38] The last one requires the unity of China maritime rights and interest safeguarding institutes, including the CCG and the PLAN.

In 2016, China's national Thirteen Five Year Plan (FYP, 2016–2020), while focusing on economic and social development, stated that the government would "Coordinate the use of all sorts of methods to protect and expand national maritime rights and interests." It includes both civilian and military areas, in which CCG and PLAN could play important roles together.

This kind of cooperation between CCG and PLAN has been noted, although sometimes criticized by other countries. For example, the annual report on Chinese military forces to the US Congress in 2015 discussed Chinese maritime law enforcement agencies' relationship with the PLAN[39]:

China identifies sovereignty as a core interest and emphasizes a willingness to assert and defend its claims in the East China Sea and South China Sea. China prefers to use its government-controlled, civilian maritime law enforcement agencies in these disputes and uses the PLA Navy in an overwatch capacity in case of escalation. China has demonstrated this model at Huangyan Island, Second Thomas Shoal, Diaoyu Islands, and CNOOC-981's drilling operations south of the Xisha Islands. China, however, uses a whole-of-government approach and also applies pressure on rival claimants using economic and political levers. China almost certainly wants to assert its maritime dominance without triggering a regional backlash.

---

[38] 习近平: 进一步关心海洋认识海洋经略海洋 推动海洋强国建设不断取得新成就 [Xi Jinping: Keep Showing Concern for the Ocean, Knowing the Ocean, Controlling the Ocean; Keep Making New Accomplishments in the Building of Maritime Great Power], *Xinhua*, July 31, 2013, http://www.xinhuanet.com/politics/2013-07/31/c_116762285.htm.

[39] Department of Defense, *Military and Security Developments Involving the People's Republic of China for 2015* (Washington, DC: Department of Defense, April 2015).

On May 20, 2018, it was reported that there was a joint navigation exercise involving the CCG, PLAN, and local comprehensive law enforcement ship [地方综合执法船] around the Xisha Islands. This report detailed the cooperative operations between all three entities. The PLAN frigate *Shaoguan* [韶关] led this 3-ship joint fleet. During this exercise which lasted for 5 days and 4 nights, whenever the *Shaoguan* found foreign fishing ships in Chinese EEZ, it transferred this information to the CCG ships immediately, and then, the latter proceeded to inspect and drive them away. The fleet inspected more than 40 ships and expelled over 10 foreign fishing ships. The command of the joint fleet said the joint exercise would make sure the different ships deal with different situations rapidly and flexibly. This is the first military–police–civilian joint navigation exercise around the Xisha Islands.[40]

The main body of CCG personnel comes from the former Border Defense Coast Guard force, whose officers and soldiers are active duty and therefore are like the personnel of PLAN. The personnel responsible for technical operations, including navigation, machinery and electronics, telecommunications, telegraph, radar, signal, gun, and sailing, share the same education and training as the PLAN personnel. The operating rules of CCG ships and their personnel training guidelines both come from the PLAN.[41]

In terms of equipment, CCG has very important cooperation with the PLAN. In March 2007, it was reported that the PLAN transferred 2 Type 728 cutters (44102, ex-509 *Changde*; 46103, ex-510 *Shaoxing*) to the coast guard and re-numbered them as 1002 & 1003. At the time, these ships were the largest vessels in the CCG inventory.

In 2017, CCG built 3 Type 818 patrol ships (CCG 46301, 46302, and 46112) which are very similar to the Type 054A frigates (*Jiangkai II* Class Frigates) of PLAN. The difference is that the Type 818 is not equipped with missiles and features a bow thruster, which provides it with more agility in MLE activities. These new ships share commonalities with PLAN ships, with reserved places for navy arms, electronic

---

[40] 军警民编队首巡西沙岛礁 驱离外籍渔船 10 余艘 [The First Military-Police-Civilian Fleet Navigates in Xisha Island More than 10 Foreign Fishing Ships Were Expelled], 环球时报网站 [Global Times web], May 20, 2018, http://mil.huanqiu.com/world/2018-05/12061593.html.

[41] 杨洋、李培志: 中国海警海军融合式发展问题研究 [Yang Yang, Li Peizhi, On Integration Development of China Coast Guard and Navy], 11.

equipment, and fire control radar. If needed, the CCG ships can be transformed into PLAN ships easily.[42]

After the restructuring in 2018, there will be an integrated command system under the CMC. Another reason for this comes from the increasing number of disputes in the East and South China Seas. Some scholars propose a "PLAN- CCG Joint Commanding Regime." In this system, the CCG and PLAN would carry out diverse maritime operations collectively and differently. The CCG would take responsibility for patrols in disputed seas, anti-smuggling, anti-piracy, and anti-terrorism, while sharing information with the PLAN. But if the situation escalated into a crisis or war, the command will be transferred immediately to the PLAN. As far efficiency is concerned, this Joint Command Regime should be based on the PLAN command system.[43] For example, although the CCP built the first SWAT team focusing on anti-terrorism in 2004,[44] the PLAN will play a major role in the possible anti-terrorism joint combat at sea. But the CCG can provide vital assistance in these operations.

The fused development of the CCG and PLAN includes information sharing. The PLAN intelligence basically focuses on the warfare, while the CCG intelligence focuses on the maritime security and safeguarding maritime sovereignty and interests. So, it is needed to build an intelligence sharing platform for both forces.

Furthermore, the CCG and PLAN can share their education and training systems. Now, the CCG has several colleges and training centers which can provide undergraduate, graduate education, and training for its personnel, like the China Maritime Police Academy located in Ningbo Province and training bases in Weihai, Guangzhou, and Chengmai. However, given the rising demand for more professional officers and soldiers, it is not enough. On the other hand, the PLAN has a much better education and training system than the CCG. After the 2017 military reform, although the number of military colleges was reduced substantially, it still runs the Naval Command College, Naval Academy,

---

[42] Ibid.

[43] 梁卫华, 严春梅: 论海军海警联合行动的装备保障 [Liang Weihua, Yan Chunmei, On the Supplies of Equipment in PLAN-CCG Joint Operation], 公安海警学院学报 [*Journal of China Maritime Police Academy*], no. 3 (2014): 47–50.

[44] 郑小平: 海警部队参与海上反恐作战的思考 [A Thinking on the Engagement of CCG in Maritime Anti-terrorism Combat], 武警学院学报 [*Journal of Chinese People's Armed Police Force Academy*] 24, no. 9 (September 2008): 57.

Naval University of Engineering, Naval Submarine Academy, Naval Aeronautical University, even Naval Medical University, and much more training bases than the CCG. So, the CCG personnel can be educated and trained in naval colleges and training bases, especially if the CCG needs the PLAN's help to train its pilots in the future because it does not have an aeronautic college so far.[45]

Conclusion

The rapid development of the CCG's capability is in accordance with China's recent ambitious strategy of becoming a MGP, in which CCG is assigned very important role of safeguarding Chinese maritime right and interest. This role is shared with PLAN. The CCG and PLAN are forging a nexus to implement a flexible but firm maritime strategy. The CCG and PLAN are going to cooperate closely in many aspects, like command and control, equipment, personnel, and information sharing.

But the rising power of the CCG raises concerns among some scholars and politicians, especially in Western countries and claimant countries which have maritime territorial disputes with China. As the editors note in the introduction to this volume, there is concern that the decision by states, most notably, but not only by, China to build up and employ coast guards as first-line defenders during territorial disputes could result in heightened tension: Rather than employing coast guards as tools of regional peace, countries are using them, as opposed to naval forces, as aggressive instruments of state power to assert territorial claims—a new and destabilizing phenomenon in maritime territorial disputes.[46] Japan claims that attention must continue to be paid to the status of CCG activities in East and South China Sea waters. Such activities by China constitute acts that unilaterally change the status quo and further advance its efforts to create a fait accompli. Japan is deeply concerned about these activities, and the concern is shared with the international

---

[45]李培志: 建设海洋强国战略背景下中国海警体制改革的思考 [Li Peizhi, Thinking about the Reform of CCG under the Strategy of Constructing Maritime Power], 武警学院学报 [*Journal of Chinese People's Armed Police Force Academy*], no. 3 (2016): 47–50.

[46]Lyle Morris makes a similar argument. See Lyle J. Morris, "The Rise of Coast Guards in East and Southeast Asia," *Naval War College Review* 70, no. 2 (2017): 75.

community, including the United States.[47] The CCG is viewed as a major vector of Beijing's maritime strategy, and Washington think tank analysts are working late into the night trying to divine a way to counter China's armada of imposing "white hulls."[48] Also, there are concerns about the latest restructuring that blurs the boundary between police and military activity.[49]

However, there is still a silver lining if one refrains from always viewing the situation from a pessimistic or negative viewpoint. That is, a big problem could be a big opportunity. A scholar proposed that Beijing and Washington could be well served by considering bilateral coast guard cooperation.[50] Washington should extend a hand in cooperation to CCG, rather than simply aiming to counter its every move.

Acknowledgements This chapter is the result of the project funded by the Social Science Fund of Jiangsu Province (Project No. 15ZZB007).

[47] Anthony H. Cordesman, *The PLA Navy*, (Washington, DC: Center for Strategic and International Studies, October 21, 2016) 53, https://csis-prod.s3.amazonaws.com/s3fs-public/publication/161024_PLAN_Final.pdf.

[48] Lyle J. Goldstein, China's Coast Guard: A Big Problem or a Big Opportunity?, *National Interest*, November 15, 2015, http://nationalinterest.org/feature/chinas-coast-guard-big-problem-or-big-opportunity-14343?page=show.

[49] MAREX, "China's Coast Guard Is Now a Military Police Unit," The Maritime Executive, March 3, 2018, https://www.maritime-executive.com/article/china-s-coast-guard-is-now-a-military-police-unit#gs.a7TdUr0.

[50] Lyle J. Goldstein, "China's Coast Guard: A Big Problem or a Big Opportunity?".

CHAPTER 3

The JMSDF and JCG: Toward Cooperation and Contribution

Takuya Shimodaira

In recent years, China is believed to be building up capabilities to conduct operations in more distant waters and airspace. Accordingly, China has rapidly expanded its maritime activities based on its sea and air power in both qualitative and quantitative terms. In the sea areas and airspace surrounding Japan, a large number of ships and aircraft operated by Chinese maritime law enforcement agencies have been observed engaging in monitoring activities and asserting Beijing's claimed maritime rights and interests. These operations include potentially dangerous activities such as a Chinese vessel's direction of a fire-control radar at a Japan Maritime Self-Defense Force (JMSDF) destroyer and the flight of Chinese military fighter jets abnormally close to Japan Self-Defense Force (JSDF) aircraft.[1]

Since September 2012, China has challenged Japan's sovereign control of the Senkaku Islands by regularly sending law enforcement vessels

---

[1] Ministry of Defense of Japan, *Defense of Japan 2017* (Tokyo: Ministry of Defense of Japan, 2017), 98.

T. Shimodaira (✉)
Security Studies Department and Policy Simulation Office,
National Institute for Defense Studies (NIDS), Tokyo, Japan

© The Author(s) 2019
I. Bowers and S. L. C. Koh (eds.), *Grey and White Hulls*,
https://doi.org/10.1007/978-981-13-9242-9_3

into Japanese territorial waters and contiguous zones. On December 2015, China elevated the stakes by sending its first armed coast guard vessel into the territorial seas of the Senkaku. Since then, there have been consistent entries by armed China Coast Guard (CCG) vessels into the seas around the Senkaku Islands.[2]

In recognition of recent security environment, the Japan Ministry of Defense (JMOD) has highlighted a tendency toward an increase and prolongation of so-called gray-zone situations that are neither pure peacetime nor full wartime contingencies over territory, sovereignty, and maritime economic interests.[3] The National Defense Program Guidelines for FY2011 and beyond first referred to so-called gray-zone disputes.[4] Dealing with these "gray-zone" situations has become a core security challenge for Japan and requires seamless management between the Japan Coast Guard (JCG) and JMSDF for the contingencies that might escalate into military conflicts.

The JCG is engaged night and day in a variety of activities, including criminal investigations, maritime security operations, search and rescue work, maritime environment preservation, disaster mitigation, oceanographic research, and maritime safety operations, and also working to strengthen collaboration and cooperation with other countries, so that Japan can securely utilize the ocean environment.[5]

The JSDF consistently engages in warning and surveillance activities in the waters and airspace surrounding Japan during peacetime so that it can respond to various contingencies immediately and seamlessly. The JMSDF patrols the waters surrounding Hokkaido, the Sea of Japan, and the East China Sea, using P-3C patrol aircraft and other aircraft.[6] The National Defense Program Guidelines for FY2019 and beyond defines the national defense objectives: first, to create, on a steady-state basis, security environment desirable for Japan by integrating and drawing on

---

[2] Lyle J. Morris, "The New 'Normal' in the East China Sea," *The RAND Blog*, February 27, 2017, https://www.rand.org/blog/2017/02/the-new-normal-in-the-east-china-sea.html.

[3] Ministry of Defense of Japan, *Defense of Japan 2017*, 43.

[4] Ministry of Defense of Japan, *National Defense Program Guidelines for FY2011 and beyond* (Tokyo: Ministry of Defense of Japan, 2010), 3.

[5] Japan Coast Guard, *Japan Coast Guard JCG: Justice and Humanity* (Tokyo: Japan Coast Guard, 2018), 1, https://www.kaiho.mlit.go.jp/e/english.pdf.

[6] Ministry of Defense of Japan, *Defense of Japan 2017*, 318.

the strengths at the nation's disposal; second, to deter threat from reaching Japan by making opponent realize that doing harm to Japan would be difficult and consequential; and finally, should threat reach Japan, to squarely counter the threat and minimize damage. Japan will strengthen each of the means by which to successfully achieve these national defense objectives: Japan's own architecture for national defense; the Japan-US Alliance; and international security cooperation.[7]

China has challenged the status quo of the current regional maritime order. On April 11, 2016, the G7 Ministers expressed concern about the situation in the East and South China Seas, where unilateral changes to the status quo that raise tensions are being witnessed. Japan also expressed its concerns about the unilateral alteration of status quo in these waters and reaffirmed the commitment to further strengthening international cooperation on maritime security and safety in the "G7 Foreign Ministers' Statement on Maritime Security."[8] Tokyo strongly recognizes the importance of addressing maritime security issues in the East and South China Seas, from the standpoint of supporting the principle of rule of law and freedom of navigation under Japan's security banner "Proactive Contribution to Peace."

This chapter asks what kind of cooperative contribution should the JMSDF and the JCG provide to maintain the rule-based regional order? Cooperation between the JMSDF and the JCG could deliver a favorable influence in the Indo-Pacific region, together with partner nations. Maximizing Japanese capabilities from the sea will be one of the most important practical means for maintaining the rule-based regional order.

CHINESE MARITIME POWER

China's Armed Forces are composed of three major organizations, each of which has a maritime subcomponent: The People's Liberation Army (PLA) contains the People's Liberation Army Navy (PLAN); the People's Armed Police (PAP), which now leads China's Maritime Law Enforcement (MLE) forces, including the CCG; and the Militia, which contains a growing proportion of sea-based units, the People's Armed

---

[7] Ministry of Defense of Japan, *National Defense Program Guidelines for FY2019 and Beyond* (Tokyo: Ministry of Defense of Japan, 2018), 8.

[8] Ministry of Foreign Affairs, *G7 Foreign Ministers' Statement on Maritime Security*, April 14, 2016, http://www.mofa.go.jp/mofaj/files/000147444.pdf.

Forces Maritime Militia (PAFMM). Each of China's three sea forces is the world's largest of its type.[9] From January 1, 2018, the PAP has come under the command of the Communist Party of China (CPC) Central Committee and the Central Military Commission (CMC).[10] The PAP will fight side by side with PLA and the PAFMM, giving full play to the might of people's war.

China has the world's largest navy. The PLAN currently has just over 300 vessels. Bernard D. Cole analyzed that China has both domestic political goals, especially sovereignty concerns, and traditional economic objectives. Beijing has emphasized the navy's increasing role in international efforts in general, striving to maintain maritime security through multiple peaceful ways and means. China is building and deploying a twenty-first-century navy to be able to defend its interest at sea.[11] China is forecast to have a larger navy than the United States in five years or so if one simply counts numbers of principal combatants and submarines—virtually all of which will be available in East Asia, facing only a portion of the US Navy in these waters on a day-to-day basis. If current trends continue, China will have a growing quantitative advantage in the Western Pacific while gradually closing the qualitative gap.[12]

China also operates the world's largest coast guard by a sizable margin. Today, the CCG has 225 ships over 500 tons capable of operating offshore, and another 1050+ confined to closer waters, for a total of over 1275 vessels. Lyle J. Morris analyzed several shifts in CCG capabilities and operations in the South China Sea. First, he observed, China is employing larger, more heavily armed, and more capable offshore patrol vessels for longer periods of time in disputed waters in the South China Sea. Second, the CCG patrols in the South China Sea now operate more widely, more regularly, and apparently also more assertively. Third, the

[9] Andrew S. Erickson, "Understanding China's Third Sea Force: The Maritime Militia," *Harvard Fairbank Center Blog Post*, September 8, 2017, https://medium.com/fairbank-center/understanding-chinas-third-sea-force-the-maritime-militia-228a2bfbbedd.

[10] Wang Qiang, "Armed Police Move Heightens Central Control," *Global Times*, January 3, 2018, http://www.globaltimes.cn/content/1083146.shtml.

[11] Bernard D. Cole, "What Do China's Surface Fleet Developments Suggest About Its Maritime Strategy," in *China's Evolving Surface Fleet* [China Maritime Studies No. 14], ed. Peter A. Dutton and Ryan D. Martinson (Annapolis, MD: US Naval War College, 2017), 19, 22, 28.

[12] Michael McDevitt, *Becoming a Great "Maritime Power": A Chinese Dream* (Richmond, VA: Center for Naval Analyses, 2016), ix.

CCG now coordinates intelligence, command, and control to a greater degree with Chinese fishing, maritime militia, and PLAN vessels.[13] The US Office of Naval Intelligence report points out that China prefers to use its coast guard as the primary agency to enforce its maritime rights and interests. By keeping the PLAN in the background, China hopes to limit the escalation potential of maritime confrontations in the Yellow, East China, and South China Sea.[14]

Third, China has the world's largest maritime militia. Andrew S. Erickson identified the maritime militia as China's third sea force. These units typically answer to the PLA chain of command and are certain to do so when activated for missions at sea. They are a critical enabler for China's prosecution of "gray-zone" operations to increase Chinese control over the East and South China Seas through coercion short of escalation to war. In the East and South China Seas, together with the CCG, the maritime militia can engage in entire levels of finely calibrated escalation that the United States could find difficult to match.[15]

JAPANESE MARITIME POWER

The JCG

Since its establishment as the Maritime Safety Agency (MSA) in May 1948 and after being officially its English name changed to the JCG in April 2000, the JCG has conducted day-and-night surveillance and control of official vessels, oceanographic research vessels, vessels carrying foreign activists seeking to stake territorial claims, and fishing boats from foreign countries.[16] Its roles and missions have expanded to include not only guarding Japan's enormous coastline and providing search and

[13] Lyle J. Morris, "The Era of Coast Guards in the Asia-Pacific Is Upon Us," *Asia Maritime Transparency Initiative*, March 8, 2017, https://amti.csis.org/era-coast-guards-asia-pacific-upon-us/.

[14] Office of Naval Intelligence, *The PLA Navy: New Capabilities and Missions for the 21st Century* (Washington, DC: US Office of Naval Intelligence, 2015), 46, http://www.oni.navy.mil/Portals/12/Intel%20agencies/China_Media/2015_PLA_NAVY_PUB_Print_Low_Res.pdf?ver=2015-12-02-081233-733.

[15] Andrew S. Erickson, "Understanding China's Third Sea Force: The Maritime Militia."

[16] Japan Coast Guard, *Japan Coast Guard JCG: Justice and Humanity*, 9.

Table 3.1 JCG patrol vessels and patrol craft

Type	Number	Vessels and craft
Patrol vessels	134	
PLH-type (Large with helicopter)	14	Akitsushima, Yashima, Soya
PL-type (Large)	48	Izu (3500t), Hida (2000t), Kurikoma (1000t), Suzuka (1000t), Yonakuni (1000t), Wakasa (1000t)
PM-type (Medium)	38	Katori (500t), Natsui (350t)
PS-type (Small)	33	Kaimon, Sanrei (180t), Shimoji (180t)
FL-type (Fire fighting boat)	1	Hiryu
Patrol craft	238	
PC-type (Patrol craft)	69	Nachi (35 m), Nagozuki (30 m)
CL-type (Craft large)	169	Satsukaze (20 m)
Total	372	

Source Japan Coast Guard, March 2018, 3–6, http://www.kaiho.mlit.go.jp/e/english.pdf

rescue services, but also constabulary operations in the sea lanes and high seas for anti-piracy mission.[17]

With its headquarters in Tokyo, the JCG has divided the nation into 11 operational regions to facilitate its operations. Each region has a Regional Coast Guard Headquarters under which there are various Coast Guard Offices, Coast Guard Air Stations, Coast Guard Stations, Traffic Advisory Service Centers, Air Stations, and Hydrographic Observatories. As shown in Table 3.1, the total number of vessels and craft for the JCG is 457 which include 134 patrol vessels and 238 patrol craft.[18]

Table 3.2 demonstrates that when compared with the CCG, the JCG suffers from substantial and increasing disadvantage in terms of total tonnage. Further, as the US Office of Naval Intelligence estimates, this tonnage differential also translates into ship numbers. Japan has approximately 53 large and 25 small vessels, totaling 78 whereas China has approximately 95 large and 110 small vessels, totaling 205.[19]

---

[17] Richard J. Samuels, "New Fighting Power!: Japan's Growing Maritime Capabilities and East Asian Security," *International Security* 32, no. 3 (Winter 2007/2008), 84–112.

[18] Japan Coast Guard, *Japan Coast Guard JCG: Justice and Humanity*, 3–6.

[19] Office of Naval Intelligence, *The PLA Navy: New Capabilities and Missions for the 21st Century*, 45.

Table 3.2 Total coast guard tonnage increases for Japan and China, 2010–2016

Country	Total tonnage (2010)	Total tonnage (2016)	Total tonnage increase
Japan	70,500	105,500	50% increase
China	110,000	190,000	73% increase

Source Lyle J. Morris, "Blunt Defenders of Sovereignty: The Rise of Coast Guards in East and Southeast Asia," *Naval War College Review* 70, no. 2 (Spring 2017), 78

Notably, the JCG's PLH-class cutters are only equipped with two Oerlikon 35–40 mm autocannon and two M61 Vulcan 20 mm six-barrel Gatling-style guns, compared with the 76 mm cannon on China's largest cutter, *Haijing* 3901.[20] In terms of aviation assets, the JCG has by far the largest fleet in the Indo-Pacific region, second only to the US Coast Guard in the world, boasting 31 fixed-wing aircraft and 52 helicopters, totaling 83.[21]

The JMSDF

The JMOD ensures security in territorial waters, airspace, as well as in the surrounding areas and conducts surveillance and reconnaissance activities therefor in surrounding sea areas. The JSDF is tasked with swiftly responding to various contingencies around Japan.

The JMSDF has a total of 114 warships and 45,800 volunteer personnel. It has a large fleet of fast, powerful destroyers, modern diesel-electric attack submarines, and amphibious ships that can transport tanks and other ground forces.[22] The National Defense Program Guidelines for FY2019 and beyond Annex Table outlined in Table 3.3 shows the JMSDF current and planned force structure.[23]

---

[20] Lyle J. Morris, "Blunt Defenders of Sovereignty: The Rise of Coast Guards in East and Southeast Asia," *Naval War College Review* 70, no. 2 (Spring 2017), 89.

[21] Japan Coast Guard, *Japan Coast Guard JCG: Justice and Humanity*, 8.

[22] Kyle Mizokami, "Sorry, China: Why the Japanese Navy Is the Best in Asia," *The National Interest*, October 16, 2016, http://nationalinterest.org/blog/the-buzz/sorry-china-why-the-japanese-navy-the-best-asia-18056.

[23] Ministry of Defense, *National Defense Program Guidelines for FY2019 and Beyond*, 33.

Table 3.3 Future JMSDF force structure outlined in the National Defense Program Guidelines for FY2019 and beyond

Category		Present	Future
Major units	Destroyer units	4 flotillas (8 divisions) 6 divisions	4 groups (8 divisions)
	Minesweeper units (Destroyer and minesweeper in future)	1 flotilla	2 groups (13 divisions)
	Submarine units	6 divisions	6 divisions
	Patrol aircraft units	9 squadrons	9 squadrons
Major equipment	Destroyers (Aegis-equipped)	54 (8)	54 (8)
	Submarines	22	22
	Patrol vessels	–	12
	Combat aircraft	Approx. 170	Approx. 190

Source Ministry of Defense, *National Defense Program Guidelines for FY2019 and Beyond*, December 18, 2018, 33

The JMSDF grew out of the MSA, and for its first four months, from April to August 1952, it was organized as the Maritime Security Force within the MSA.[24] The JMSDF has three primary missions: to defend Japan's maritime domain, to engage in noncombatant operations overseas (defense diplomacy), and to respond to call for search and rescue activities within Japanese territorial waters in case of maritime incidents.[25] Furthermore, surveillance activities are conducted with the flexible use of ships and aircraft as required. In addition, the Japan Ground Self-Defense Force (JGSDF) coastal surveillance units and JMSDF security posts conduct 24-hour surveillance activities in the major sea straits.[26] The JMSDF can step into conduct "maritime security operations" in support of the JCG according to Article 82 of the Self-Defense Forces Law.

[24] James E. Auer, *Postwar Rearmament of Japanese Maritime Forces, 1945–71* (New York: Praeger, 1973), chapter 5.

[25] Andrew L. Oros and Yuki Tatsumi, *Global Security Watch Japan* (Santa Barbara: Praeger, 2010), 60.

[26] Cabinet Secretariat, "Government Initiatives," *Office of Policy Planning and Coordination on Territory and Sovereignty*, https://www.cas.go.jp/jp/ryodo_eg/torikumi/torikumi.html.

North Korean Incursion Incidents

Because the JMSDF and the JCG are different in nature, there has not historically been a culture of close cooperation and coordination between the two institutions. However, this operational distance has gradually closed as Japan's maritime operational environment changed. Two incidents in 1999 and 2001 when suspicious North Korean boats entered Japanese territorial waters provided the initial impetus for closer operational coordination.

The 1999 Suspicious Boat Incursion[27]

On March 21, 1999, the Defense Intelligence Headquarters of the Japan Defense Agency (JDA, current JMOD) received information of two North Korean fishing boats leaving the port of Chongjin, known to be frequented by North Korean spy operations vessels. The two North Korean boats were disguised as Japanese fishing trawlers but did not have fishing nets and were bristling with an array of antennas. On March 22, JMSDF destroyers *Haruna*, *Miyako*, and *Abukuma* got underway. JMSDF P-3C patrol aircraft began precautionary surveillance off the Noto Peninsula in Northern Ishikawa prefecture of the central Japan and discovered the two North Korean suspicious boats in Japanese territorial waters on March 23. The area of incursion was off the coastal region where the abduction of Japanese nationals by North Korean agents reportedly took place in the 1970s and 1980s.

Generally, responses to suspicious boats are the chief responsibility of the JCG; however, it was deemed extremely difficult or impossible for the JCG to deal with the situation. The JCG vessels ordered them to halt and fired warning shots upon the boats, but they ignored and ran away. Early in the morning of March 24, orders were issued to the JMSDF to conduct "Maritime Security Operations" for the first time in the Japanese history.[28] The JCG patrol vessel took measures against

---

[27] Japan Coast Guard, *Kaijo Hoan Hakusho Heisei 12Nen Han* [海上保安白書 平成12年版: Japan Coast Guard White Paper 2000] (Tokyo: Japan Coast Guard, 2000), 51–53; Japan Coastguard, *Kaijo Hoan Report 2001* [海上保安レポート2001: Japan Coast Guard Report 2001] (Tokyo: Japan Coast Guard, 2001), 42–44; and Ministry of Defense of Japan, *Defense of Japan 2002* (Tokyo: Ministry of Defense of Japan, 2002), 124–131.

[28] Japanese Maritime Self Defense Force, *Precautionary Surveillance*, http://www.mod.go.jp/msdf/formal/english/surveillance/index.html.

the suspicious boat, including firing warning shots, but pursuit became difficult. For more the 24 h, the JMSDF ships and aircraft chased the two suspicious boats while firing warning shots and dropping explosive charges to persuade the two boats to stop. The military action marked the first time Japan has fired warning shots since 1953, when it intercepted a suspected Soviet submarine, and the first use of a 1954 law that allows the prime minister to call out the JMSDF to counter a naval threat.[29]

The pursuit of the two suspicious boats was called off when they crossed Japan's Air Defense Identification Zone (ADIZ), because, in general, out of ADIZ, further air defense capabilities are required. US satellite surveillance confirmed the two suspicious boats fled into the North Korean port of Chongjin. North Korea denied its involvement in the reported incident.

As this was the first time, the JMSDF formally carried out "Maritime Security Operations" a number of lessons were learned from this incident. These included the timing of orders, limited pursuit capability, and the lack of a common operational manual for mutual cooperation between the JMSDF and JCG. Based on these lessons, the JDA and the JSDF took the following action.[30]

First, in terms of developing capabilities equipment to deal with suspicious vessels, the JMSDF undertook the following initiatives:

1. Increased the speed of construction of a new-type missile patrol craft.
2. Established a new Special Boarding Unit organization.
3. Equipped destroyers with machine guns.
4. Furnished forcible maritime interdiction equipment (flat-nosed shells).
5. Improved manning to ensure crew availability.

Second, to strengthen cooperation with the JCG, the JDA and the JCG jointly developed the "Manual for Joint Strategies concerning Suspicious Boats" and delimited each role that they should play in taking action

---

[29] Sonni Efron, "Japan Gives Up Chase of Suspected N. Korean Spy Ships," *Los Angeles Times*, March 25, 1999, http://articles.latimes.com/1999/mar/25/news/mn-20861.

[30] Ministry of Defense of Japan, *Defense of Japan 2006* (Tokyo: Ministry of Defense of Japan, 2006), 175–176.

after suspicious boats are found and in taking action after an order for "Maritime Security Operations" is issued. The manual asserts that the JDA and the JCG shall jointly take the following actions to deal with suspicious boats.

1. *Liaison system*: The JDA and the JCG shall establish an appropriate communication system and shall communicate information about operations from initial to final stages in an appropriate manner.
2. *Joint operations before a maritime security operation order is issued*: The JCG shall initially deal with suspicious boats by dispatching necessary forces. The JMSDF shall cooperate with the JCG as required.
3. *Joint operations after a maritime security operation order is issued*: When an order for "Maritime Security Operations" is issued, the JMSDF shall take action to stop suspicious boats in cooperation with the JCG.
4. *Joint training*: The JDA and the JCG should conduct periodical mutual visits, information exchange, and joint training exercises. Also, according to the manual, the JMSDF should conduct joint exercises with the JCG, regarding communications and procedures to track and seize suspicious boats in order to strengthen their cooperation.

Third, the Japanese government made amendments to the Self-Defense Forces Law to respond to suspicious boats. Legislative reviews were conducted, which focused on the authority of use of weapons to stop suspicious boats. Following the reviews, the Self-Defense Forces Law was amended in 2001 to add the following provisions for the use of weapons in maritime security operations.

Despite repeated orders to stop the vessel for required inspection in maritime security operations, the crew of the vessel may refuse to follow the order or attempt to flee. In such a case and when the JDA determines that the incident meets certain requirements, JMSDF personnel engaged in such operations are allowed to use weapons within limitations considered reasonably necessary depending on the incident, provided that they have adequate and legitimate reasons to believe that they have no other means but to use weapons to stop the boat. This use of weapons will be considered to be a lawful act even when it results in injury to the crew of the boat.

The 2001 Suspicious Boat Incursion[31]

On December 22, 2001, a JMSDF P-3C patrol aircraft located a North Korean suspicious boat, disguised as Chinese fishing boat but without fishing gear, off Amami-Oshima in Kagoshima prefecture of the southern Japan, within Japanese Exclusive Economic Zone. The JMSDF and the JCG immediately dispatched vessels and planes. The JCG patrol vessel *Inasa* contacted and ordered the suspicious ship to stop for inspection. As the suspicious boat ignored the order, the *Inasa* fired warning shots into the air and sea. The JCG patrol vessel *Mizuki* joined and began to target the suspicious boat directly. This was the first time since 1948 that a JCG vessel took such action, and it did so in accordance with the Article 20, Paragraph 1 on the JCG Law revised based on the experience of 1999 North Korea suspicious boat incident.

As the JMSDF destroyer *Kirishima* and the JCG patrol vessel *Amami* joined the chase and approached, the suspicious boat opened fire with automatic weapons and anti-tank RPG launchers causing the *Inasa* and *Amami* to return fire in self-defense. The *Inasa* and *Amami* damaged the suspicious boat, which was scuttled to avoid capture. The clash was known as the battle of Amami-Oshima, and it resulted not only in the sinking of the North Korean boat but also the deaths of fifteen North Korean crewmembers.[32] The incident remains the largest Japanese maritime confrontation since the Pacific War and thrust the JCG and JMSDF into the spotlight as standing in the first line of defense for Japan.

Although the interoperability between the JMSDF and the JCG improved and each maritime force updated their response capability following the 1999 North Korean suspicious boat incursion, the 2001 incursion exposed the need for further improvements including the need for seamless operations and a better information exchange mechanism.

---

[31] Japan Coast Guard, *Kaijo Hoan Report 2003* [海上保安レポート2003: Japan Coast Guard Report 2003] (Tokyo: Japan Coast Guard, 2003), 24–31; Toso, Jugeki, Soshite Jibaku Amami-Oshima Kousakusen Jiken [「逃走、銃r、そして自爆 奄美大島工作船事件」: Flee, Exchange Fires, Scuttled: Suspicious Boat Incident off Amami-Oshima] *JIJI.COM News*, July 17, 2013, https://www.jiji.com/jc/v4?id=kosakuten0001; and Ministry of Defense of Japan, *Defense of Japan 2002*, 124–131.

[32] James Brooke, "Koizumi Calls for Vigilance After Japan Sinks Suspicious Boat," *The New York Times*, December 24, 2001, www.nytimes.com/2001/12/24/world/koizumi-calls-for-vigilance-after-japan-sinks-suspicious-boat.html.

Based on the lessons learned from the 2001 suspicious boat incursion, the JDA and the JSDF took the following action.[33] First, it strengthened the in-flight capability of P-3C patrol aircraft to transmit photos to JMSDF bases, as well as the JMSDF bases to make large data transmissions to the central command organizations. Second, it undertook share information on suspicious boats, though it may be uncertain, between the Chief Cabinet Secretary, the JDA and the JCG at the earliest possible time.

Third, it decided, as government policy, to dispatch JMSDF vessels at the earliest possible time to deal with possible spy ships, in order to mitigate against unexpected incidents. Fourth, it acquired accurate and long-range weapons.

CHINA'S GRAY-ZONE CHALLENGE

China is pursuing a "salami-slicing" strategy, and its actions look like an attempt to gradually and systematically establish legitimacy for its claims in the South China Sea. The goal of Beijing's salami-slicing would be to gradually accumulate, through small but persistent acts, evidence of China's enduring presence in its claimed territory.[34] James Kraska explains this approach as a form of "hybrid warfare," by which China uses fishing vessels in combination with paramilitary units such as CCG vessels to gain control of disputed territories.[35]

In the East China Sea, the government of Japan's purchase of three of the Senkaku Islands from their private Japanese owner on September 11, 2012, set off a diplomatic issue that continues today. By the end of 2012, CCG ships had intruded into Senkaku territorial waters 68 times since September 11, an unprecedented spike in intrusions from previous years.[36] Huge White said that it is clear that an armed clash between

---

[33] Ministry of Defense of Japan, *Defense of Japan 2006*, 176.

[34] Robert Haddick, "Salami Slicing in the South China Sea," *Foreign Policy*, August 3, 2012, http://foreignpolicy.com/2012/08/03/salami-slicing-in-the-south-china-sea/.

[35] James Kraska and Michael Monti, "The Law of Naval Warfare and China's Maritime Militia," *International Law Studies* 91 (2015), 450–467, https://stockton.usnwc.edu/cgi/viewcontent.cgi?article=1406&context=ils.

[36] Ministry of Foreign Affairs of Japan, *Trends in Chinese Government and Other Vessels in the Waters Surrounding the Senkaku Islands, and Japan's Response: Records of Intrusions of Chinese Government and Other Vessels into Japan's Territorial Sea*, December 13, 2018, http://www.mofa.go.jp/region/page23e_000021.html.

Japan and China over the Senkaku Islands is a real possibility.[37] The numbers of CCG ships intruded into Senkaku territorial waters decreased from 29 days 108 times in 2017 to 19 days 80 times in 2018. There was nothing in December 2018 for the first time.[38]

On August 6, 2016, an armada of 230 Chinese fishing boats, accompanied by 7 CCG vessels, was spotted near Japanese waters around the Senkaku Islands.[39] This could have been the starting point of a nightmare scenario for Japan in which Japanese islands are taken by armed Chinese fishermen backed by large CCG vessels and PLAN destroyers. As this incident made clear, China has the capability to inundate the Senkaku waters with government and civilian vessels in such a way as to greatly challenge the JCG's capability to respond.

Given Chinese maritime activities in Japanese waters, the JMSDF and the JCG are both on alert to counter Chinese actions in the East China Sea which might replicate its approach to the South China Sea. Greater interoperability between the JMSDF and the JCG is desirable. Japan's maritime security forces need the capability to prepare for and respond to these challenges at the minimum feasible level of escalation.

The specific challenges posed by the Chinese strategy of reactive assertiveness in the East China Sea are that it tends to blur the lines between law enforcement and warfare. Because Japan's security system strictly divides the civilian and military corps and activities, the country has struggled to adapt its institutions to this new reality.[40]

---

[37] Hugh White, "Asia's Nightmare Scenario: A War in the East China Sea Over the Senkakus," *National Interest*, July 5, 2014, http://nationalinterest.org/feature/asias-nightmare-scenario-war-the-east-china-sea-over-the-10805?page=3.

[38] Ministry of Foreign Affairs of Japan, *Trends in Chinese Government and Other Vessels in the Waters Surrounding the Senkaku Islands, and Japan's Response: Records of Intrusions of Chinese Government and Other Vessels into Japan's Territorial Sea*, December 13, 2018.

[39] "Japan Protests After Swarm of 230 Chinese Vessels Enters Waters Near Senkakus," *Japan Times*, August 6, 2016, https://www.japantimes.co.jp/news/2016/08/06/national/japan-ramps-protests-china-fishing-coast-guard-ships-enter-senkaku-waters/#.WkICOkxuLIU.

[40] Céline Pajon, "Japan's Coast Guard and Maritime Self-Defense Force in the East China Sea: Can a Black-and White System Adapt to a Gray-Zone Reality?" *Asia Policy* 23 (January 2017), 129.

However, as has been shown, the JMSDF and the JCG have improved their capabilities and enhanced their cooperation and coordination at the operational level through the experiences of 1999 and 2001 North Korean suspicious boat incidents. Additionally, in March 2016, the JCG inaugurated on Ishigaki Island a special unit dedicated to safeguarding the waters around the Senkaku Islands: 606 personnel, ten large 1500-ton patrol ships with 20 mm guns and water cannons, and two helicopter-equipped patrol vessels are now stationed on the small island, located only 170 km from the Senkaku Islands, where Naha is 410 km away. In addition to the twelve new ships based on Ishigaki, the Naha headquarters has six 1000-ton or larger patrol ships and one helicopter-equipped patrol vessel for other operations. With 1722 personnel in total, the 11th regional division is now the largest in Japan.[41] The JMSDF could be called on to conduct "Maritime Security Operation" if a foreign warship entered Japanese territorial waters for purposes other than innocent passage, if the JCG was outgunned, or if it became difficult for the JCG to deal with the matter.

FROM COOPERATION TO CONTRIBUTION

Céline Pajon proposed the next steps for closer cooperation between the JMSDF and the JCG. First, they could update their communication systems and secure channels. Second, the two fleets should share technology for fully integrated, comprehensive MDA (maritime domain awareness). Third, a common unified C4ISR (command, control, communication, computer, intelligence, surveillance, and reconnaissance) system is being developed to serve the three branches of the JSDF (Ground, Maritime, and Air). Plans should be made for a similar JCG upgrade. Fourth, the JCG and JMSDF need to engage in more joint exercises and training to ensure smooth joint operations should a "gray-zone" situation worsen.[42]

[41] "Japan Coast Guard Inaugurates Special Senkaku Patrol Unit," *Japan Times*, April 17, 2016; "Japan Coast Guard Deploys 12 Ships to Patrol Senkaku," *Japan Times*, April 4, 2016.

[42] Céline Pajon, "Japan's Coast Guard and Maritime Self-Defense Force: Cooperation among Siblings," *Maritime Awareness Project Analysis*, December 1, 2016, 4.

In response to the unpredictable and increasingly severe security environment, it is crucial to have both domestically and internationally enhanced cooperation for both the JMSDF and the JCG. Domestically, both the JMSDF and the JCG have continued to update their response capabilities and enhance interoperability based on the experiences of the 1991 and 2001 intrusions by North Korean boats.

Internationally, from now on, Japan should act more proactively for the regional maritime security issues with the following mind-set: from cooperation to contribution. This is necessary because the two Japanese maritime forces have limited resources, and partner countries in the Indo-Pacific region now also face "gray-zone" disputes in their sovereign waters.

Therefore, there is a good incentive to move beyond cooperation and toward contribution in cooperation with multilateral forces. It is the US-initiated North Pacific Coast Guard Forum (NPCGF) in 2000 stands out as an important success story with potential applicability to Southeast Asia. NPCGF brings together the coast guards of Canada, China, Japan, Russia, South Korea, and the United States for annual meetings, information sharing, and multilateral multi-mission exercises. Such a forum could go a long way toward promoting professionalism across coast guard fleets and perhaps lessen the use of some of the destabilizing tactics those coast guards have been employing.[43]

In 2005, the NPCGF published the Combined Operation Manual, which is very similar to the Code for Unplanned Encounters at Sea (CUES) in that it provides for voluntary safety, maneuvering, and communication procedures. As with the NPCGF, the Arctic Coast Guard Forum (ACGF) and the Western Pacific Coast Guard Forum (WPCGF) were formed to foster safe, secure, and environmentally responsible maritime activity in their region. All these forums likely would bolster current cooperation efforts in the region, including rules of behavior negotiations with the CCG.[44]

---

[43] Lyle J. Morris, "Blunt Defenders of Sovereignty: The Rise of Coast Guards in East and Southeast Asia," 104.

[44] Kevin Bruen, "Cooperate Through Coast Guards in the Western Pacific," *Proceedings*, Vol. 143/9/1, 375 (September 2017), 60.

Coordinating activities through a South China Sea Coast Guard Forum and conducting operations from US Coast Guard and regional maritime law enforcement vessels rather than US Navy vessels can mitigate these concerns. One option to address the lack of US Coast Guard capacity is for US Pacific Command to provide a Navy surface combatant to conduct patrols in the eastern Pacific with an embarked law enforcement detachment as a Coast Guard national security cutter carries out joint operations and exercises with South China Sea nations.[45] It is getting more important to have close cooperation between the Navy and law enforcement force in the Indo-Pacific region.

Due to the increase of piracy attacks in the seas around Somalia, on July 24, 2009, the government of Japan decided to participate in international counter-piracy initiatives and enacted "Act of Punishment and Countermeasures against Piracy," which criminalizes acts of piracy and enables Japan's naval vessels to protect any ship from pirates regardless of her flag. The JMSDF destroyers with the JCG officers on board have conducted operations to escort merchant ships to deter pirates in the Indian Ocean from March 2009. Apart from the direct threat of piracy to shipping, there is also a wider strategic context. Piracy has served the broader strategic interests of the great powers of Indo-Pacific region—the United State, Japan, India, and Australia as well as China. All these countries have sought to play a role in anti-piracy operations both off Somalia and in Southeast Asia in the Indo-Pacific region.

These regional practical forms should be considered as a prescription to reduce tension and build trust. These efforts stipulate the incentives from the cooperation to the contribution for creating rule-based regional order. They help maximize the multilateral capability and cooperation aiming to proactive contribution to the rule-based regional order.

Conclusion

Japan has long been a strong and active advocate for the rule of law in the seas and has contributed to capacity building efforts in the Indo-Pacific region. However, the security environment in the waters around

---

[45] Shawn Lansing, "The Coast Guard Can Reduce Risk in The South China Sea," *Proceedings*, Vol. 143/8/1, 374 (August 2017), 31.

Japan has become direr as China's maritime ambitions have resulted in the incursions into Japanese waters.

Prime Minister of Japan Shinzo Abe delivered an address at the Welcome Reception for the Coast Guard Global Summit on September 2017, "during this summit, you will reach a shared understanding on common values such as the free seas, and that strong unity will be established among the coast guard agencies. The common values and strong unity will become a motivating force, acting as a lighthouse that will guide you through the darkness."[46]

Japan needs to adopt a "whole of government" and "multilateral" approach for enhancing cooperation in maritime domain to ensure its security in the new regional context of "gray-zone" situations. The internal cooperation symbolized as "whole of government" approach will be activated through the enhanced relationship between the JMSDF and the JCG. The external cooperation symbolized as "multilateral" approach will be realized through the active participation of the United States and China.

Cooperation among maritime forces around the world is crucial in order to realize free and open waterways in the Indo-Pacific region. Japan must be prepared and feel comfortable operating in a shared command and control environment. The JMSDF and the JCG should have collective responsibility for maintaining maritime commons and supporting a rule-based order as active maritime security guardian.

---

[46] Prime Minister of Japan and His Cabinet, *Welcome Reception for the Coast Guard Global Summit*, September 12, 2017, https://japan.kantei.go.jp/97_abe/actions/201709/12article2.html.

CHAPTER 4

Establishing a Maritime Security Joint-Force Partnership Between the Republic of Korea Navy and the Korea Coast Guard

Sukjoon Yoon

This chapter examines how the Republic of Korea (ROK) can implement a maritime security joint-force partnership between the Republic of Korea Navy (ROKN) and the Korea Coast Guard (KCG). In doing so, it explores the nature of the current ROK navy-coastguard nexus and argues that this can be optimized for closer cooperation between the two services. Previous intermittent attempts at cooperation between the ROKN and the KCG have revealed significant structural and operational difficulties, leading to a gap between declared intentions about the advantages of a maritime security joint-force partnership and its actual implementation in real-world maritime security situations.

Since 2016, the debate about the ROK's navy-coastguard nexus has centered around the concept of *One National Fleet* (ONF). It has also become clear that significant disparities and differences of opinion exist between the ROKN and the KCG. A variety of issues and problems are pertinent to the process of establishing an effective maritime security

S. Yoon (✉)
Korea Institute for Military Affairs (KIMA), Seongnam City,
Gyeonggi Province, South Korea
e-mail: sjyoon6680@kima.re.kr

© The Author(s) 2019
I. Bowers and S. L. C. Koh (eds.), *Grey and White Hulls*,
https://doi.org/10.1007/978-981-13-9242-9_4

joint-force partnership, including: characterizing maritime security functions in the seas off the Korean Peninsula, where there is often ambiguity between war-fighting and peacetime roles and missions; adapting to recent and likely future changes in the type of maritime threats facing the ROK; determining who are the major actors affecting the maritime security commons, and the appropriate stance toward them; how should both the ROKN and the KCG adapt to the twenty-first-century maritime security environment, particularly in ambiguous contexts; and how best to formulate the shape and structure of a maritime security joint-force partnership between the ROKN and the KCG.

Problems Facing the ROKN and the KCG

The seas around the Korean Peninsula are subject to numerous problems, which are compounded by the lack of agreed maritime geographic boundaries. The semi-enclosed seas of the region have resulted in overlapping exclusive economic zones (EEZs), giving rise to conflicts with regional neighbors particularly over fishing rights. There is also the issue of the Northern Limit Line (NLL), the de facto maritime boundary between North Korea and the ROK. The NLL was unilaterally imposed by the United Nations Command (UNC) after the Korean War but not accepted by the North.[1] The United Nations Convention Law of the Sea (UNCLOS) is the dominant legal framework, but for the ROK significant ambiguities complicate the maritime security environment and therefore the operations of the ROKN and the KCG.[2]

The Korean Peninsula is technically still at war, because the Korean War ended with an armistice rather than a peace treaty. This has led to frequent naval skirmishes between the two Koreas in the vicinity of the NLL. Both the ROKN and the KCG are committed to full compliance with UNCLOS, but preserving maritime security entails complex and onerous challenges in dealing with daunting and multifaceted threats.[3]

---

[1] Republic of Korea Navy, *North Limit Line: De facto Maritime Boundary* (Kyeoyoungdae: March 26, 2011), 11–12.

[2] Korea Coast Guard, *Korea Coast Guard 2012 White Paper* (Incheon: KCG, 2012), chapter 1.

[3] Korea Coast Guard, *Korea Coast Guard 2013 White Paper* (Incheon: KCG 2013), chapter 1.

Moreover, they operate in the context of the so-called Joint Interagency Intergovernmental and Multinational (JIIM) environment, which obliges the ROKN and the KCG to take account of multiple stakeholders, including those of neighboring nations, beyond simply meeting their mission requirements of law enforcement and combat readiness in the seas around the Korean Peninsula.

There is also a structural problem between the ROKN and the KCG. During the Cold War, the relationship between the ROKN and the Korean Maritime Police (KMP, later replaced by the KCG on August 8, 1996) was limited to countering espionage attempts by North Korea. The KMP was subordinate to the Korean Police authority, and its primary role was concerned with homeland defense, to prevent North Korean activities intended to collect information and intelligence.[4] There was little scope for close maritime security cooperation between the ROKN and the KMP: the ROKN deployed its assets on the high seas for counter-infiltration operation, whereas the KMP focused on port patrols and onshore interdiction of North Korean espionage activities.

Since the end of the Cold War, however, and especially since the 1994 implementation of UNCLOS, maritime security missions have expanded beyond homeland defense, requiring both the ROKN and the KCG to conduct a much wider variety of operations.[5] They must now deal with Illegal, Unreported, and Unregulated (IUU) fishing, illegal immigration and smuggling, maritime pollution, search and rescue (SAR), and humanitarian assistance and natural disaster relief (HA/DR).[6]

The twenty-first-century maritime security environment requires the ROKN and the KCG to establish a new type of national security partnership between them: a capability-based cooperative joint-force relationship to protect the ROK's maritime rights and interests.

---

[4] Korea Coast Guard, *Korea Coast Guard 2014 White Paper* (Incheon: KCG, 2014), appendix.

[5] Seong-Jin Kim, "The Ocean, A New Territory of the 21st Century," *Dokdo Research Journal* 15 (Autumn 2011): 13–19.

[6] Commander Shawn Lansing, "The Coast Guard Can Reduce Risk in the South China Sea," *USNI Proceedings*, August 2017, 26–31.

Challenges in Establishing a Maritime Security Joint-Force Partnership Between the ROKN and the KCG

The unique maritime security environment in which they operate means that the ROKN and the KCG face very different challenges if they are to integrate their approaches and capabilities to prepare for a new kind of twenty-first-century maritime strategy.[7] There are three maritime security issues where the ROKN and the KCG diverge markedly: their perceptions of maritime threats, their disparate roles in far-sea and coastal environments, and the operational gaps between national defense operations and law enforcement operations.

First, the difference in threat perception stems from the Cold War era, when the infiltration by North Korean spy boats in the coastal littorals off the southern Korean Peninsula and North Korean incursions near the NLL posed a serious and continuous threat to national security.[8] Nowadays, however, a variety of new non-military maritime threats are emerging off the Korean Peninsula including: disputes over jurisdictional rights where EEZs overlap, proliferation of Chinese IUU fishing activities, increasing illegal immigration to South Korea, SAR and HA/DR requirements, and proliferation security intercepting materials relating to weapons of mass destruction. These are general challenges not only for the ROK's defense strategy, but also to its maritime security.

Second, traditional roles and capabilities need to change. The ROKN has generally been responsible for both near- and far-sea operations while the KCG has focused its substantial support force on operations in the littoral areas of the Korean Peninsula. Now that the KCG is also capable of far-sea operations, a degree of friction between the two organizations has arisen creating something of a turf war. The KCG is now slated to play a leading role in maritime security as the sole law enforcement enabler, and it is changing its emblem and the color of KCG cutters, to make them similar to those of US Coast Guard (USCG). This is part of the ambitious whole-of-government national maritime security strategy articulated by the 'Korean Maritime Power' slogan from the

---

[7] Republic of Korea Navy, *Navy Vision 2030* (Kyeoyoungdae: ROKN, 2008), 36.

[8] *The Korea Maritime News*, November 12, 2019, 10; *The Korea Maritime News*, November 18, 2018, 10.

administration of President Kim Young-sam. It will mean developing a cooperative relationship between the ROKN and the KCG that encompasses both military and non-military missions, working together as partners to address national security imperatives and provide maritime order and stability.

Third, there are poorly understood operational gaps between the ROKN and the KCG which pose a serious challenge to improving maritime security.[9] During the twentieth century, the ROKN deployed to frontline Areas of Responsibility to maintain deterrence while the KCG focused on coastal defense and managing fishing activities. This distinct history means that the two forces are now unprepared for joint maritime force operations or combined military/non-military maritime security missions because they have been used to dealing with dissimilar kinds of maritime threats, and also their command chains and bureaucratic hierarchies have become inflexible.[10]

COMMONALITIES AND DISPARITIES BETWEEN THE ROKN AND THE KCG

In the twenty-first century, maintaining the rule of law in the seas off the Korean Peninsula often requires a less provocative, but well-equipped law enforcement arm, and also necessitates maritime security coordination between the ROKN and the KCG. From the coastal littoral to the 200-mile EEZ, and in international waters where maritime zones overlap, law enforcement operations between the ROKN and the KCG make the seas safe in this era of globalization. The best example is their maritime security joint force tasked with implementing the UN Sanctions against North Korea.

If the ROKN and the KCG are to work effectively toward creating a special maritime security partnership in such a complex maritime environment, they will be able to take advantage of some commonalities, but they will also need to tackle some structural and operational disparities.

---

[9] Geoffrey Till, "Letter of the Law: Wresting with Law and National Interest," *Jane's Navy International*, November 2016, 14–19.

[10] *The Korea Maritime News*, October 29, 2019, 9.

There are some basic conceptual commonalities between the ROKN and the KCG which should facilitate joint maritime security operations. First, their administrative and bureaucratic systems provide a similar structure for their roles and missions and could facilitate a coordinated approach to dealing with ambiguous threats in ROK maritime domains. Second, their mission completion requirements are similar for military and non-military functions. Third, they share fundamental doctrines and operational rules of engagement and are equally committed to the rule of law. Finally, both services are also committed to enhancing relations with regional coastal states through maritime security confidence-building measures.

To credibly meet twenty-first-century maritime threats, both the ROKN and the KCG are currently acquiring new assets and platforms to enable effective long-endurance operations for a multiple and diverse roles and missions. These missions include controlling Chinese IUU fishing activities in the Yellow Sea, safeguarding national maritime sovereignty around Dokdo and Ieodo, ensuring the maintenance of international law, and contributing to regional and global maritime security. In line with a more cooperative maritime strategy, the ROKN is acquiring more forward-deployed naval assets, such as destroyers, frigates, corvettes, and fast patrol vessels; the KCG has also developed far-seas operational capacities in the form of 3–5000 ton cutters. The KCG needs to build experience of more complex maritime missions by expanding their maritime patrol operations to encompass intelligence gathering and conducting combined military/non-military missions together with the ROKN.[11] The ROKN's naval force improvement plan, *The Path Ahead, The Way to the Future* (2014), aims for extended multiple maritime security capability. The KCG's *2014 White Paper* proposed long-endurance maritime security capabilities to deal with intractable tensions and unpredictable non-military threats.[12] The current Joint Military Strategy

---

[11] There are very few publications on this problem between ROKN and KCG. However, similar issues between USN and USCG would be relevant case studies. See "Special Issue: Coast Guard," *USNI Proceedings*, August 2008; "Special Issue: Homeland Security," *USNI Proceedings*, October 2014.

[12] See Republic of Korea Navy, *The Path Ahead, The Way to the Future* (Gyeoyong City: ROK Navy HQ, 2014); Korea Coast Guard, *Korea Coast Guard 2014 White Paper* (Incheon, South Korea: Korea Coast Guard, 2014), chapter 14. Note that this is the most recent KCG White Paper.

for the ROK, issued by the Joint Chiefs of Staff, requires the ROKN to conduct joint maritime security operations with other services including security-related organizations such as the KCG; the ROKN has been hoping that the KCG will expedite joint maritime security cooperation with the ROKN.

There are, however, significant structural and operational disparities between the ROKN and the KCG. Even though the forging of much closer maritime security cooperation between them is now seen as a vital national security goal, the actual process of establishing common roles and missions for the ROKN and the KCG, which depends upon developing a shared conceptual framework, is far from straightforward.

At present, they have separate roles and missions, an essential aspect of which is that the ROKN is much more heavily armed than the KCG, which primarily functions as a maritime law enforcement agency. This separation has recently been blamed for some notable problems, the clearest case being the sinking of the civilian ferry *Sewol* in 2014 in a very narrow channel south of the Korean Peninsula. The ROKN and the KCG conspicuously failed to conduct timely and cooperative SAR operations. The sinking of the *ROKS Cheonan*, a corvette, and the North Korean artillery bombardment of Yeonpyeong Island (both incidents took place in 2010) are other examples where the two maritime security agencies failed to adequately deal with the complex maritime security situations which arise in the seas around the Korean Peninsula.[13]

THE CONCEPT OF THE ONF AND DISAGREEMENT BETWEEN THE ROKN AND THE KCG

The concept of ONF, comprising the ROKN and the KCG, was an important slogan originally proposed by ROK Chief of Naval Operations (CNO), Admiral Jung Ho-sup. It was meant to describe the concept of a single joint task fleet charged with protecting national defense and preserving maritime security, including ambiguous operations: sea control and denial, fisheries protection, enforcement of maritime agreements, implementation of embargoes and sanctions, SAR, HA/DR, anti-piracy, etc. ONF was first proposed at an academic seminar discussing maritime

---

[13] Captain David Ramassini, "Build a Great White Fleet for the 21st Century," *USNI Proceedings*, May 2018, 62–66.

cooperation, *Enhancing the National Maritime Security and Safety Capacities between the ROKN and the KCG*, co-hosted by the ROKN and the KCG, together with a private institution, the Korea Institute for Maritime Strategy (KIMS), on September 16, 2015.[14]

The requirements for joint-force maritime security operations between the ROKN and the KCG are generally acknowledged as particularly challenging, given the Korean Peninsula's complex maritime security situation. The KCG had initially appeared to suggest the emulation of the US conceptual model, based upon '*A National Fleet: A Joint Navy/Coast Guard Statement*' (March 2013), and its implementation document '*A National Fleet Plan Between the USN and the USCG*' (August 2015). These documents have been the main inspiration for discussions about the ROKN-KCG maritime security partnership.[15]

Thus, there was a seminar led by the ROKN that focused on adopting the US Navy(USN)-USCG concept for the '(One) National Fleet Plan.'[16] Also discussed was the 2015 framework for US Maritime Strategy involving the USN, Marine Corps, and Coast Guard, '*A Cooperative Strategy for 21st Century Seapower: Forward, Engage, Ready.*'[17] Following these discussions, in early August 2016 a joint policy document '*Memorandum on Policy Coordination for Strengthening the One National Maritime Power*' was signed by Admiral Jung Ho-sup, and the Commissioner-General of the KCG, Hong Ik-tae. This document was intended to specify how the various aspects of the 'One National Fleet Plan' between the ROKN and the KCG could be implemented. It covered the enhancement of joint maritime security operations and included steps toward achieving interoperability between the ROKN

---

[14] See Proceedings of the ROKN-KCG Maritime Security and Safety Cooperation Seminar *Enhancing the National Maritime Security and Safety Capacities Between the ROKN and the KCG*, held in Seoul, September 16, 2015.

[15] Commander Brain Smicklas, "Guard the Coast from High-End Threats," *USNI Proceedings*, February 2019, 44–49.

[16] Lieutenant Commander Kevin Duffy, "Indispensability Is Not Enough," *USNI Proceedings*, January 2017, 34–37.

[17] Captain Kevin Bruen, "Cooperative Through Coast Guards in the Western Pacific," *USNI Proceedings*, September 2017, 60–62.

and the KCG. Then, on September 12, 2016, the first-ever Navy-Coast-Guard Staff Talks were held, with a view to enhancing strategic and operational cooperation between the ROKN and the KCG. These talks discussed joint maritime security exercises and training operations, based on the US experience.

In practice, however, the ROKN and the KCG face significant conceptual constraints and differences which make operating a maritime joint force partnership more problematic when compared with the USA. During the September 16 seminar, it became clear that most aspects of the US model for joint maritime security cooperation were not relevant to the ROKN-KCG.[18] There are also significant differences in perception between the ROKN and the KCG which hinder the prospects for cooperation. The KCG is proving reluctant to progress the project, being suspicious that the ROKN's interpretation of a national maritime security strategic partnership relies upon the concept of the ONF. The most serious sticking point is the dominant role that the ROKN would hold in such an arrangement if the concept of a high-end ROKN-KCG maritime security partnership with similar principles and guidelines to those of the USN-USCG partnership was adopted.

The ROKN clearly expects to take ultimate charge of KCG assets in politically sensitive seas, especially near the NLL and the Korea-China Provisional Waters Zone (a fishing area in the Yellow Sea), since combat readiness is required in these areas where North Korean maritime threats are most likely. Moreover, in NLL littoral areas and on the high seas around the Korean Sea Lines of Communication (SLOC), the issue of whether the ROKN or the KCG should take the lead in safeguarding the ROK's maritime security is politically sensitive, with both seeking popular and presidential support: a quarrel which could potentially impede close coordination between the ROKN and the KCG.

---

[18]The USN-USCG model includes: refueling at sea, ports, waterways and coastal security, joint air operations and joint operational exercises, joint law enforcement operations, drug interdiction by submarines, international training, and joint naval exercises.

New Initiatives on the Practical Implementation of ONF Between the ROKN and the KCG

The concept of the ONF remains on the table for discussion between the ROKN and the KCG, but the formulation of a more practical maritime security joint-force partnership between the ROKN and the KCG will require a serious rethink.[19]

Korea needs to develop its own distinctive approach, rebalancing its maritime security joint-force composition to enable distributed-missions, cost-effective joint operations based on integrated capabilities and strategies, as well as facilitating international engagement.

First, the ROKN should recognize the KCG as a full national, international, and diplomatic partner: This will allow a more adaptive and interoperable maritime security joint-force composition. Also common standards for operational and diplomatic capabilities, tactics, techniques, procedures, and terminology must be agreed, so that any security joint task force operation, whether by a standing force or an ad hoc one, would not trip over its own bootlaces. In this regard, some recent interactions between the ROKN's three fleet commands and the KCG's regional district headquarters have demonstrated promising levels of cooperation between on-scene commanders, allowing an agile and flexible implementation of the concept of the ONF as put forward in 2016.

If an equal administrative status is granted to the ROKN and the KCG, they can become legal and operational partners beyond the sphere of maritime security. While a situation of technical war persists, the ROKN sometimes operates in ambiguous contexts which are not clearly distinguishable as war-fighting or peacetime situations, and this is a potential hindrance for future maritime security cooperation between the ROKN and the KCG. For this reason, the KCG is currently seeking legal changes to allow it to conduct maritime law enforcement missions as a more autonomous entity. In 2017, in response to the *Sewol* disaster of 2015, the KCG, then subordinate to the Ministry of National Safety and Public Affairs (NSPA), was formally disbanded and then re-established as an independent entity under the auspices of the Ministry of Ocean and Fishery Affairs (MOFA).[20]

---

[19] Lieutenant Commander Brooke Millard, "Innovative Thinking to Retain Women," *USNI Proceedings*, August 2018, 44–49.

[20] *The Korea Maritime News*, February 11, 2019, 1.

Second, the KCG's newly acquired capability to conduct distributed far-sea security missions should allow maritime security task forces between the ROKN and the KCG to be more practically useful. Heavily armed ROKN assets are not cost-effective for non-military maritime security missions, so the combatant commanders of ROKN's three district naval fleets will need KCG support to meet the new operational requirements of maritime security. The ROKN should therefore work with the KCG, endorsing its up-arming as independent maritime law enforcement operational partner. The KCG's well-equipped and well-designed new platforms can then deal with high seas patrols and operations, such as against Chinese IUU fishing vessels.

Since its re-establishment, the KCG has developed its own independent capacities for logistics, and for education and training. Under the leadership of Park In-young, a retired ROKN four-star Admiral, the KCG has significantly expanded its maritime security capability. A good example of distributed/interoperable functions between the ROKN and the KCG is a recent far-seas SAR operation in which the KCG 5000-ton *KCGS Sambong* provided close support to *ROKS Kwanggyeto the Great* (DDG 750) in the East Sea to assist a distressed North Korean vessel.[21]

Third, the ROKN should recognize that the KCG has an independent claim to national defense funding, as a maritime law enforcement agency, distinct from the ROKN's funding competition with the ROK Army and Air Force in the so-called Pie Game. For the ROKN and the KCG to implement a viable concept of ONF, whether as a standing force or for an ad hoc joint maritime security force, it must be an affordable, accountable, and reliable instrument of ROK's national maritime power.[22] By cooperating more closely both the ROKN and the KCG can play to their strengths. For example, the KCG is a more effective and adaptable instrument for controlling fishing areas near the NLL, namely the waters of the Five Islands off the west coast of the Korean Peninsula, where some Chinese vessels have been licensed by North Korea, whereas the ROKN stands ready to deal with any military incident with major national or international repercussions in the same area.

---

[21] Sukjoon Yoon, "Japan and South Korea's Unnecessary Squabble," *The Diplomat*, January 12, 2019, https://thediplomat.com/2019/01/japan-and-south-koreas-unnecessary-squabble/.

[22] *The Korea Maritime News*, December 24, 2018, 9.

Fourth, both the ROKN and the KCG are involved in various forms of regional and global international engagement, whether for national defense or multinational maritime law enforcement, and closer maritime security joint force cooperation between them will leverage the effectiveness of these forums. The ROKN conducts bilateral Navy-to-Navy staff talks with regional partners and also participates in multi-naval cooperation forums, such as the Western Pacific Naval Symposium (WPNS) and International Fleet Reviews. The KCG has various bilateral cooperative endeavors with neighboring Coast Guards and with ASEAN maritime security agencies and also takes part in multinational coast guard forums, such as the North Pacific Coast Guard Forum (NPCGF) and the Heads of Asian Coast Guard Agencies Meeting (HACGAM).[23]

International cooperation is also essential to enforce UNSC Resolutions against North Korea's illegal nuclear weapons and ballistic missiles. The ROKN is part of a multinational task force (together with the navies of the USA, the UK, France, Australia, New Zealand, Canada, and Japan) which monitors North Korea's illegal ship-to-ship fuel transfers: These violate inter-Korean cooperation agreements as well as UNSC sanctions. The US Coast Guard has recently sent an advanced modern national security cutter, *USCGC Bertholf* (WMSL-750), to the US 7th Fleet to enhance UNSC law enforcement capability in the East China Sea and the South Sea off the Korean Peninsula.[24] A modern Korean cutter, *KCG Lee Chang-ho*, conducted bilateral combined maritime security joint exercises with the *USCGC Bertholf*, comprising SAR, HA/DR, and maritime interdiction on the high seas off the Korean Peninsula, demonstrating the growing independence of the KCG and its capacity to deal with maritime security and national defense matters.[25]

---

[23] Korea Coast Guard, *Korea Coast Guard 2014 White Paper*, Part III; *The Korea Maritime News*, September 17, 2018, 9; and *The Korea Maritime News*, February 2019, 9.

[24] Ankit Panda, "US Sheds Light on Sanctions-Busting North Korean Ship-to-Ship Transfer Activities," *The Diplomat*, October 30, 2018, https://thediplomat.com/2018/10/us-sheds-light-on-sanctions-busting-north-korean-ship-to-ship-transfer-activity/; *Joongang Ilbo*, March 29, 2019, 1.

[25] Lee Cheongjae, "USCGC Bertholf in Seas off the Korean Peninsula," *Joongang Ilbo*, March 21, 2019, 10.

Fifth, the KCG is more independent and adaptable than the ROKN in the twenty-first-century maritime security environment. Since the recent détente between North and South Korea, and with progress toward peace and stability during 2018, maritime security now appears to be more relevant than military sea control. In 2019, President Moon announced his Korean Peninsula Peace Initiative as central to his National Security Strategy, and the KCG is now more adaptable and appropriate than the ROKN in responding to non-traditional threats.[26] Many security-related institutions in South Korea have started to focus more of their attention upon transnational threats, such as illegal fishing, environmental protection, refugee crises, energy security, and maritime security.[27]

There was a recent incident in which a Japanese Maritime Self-Defense Force (JMSDF) P-1 patrol aircraft intervened in a ROK joint SAR operation. The JMSDF subsequently claimed that the destroyer *ROKS Kwanggyeto the Great* had tracked the P-1 and locked its fire control radar onto it, protesting this as a hostile act. The KCG, however, was able to provide video evidence confirming that the P-1 had flown dangerously close to the destroyer. There followed an extended rift between the Japanese and ROK governments.[28] This shows how, when dealing with contentious issues and in sensitive seas, mission-completed cooperation between the ROKN and the KCG can prove invaluable.[29]

Although the ROKN and the KCG are proposing alternative strategies for any cooperative partnership between them, it is clear that due to recent changes in the maritime operational environment, the ROKN national defense roles and missions can usefully be supplemented by a broad range of the KCG's operational utilities and functions. In the twenty-first century, maintenance of maritime good order and security in the seas off the Korean Peninsula *requires* more joint-force cooperation: The relation between the ROKN and the KCG, instead of being led by the navy, should transition toward a coequal and complementary maritime security partnership.

[26] Blue House, *President Moon Jae-in's National Security Strategy* (Seoul: Blue House, 2019), preface.
[27] See contributor's op-ed articles in *The Studies of New Security Challenges* 193, no. 2 (Winter 2018).
[28] Sukjoon Yoon, "Japan and South Korea's Unnecessary Squabble".
[29] *Kookbang Ilbo* [Defense Daily], January 17, 2019, 2.

Some progress in this direction is ongoing. The KCG is expanding its backup capacity by enhancing its high seas maritime security operations, reducing the gap between its own and the ROKN's capabilities. The KCG is also constructing its own repair facilities and conducting its own education and training programs. And in February 2019, ROKN CNO Admiral Sim Seung-seob visited the headquarters of the ROK Coast Guard to consult with the KCG Commissioner-General Cho Hyun-bai, about closer cooperation on maritime security and defense.[30]

Conclusion

The ROKN nor the KCG should no longer see themselves as competitors. Instead, they should strive to become effective operational partners in maintaining maritime security, albeit with distinct perspectives and different histories, but both working toward common policy goals. In the challenging security environment of the seas around the Korean Peninsula, which is still technically in a state of war, but which also confronts many non-military threats, both the ROKN and the KCG will benefit from establishing a maritime security joint-force partnership.

Having recently enhanced its high seas capabilities, the KCG is well placed to complement some of the functions of the ROKN, and can provide considerable relief from the heavy burdens which the ROKN carries in conducting its current roles and missions. In its military function, the ROKN must maintain constant sea combat readiness and requires comprehensive war-fighting capabilities against North Korean maritime provocations. There is also much to be gained from a reassessment of the relationship between the ROKN and the KCG in terms of who should do what in implementing UNSC resolutions against North Korea.

The national interest would clearly be served by closer cooperation between the ROKN and the KCG, but there is significant disagreement between them. Each would prefer to take the credit, independently, for any non-military maritime security missions achieved, which stems from a fundamental culture clash between the Army-influenced attitudes of the ROKN and the police force mentality of the KCG. This results in an unfortunate tussle for independent control over manpower and budgets which reflects little credit upon the inner circles of either institution.

---

[30] *Kookbang Ilbo* [Defense Daily], February, 19, 2019, 6.

In dealing with emergent maritime threats, there are obvious advantages to having a single coherent unified command and control structure. And though the ROKN and the KCG disagree on some particularly charged issues, they also agree on many points, so that with goodwill, and with further diligent efforts, it should be possible to build an effective maritime security partnership between them. Some progress has already been made toward the establishment of a joint maritime security task fleet by integrating their capacities at the operational level for non-executive military missions.

The concept of ONF is the central organizing principle guiding the process of how two distinct maritime security entities, one with a primary military function and another as a constabulary instrument of maritime law enforcement, can broaden and deepen their cooperation, so that each can play to their strengths without getting hung up on structural, operational, or cultural differences. Some lessons can be learned from the US experience of the USN-USCG maritime security partnership, and perhaps from some other Asian coastal states, but the seas around the Korean Peninsula are not like anywhere else and only by resolving their differences can the ROKN and the KCG create a maritime security joint-force partnership for the twenty-first century which this uniquely challenging security environment requires.

PART II

Southeast Asia

CHAPTER 5

Navy-Coast Guard Emerging Nexus: The Case of Vietnam

Truong-Minh Vu and The Phuong Nguyen

The Vietnam Coast Guard (VCG) has been significantly rising as the new vanguard of Vietnam's maritime sovereignty against aggressive external forces. Its development and modernization in the last couple of years are unprecedented, especially in terms of capabilities and physical strength. In just a few years, the VCG has grown up remarkably from a force with just a few small and second-handed vessels in its service to a force whose rank at the moment is second to none in Southeast Asia in terms of both the number of vessels and overall capabilities. Recent incidents also showed to the public an increasing presence of a law enforcement service that was previously unknown in the country's geo-strategic mindset.

Understanding this remarkable development and modernization of the VCG, as well as other components of Vietnam's maritime security forces, is essential in order to comprehend the future maritime security strategy of Vietnam, in the context of increasing Chinese encroachment and assertiveness in the South China Sea. China's pursuit of "gray zone revisionism" in the South China Sea has revealed

---

T.-M. Vu · T. P. Nguyen (✉)
Center for International Studies (SCIS),
University of Social Sciences and Humanities,
Ho Chi Minh City, Vietnam

© The Author(s) 2019
I. Bowers and S. L. C. Koh (eds.), *Grey and White Hulls*,
https://doi.org/10.1007/978-981-13-9242-9_5

Beijing's desire for regional hegemony to gain control of specific resources and counterbalance, and eventually replace, US geopolitical preeminence in maritime East Asia.[1] Gray zone strategies and its subsequent impact have created new challenges as well as opportunities for the VCG to redefine and adjust itself to a new operational paradigm and security environment that is brand new and constantly changing. This chapter has the intention to explain the establishment as well as the modernization of the VCG, its adaptation to the new security environment where coercive gradualism is excessively exploited by a "moderate" revisionist power and the current problems it is facing to fulfill particular conventional strategic objectives and to pursue other secondary roles in protecting Vietnam's sovereign waters.

In the first section of this chapter, we will review the VCG's modernization process since 2010. This process officially took off late after the service was established around 1998, due to the country's complicated maritime security environment. Since then, the VCG has improved significantly in terms of both quality and quantity with the deployment of several new domestic constructed vessels, some of which displace between 2000 and 3000 tons. This time also marks the formation of an integrated network of security partnerships between Vietnam and other regional powers, through which the VCG has hugely benefited by admitting into service dozens of coast guard vessels acquired through foreign assistances. Also, in this section, the main responsibilities of the VCG are highlighted.

Section "Vietnam's Maritime Security Strategy and the VCG" analyzes the important position of the VCG in Vietnam's overall maritime security strategy, juxtaposed with that of the Vietnam People's Navy (VPN). This section shows that the VCG has become an important element of Vietnam's maritime strategy in the context of growing naval asymmetries between China and Vietnam in the dispute over the South China Sea, both in peacetime and in wartime scenarios. The tight cooperation between the two services is the key component of a

---

[1] See, for example, Nayan Chanda, "China's Long-Range Salami Tactics in East Asia," *Huffington Post*, January 27, 2014; John Chen, "Get Comfortable Being Uncomfortable: Uncertainty, Brinkmanship, and Salami-Slicing in East Asia," *Georgetown Security Studies Review*, February 1, 2015.

Vietnamese way to counter China's coercive gradualism threatening the country's maritime rights and interests. Coming up with such a strategic approach would not only help Vietnam effectively protect its interests, but it could also potentially contribute to our understanding of the literature of "gray zone strategies."

The last section tries to build up some insights about the obstacles the VCG is currently facing in its modernization efforts. Those hurdles are both subjective and objective, thus require careful consideration and discussions from which meaningful solutions can be drawn out. Similar to their naval counterpart, the lack of resources and inadequate policies are the two main reasons hindering modernization.

THE VIETNAM COAST GUARD: THE RISE OF A NEW SERVICE

In November 2016, the *Coast Guard Journal* was officially announced as a forum for officials and scholars to exchange their ideas and initiatives about the future operation and administration of the VCG. This journal has also become the first channel where academic writings from researchers both inside and outside the ranks of the VCG could be widely published and discussed. The birth of the *Coast Guard Journal* was one step further in an attempt to build up a "revolutionary, professional and modern" VCG.[2] This was also an indicator suggesting the rising importance of the VCG in Vietnam's overall maritime strategy, the youngest branch of the Vietnam People's Army (VPA), which was first set up in 1998. Falling under the direct management of the Ministry of National Defense (MoND), the VCG has been playing an important role in maintaining security and stability in the vast exclusive economic zone and continental shelf of the country.

The VCG was first established through then President Tran Duc Luong's order on April 7, 1998, announcing the Ordinance on the VCG, which had been accepted by the Tenth National Assembly of Vietnam on March 28, 1998. Previously, Vietnam did not have any dedicated coast guard. It was the VPN at the time that conducted offshore

---

[2] Canhsatbien.vn, *Ra mắt Tạp chí Cảnh sát biển Việt Nam* [*Coast Guard Journal* Officially Launched], November 15, 2016, http://canhsatbien.vn/portal/cong-tac-canh-sat-bien/ra-mat-tap-chi-canh-sat-bien-viet-nam. Accessed January 1, 2019.

patrol and related military activities, along with the Vietnam Border Defense Force, which has checkpoints in estuarine and littoral areas. In its early days, the VCG faced many problems including the lack of financial and human resources, inadequate infrastructure and equipment along with the huge range of missions it had to execute. According to retired colonel Ho Minh Giap, the first commander of the VCG, there were only 34 personnel in the very beginning who were deployed to just two coast guard regions with almost no barracks, vessels or ports.[3]

Facing immense difficulties in its early days, the VCG since then has improved in terms of both quality and quantity. Since 2010, more resources were invested in the VCG in order to enhance its overall strength in the context of increasing Chinese assertiveness in Vietnamese waters and Beijing's strategy of using "white hulls." This particular year also marked an increase of China's intrusion into Vietnam's waters in the South China Sea, through clashing with Vietnamese law enforcement agencies or harassing Vietnamese fishermen. Besides, non-traditional security issues have also arisen, such as piracy, sea robberies and other transnational maritime crimes, requiring the presence of a more robust, effective and modern VCG in sovereign waters.

It is not a myth to conclude that China's use of gray zone strategy in the disputed South China Sea waters is the main reason behind the rapid modernization of the VCG.[4] The never-before-seen improvement and growth of China's coast guard and its deployment of a sizeable maritime militia have set up a new security paradigm not just in the South China Sea but also in maritime East Asia. Besides the navy and the paramilitary forces, China's permissive attitude toward its fishing fleet has also played a role in complicating the security environment.[5] We will mention in more details about China's strategic maritime mindset and its gray zone

---

[3] Vietnamnet.vn, *Gặp tư lệnh đầu tiên của cảnh sát biển VN* [Meet the First Commander of the Vietnam Coast Guard], May 22, 2014, http://vietnamnet.vn/vn/tuanvietnam/gap-tu-lenh-dau-tien-cua-canh-sat-bien-vn-176696.html. Accessed January 1, 2019.

[4] Green, Michael, eds., *Countering Coercion in Maritime Asia: The Theory and Practice of Gray Zone Deterrence* (Washington, DC: Rowman, May 2017).

[5] Hongzhou Zhang and Sam Bateman, "Fishing Militia, the Securitization of Fishery and the South China Sea Dispute," *Contemporary Southeast Asia* 39, no. 2 (August 2017): 288–314.

strategy, as well as Vietnam's effort in searching for a countermeasure, in the next part. However, there is also another important motive behind the rise of the VCG: the Vietnamese strategic shift to the ocean as a new environment to sustain the country economic growth, accompanied by the mentality and strategic objective of keeping the surrounding environment as peaceful as possible for decades to come.

Although not regarded as a security strategy, the *Resolution on Vietnam Maritime Strategy to 2020*, with the goal of turning Vietnam into a prosperous country that benefited from the sea, set the principles for the Vietnamese people to look outward into the sea for their future economic prosperity. Main objectives include raising the contribution of the marine economy to 53–55% of the economy or improving the standard of living of coastal residents up to two times compared to the general living standards of the people who do not live in coastal areas and islands.[6] In the 8th Plenum of the 12th Party Central Committee in October 2018, the new *Resolution on Vietnam Maritime Strategy to 2030, with the vision to 2045*, was officially announced, continuing to emphasize turning Vietnam into "a strong maritime country, enriched by the sea, relying on and looking towards the sea."[7] Similar to the previous Resolution, the new one focuses most of its attention on the economic realm and sets up the overall strategic guidelines for the development of maritime economy in Vietnam. Although it is not a security strategy, the new Resolution mentions briefly the missions of Vietnam's armed forces, emphasizing the protection of the nation's sovereignty and the pro-active policies of enlarging the cooperation between Vietnam and other maritime countries in the region.[8]

---

[6] Vietnamnet.vn, *Challenges for Vietnam Sea Strategy*, August 10, 2016, http://english.vietnamnet.vn/fms/business/161811/challenges-for-vietnam-sea-strategy.html. Accessed January 1, 2019.

[7] Nhân Dân Online, *Xây dựng nước ta mạnh và giàu từ biển* [Building Our Country into a Strong Maritime Nation, enriched by the sea], http://www.nhandan.com.vn/cuoituan/item/37908602-xay-dung-nuoc-ta-manh-va-giau-len-tu-bien.html. Accessed January 1, 2019.

[8] See more of the contents of this Resolution at *Nguoi Lao Dong* Newspaper, Nghị quyết trung ương 8 về chiến lược phát triển kinh tế biển [The 8th Plenum Resolution on Maritime Economic Development Strategy], https://nld.com.vn/thoi-su/nghi-quyet-trung-uong-8-ve-chien-luoc-phat-trien-kinh-te-bien-20181025082833366.htm. Accessed December 1, 2019.

In 2013, the Vietnam Marine Police was officially renamed as VCG; the Bureau of Marine Police was changed to Coast Guard Command; and the Chief of the Bureau became Coast Guard Commander.[9] Additionally, each coast guard region also had its own command indicating that the regions would now have their own autonomy in dealing with various incidents at sea. These changes in name and organizational structure marked the beginning of a new wave of investment from the state aimed at turning the VCG into an internationally recognized and capable force, not only able to protect the country's maritime rights and interests, but also to promote international cooperation and trust building approach.

Until 2016, the VCG has in its service more than 50 vessels of different classes, ranging from light vessels such as the 120-ton *TT-120* class patrol vessel to the giant 2900-ton *H-222* class replenishment/transport vessel.[10] VCG also operates 3 CASA C-212 patrol aircraft. The backbone of the VCG's fleet comprises four 2000-ton *DN-2000* offshore patrol vessels, which were built by domestic shipyards with technical support from DAMEN group. More vessels of this class will be commissioned in the near future. It is also worth noting that a brand-new class of vessel, codenamed *DN-4000*, which could displace around 4000 tons, will be soon under construction. When deployed, this class will be the largest coast guard vessel in Southeast Asia. Currently, most of the VCG's vessels are constructed by domestic shipbuilders, and this trend will definitely carry on as domestic shipbuilding capabilities continue to be improved.

Additionally, as the relationship between Vietnam and other countries has been strengthening in recent years, especially in security and military affairs, more international donors are willing to give the VCG second-hand vessels. For instance, Japan and South Korea already

---

[9] *Tien Phong Newspaper*, Đổi tên cục cảnh sát biển thành Bộ tư lệnh Cảnh sát biển [Bureau of Marine Police Was Changed to Coast Guard Command], http://www.tienphong.vn/xa-hoi/doi-ten-cuc-canh-sat-bien-thanh-bo-tu-lenh-canh-sat-bien-643382.tpo. Accessed January 1, 2019.

[10] Soha.vn, *Nghiệm thu tàu vận tải đa năng lớn nhất của Cảnh sát biển VN* [Acceptance of the Largest Multirole Transport Ship of Vietnam Coast Guard], http://soha.vn/nghiem-thu-tau-van-tai-da-nang-lon-nhat-cua-canh-sat-bien-vn-20160508103035773.htm. Accessed January 1, 2019.

transferred to the VCG several of their old ships. Cooperation with the US in this particular area has also shown signs of great potential, when Washington provided 18 Metal Shark high-speed boats to the VCG. The US would also aid in training as well as provide other necessary equipment, such as the Long Range Acoustic Device (LRAD) equipping the *DN-2000* vessels.[11]

In 2017, through the Excess Defense Articles (EDA) program agreed under the then Barack Obama administration, the VCG added its largest vessel to date: a 3250-tons, refurbished former US Coast Guard *Hamilton*-class cutter which now has a new codename CBS-8020. Additional two vessels of this class are rumored to be delivered to the VCG in the next few years through a negotiating process currently underway. It is noteworthy that the VCG replaced the Phalanx close-in weapon system (CIWS) previously installed in the vessel with its own Soviet-made ZU 23-2 autocannon (this Vietnamese version of ZU 23-2 is modified by Israel and licensed to Vietnam for mass-production, enhanced with CONTROP-iSEA day/night observation/payload systems). The year 2017 is also considered the most prolific year for the VCG in terms of expanding its fleet. Vietnam has constructed eight vessels, received one from South Korea and six from Japan. From 2018 to 2020, it is estimated that the VCG is going to acquire more large vessels from the US, South Korea and Japan due to the rising maritime cooperation between Vietnam and those countries.[12] Vietnam has also signed a contract with Poland for six additional search-and-rescue vessels with a total value of 235 million USD.[13]

In November 2018, Vietnam's National Assembly passed the new Coast Guard Law, in which the definition and the roles of the VCG are clarified. Similar to other coast guards around the world, the VCG has

---

[11] Soha.vn, *Khám phá vũ khí đặc biệt của Mỹ trên tàu cảnh sát biển Việt Nam* [See More About the New US's Equipment on Vietnam Coast Guard Vessels], http://soha.vn/quan-su/kham-pha-vu-khi-dac-biet-cua-my-tren-tau-canh-sat-bien-viet-nam-20140102234623671.htm. Accessed January 1, 2019.

[12] Baodatviet.vn, *Những tàu tuần tra Việt Nam có thể nhận năm 2018* [Patrol Vessels That Vietnam Can Possibly Receive in 2018], http://baodatviet.vn/quoc-phong/quoc-phong-viet-nam/nhung-tau-tuan-tra-csb-viet-nam-co-the-nhan-nam-2018-3350455/. Accessed January 13, 2019.

[13] Ibid.

three basic responsibilities. First, the VCG plays a role in protecting the lives and safety of the Vietnamese citizens, whether in natural disasters or man-made catastrophes. Especially, given the Resolution on Vietnam Maritime Strategy to 2030, the VCG will advance the safety of recreational and commercial activities in the maritime domain, using prevention or response programs.

Second, the service has the responsibility to maintain and protect Vietnam's maritime sovereignty, which means exerting and safeguarding the country's internal waters, ports and waterways, and littorals and other important national interests in the South China Sea. The 2018 Coast Guard Law also gives the service unprecedented flexibility to operate in the seas. For instance, the bill allows VCG's personnel to open fire to warn ships illegally operating in Vietnam's waters.[14] The third responsibility, which is unique to coast guard service in general, is to ensure the balanced and sustainable use of coastal and ocean waters and resources. The service would deploy various means to protect the marine environment against pollution, environmental degradation and illegal harvesting of marine resources. Marine resources and environmental protection roles are basic staples of coast guards, something that navies would prefer not to take on as their daily activities.

Nevertheless, we are not clear about how these flexibilities can be translated into real operational maneuvers. The 2018 Coast Guard Law indeed gives an official declaration about the roles of the VCG, but it still cannot deliver any information about the service's operational guidelines, especially regarding how other services such as the VPN will play into all of this. In the next part, we will try to elaborate the relationship between these two important services of the Vietnamese armed forces in the context of current strategic challenges.

Vietnam's Maritime Security Strategy and the VCG

Regarding the second responsibility, we argue that the VCG has become an important element of Vietnam's maritime strategy in the context of growing naval asymmetries between China and Vietnam in the South

---

[14] Prashanth, Parameswaran, "Why Vietnam's New Coast Guard Law Matters," April 14, 2018, https://thediplomat.com/2018/04/vietnam-coast-guard-in-the-spotlight-with-new-law/. Accessed January 1, 2019.

China Sea. These "asymmetries" could be regarded as tactics helping weaker naval forces, which have inferior conventional combat power and technologies, ineffectively prevailing against a more technologically advanced opponent, both tactically and strategically. The main rationales of asymmetric tactics are to "avoid the strengths and exploit the vulnerabilities" of the larger opponents, by that "weakening the adversary's resolve and ability to use its superior conventional military capability effectively to intervene" in potential conflicts.[15]

However, the asymmetric approach is just one side of a coin to understand what Vietnam is doing at the moment to prepare for a potential conflict with China in the South China Sea. A wartime strategy of "asymmetry" has to be coordinated with a peacetime "anti-gray zone" approach, which goes hand in hand with a careful calculation of the balance of force and the balance of power within the bigger maritime East Asia. Therefore, close cooperation between the VCG and the VPN is important in executing a coherent and comprehensive maritime security strategy for Vietnam in the contested waters with the overall objective of deterrence against a potential conflict as well as coercive gradualism in its territorial waters.

Asymmetrical Wartime Doctrine

Open warfare is the least expected scenario that Vietnamese strategists can think of, but nothing can be ruled out. The rapid modernization of the VPN has been considered as, first and foremost, turning the service into a credible deterrent tool in peacetime to make adversaries think twice before commencing any preemptive strike. However, in case war really breaks out, the VPN always has to prepare to counter enemies in a real naval battle at a time when advanced technologies in all fields would be deployed. Therefore, the wartime strategy of Vietnam's maritime security forces will evolve around an asymmetric doctrine with the VPN as its core. The VPN is no doubt the core element of the overall maritime security strategy, especially in wartime, through which it has been receiving lots of investment. The VPN has been able to produce

---

[15] K. C. Dixit, 2010, *The Challenges of Asymmetric Warfare* (Institute for Defense Studies and Analyses), http://www.idsa.in/idsacomments/TheChallengesofAsymmetricWarfare_kcdixit_090310. Accessed January 1, 2019.

the P5 Pyatyorka/Shaddock anti-ship missiles with an effective range up to 550 km (after upgrade). Previously, Vietnam was the only country in the world receiving this kind of missile as part of military assistance packages from the Soviet Union. The most significant step in modernizing its coastal defense force was the VPN's purchase of two sets of K-300P Bastion-P coastal defense systems with a 300 km range, capable of protecting a total of 600-km length of coastline. Additionally, the VPN is equipped with the CW-100 radars from Thales, designed for monitoring the coastline and capable of conducting "over-the-horizon" tasks.[16]

According to various defense sources and from the Stockholm International Peace Research Institute (SIPRI), Vietnam has received two more new weapon systems for its coastal defense force, including the mid-range EXTRA missile system from Israel and possibly the close-range Bal-E system from Russia, which uses Kh-35 Ural-E missile, the similar type of missile used by *Molniya*-class FACs and *Gepard*-class frigates of the VPN. Russian Tactical Missiles Corporation JSC (KTRV) announced that Vietnam is the second country, after Russia, to possibly receive the Bal-E system.[17]

The firing range of the EXTRA system is up to 150 km with a very low circular error probability (CEP) at only around 10 meters. This means that EXTRA is a highly accurate missile system. In addition, the EXTRA rockets are capable of launching from a variety of means, assembled in clusters of 2–16 launch tubes. Cluster launch tubes can be mounted on trucks or in highly mobile battlefield fixed. These missiles are contained in airtight containers, which possess a long shelf life and reduce maintenance costs. As we can acknowledge from these developments, VPN's coastal defense force can cover a wide range of protection, thus plays an indispensable role in preventing any amphibious intrusion from the sea.

---

[16] Soha.vn, *Uy lực mắt thần canh biển tối tân của Việt Nam* [The Power of Vietnam's Modern Sea-Watching Radar], http://soha.vn/quan-su/uy-luc-mat-than-canh-bien-toi-tan-cua-viet-nam-20130318175716398rf20130318175716398.htm. Accessed January 1, 2019.

[17] Soha.vn, *Nga trình diễn tổ hợp tên lửa bờ Bal-E cho Việt Nam* [Russia Presents Bal-E Missile System to Vietnam], http://soha.vn/quan-su/nga-trinh-dien-to-hop-ten-lua-bo-bien-bale-cho-viet-nam-20130816013928958.htm. Accessed January 1, 2019.

Another element of the "asymmetric tactics" is the *Molniya/Tarantul* fast attack craft (FAC), which Vietnam currently has 10 vessels in its service (including six *Molniya*-class and four older *Tarantul*-class). The *Molniya*-class FAC has high speed, powerful weapons, which is suitable for surprising "hit and run" tactics initiated from various directions that the opponents could not able to respond effectively.

This tactic is best used in an environment where there are numerous small islands and estuaries spreading along a long coastline, providing places for warships to hide and facilitate ambush and later retreat under the protection of defense platforms such as coastal defense missiles. Vietnam has also mastered the technology to build the *Molniya*-class FAC based on technology transfer from Russia. The main armaments of this class are 16 Kh-35 Ural-E anti-ship missiles with firing range of 130 km that Vietnam has successfully localized with the codename KCT-15. Thus, if the information of Vietnam acquiring the Bal-E system is correct, the KCT-15 missiles could also be used by this system.

According to Professor Carl Thayer of the Australian Defense Force Academy, Vietnam's asymmetric tactics targeting China aims to prevent Beijing deploying its warships in case low-intensity conflicts break out.[18] It means that warships of the VPN are deployed to protect paramilitary ships operating around Vietnam's islands. "Asymmetric" weapon systems render Chinese navy's activities within the distance of 200–300 nautical miles from the coastline of Vietnam dangerous.

What is the role of the VCG in the scenario of open warfare? The most important task of an asymmetrical doctrine is to deny enemy's forces to take control of the waters around strategic choke points in the South China Sea or important sea lines of communication (SLOCs). However, a key question regarding the VPN is how does an asymmetric strategy, which essentially relies on cost imposition, prevent an enemy from controlling SLOCs or distant chokepoints which many could not be in the VPN's area of responsibility (AOR)? This question is hard to concretely answer at the moment, because we do not have enough information on the detailed tactical and strategic planning of the VPN regarding the issue. However, given the current modernization trajectory,

---

[18] Thayer Carl, "Can Vietnam's Maritime Strategy Counter China?" *The Diplomat*, 2014, http://thediplomat.com/2014/09/can-vietnams-maritime-strategy-counter-china/. Accessed February 23, 2017.

at least the VPN is trying its best in order to have a comprehensive response and sound anti-access/area denial capabilities within its current AOR (which possibly extends beyond the waters of the Spratlys and Paracels but still within the boundary of the South China Sea). It is definitely the VPN's missions to deal with the conventional aspects of war, but the service at the moment still does not have enough capabilities to cover the vast territorial waters under its protection. The Navy simply has too few ships, aircraft and armaments for a vast AOR. The VCG therefore would represent the go-to guarantor of security of the less important strategic points to relieve the Navy of such tasks. Basically, the VPN would provide a backstop should serious conflict erupt. But coast guard commanders would need the capabilities and will to hold their own against rival forces until reinforcements arrived. The ultimate outcome if a naval conflict breaks out is not to "win" in its literal meaning but rather to inflict as much damage as possible to the enemy in order for the political and diplomatic channels to maximize their voices in international arena against the "aggressor." It is in this context that the role of Vietnam's armed forces and other forces relating to maritime security is just parts of a bigger and more comprehensive grand strategy to protect the country's "sacred" sovereignty.

Wartime scenarios require close working relations between the VCG and other services of Vietnam's armed forces, especially the navy. For the VPN to concentrate on their various conventional tasks and missions, the VCG would have the capable assets and equipment to deploy and conduct joint operations in support of the most critical needs required in the battlefield. These could include:

- *Maritime interception/interdiction operations*: The VCG could play a role in naval operations aim to delay, disrupt or destroy enemy forces or supplies en route to the battle area before they inflict any damage against friendly forces. This mission could be more legitimately given to the VCG due to its paramilitary nature and its possession of various heavy vessels and because the enemies could use civilian vessels to conduct logistic missions.
- *Port operations, security and defense*: Vietnam has numerous ports, both military and commercial, in strategic locations not just along its long coast but also in the Spratlys. Protecting these ports against possible intrusion would be important, as those are the main logistic hubs for any successful operations of the navy in wartime.

- *Coastal sea control operations:* This mission covers a larger geographical area than port operation, and it is very vital in wartime scenarios because of the importance of protecting the coastal towns or cities against harassment or penetration from enemies' special forces or enemies' intelligence, surveillance and reconnaissance (ISR) assets. Exerting coastal sea control is also an important task in preventing the enemies from conducting surprised amphibious landing on strategic choke points.
- *Rotary-wing air intercept operations:* Although the VCG at the moment does not possess a true aviation branch of its own, the future modernization trajectory and operational requirement suggest that it is just the matter of time the service can officially establish its own air wing. In joint-operation wartime scenarios, the role of the VCG's air wing could be essential in providing useful ISR information, alongside the Vietnam People's Air Force (VPAF) and the air wing of the VPN. It is possible that all of these forces will be put under a joint command in wartime scenarios.

Anti-gray Zone Peacetime Doctrine

China's aggressive behavior within the boundary of its so-called second ring of security has clearly pointed out that it is actively changing its geo-strategic mindset from that of a continental power to a maritime power.[19] Although obviously seeking to replace the US geopolitical preeminence in Asia, bearing characteristics of a revisionist power, China's aggression within the First Island Chain is strictly bounded by several factors. Economic interdependence does not allow China to pursue any desire to challenge global economic institutions or create spiraling new regional instability, as it would be counterproductive to China's effort to keep an acceptable economic growth rate through globalization and a stable and friendly neighborhood. Additionally, Beijing would be willing to preserve the current international order amenable to economic

---

[19] Andrew J. Nathan, "Domestic Factors in the Making of Chinese Foreign Policy," *China Report* 52, no. 3 (2016): 179–191.

growth and prosperity. In other words, although China has always had the intention to change the current regional international system, it would do so while managing risk and preserving stability.[20]

Since 2009 until recently, regional observers can identify a series of Chinese actions or steps that could be designated as parts of the gray zone strategy. Michael J. Mazarr from the US War College has defined four characteristics of a gray zone strategy as (1) pursues political objectives through cohesive, integrated campaigns; (2) employs mostly nonmilitary or non-kinetic tools; (3) strives to remain under key escalatory or redline thresholds to avoid outright, conventional conflict; and (4) moves gradually toward its objectives rather than seeking conclusive results in a specific period of time.[21] Of all, the employment of strategic gradualism is essential as it distinguishes gray zone strategy with other conventional military strategies, which are usually designed to achieve rapid and decisive results. In essence, gradualism means aspects of gray zone strategy will "unfold over time, bit by bit, each step carefully remaining below clear thresholds of response."[22] And over time, when enough on-the-ground footprint is accumulated, "the architect of such a campaign intends for these incremental steps to sum up a decisive change in the status quo."[23]

William G. Pierce et al. gives us a most comprehensive definition of the concept of coercive gradualism so far, which actually comprises of two main characteristics. Similar to Mazarr's argument, William and his colleges emphasize the gradual approaches of the strategy, indicates gradualism as "a state employing the instruments of national power in a synchronized and integrated fashion to achieve national or multinational

---

[20] Debate continues, of course, over just how limited its aspirations are, or will remain. Jonathan Holslag has argued that, to fulfill them, "China must become the most powerful country in Asia by far, and attain the power to deter other protagonists by force." He lays out four specific goals of Chinese foreign policy: Control of key frontier lands like Tibet; sustain Party rule through economic growth and stability; win respect for Chinese sovereignty; and to "recover so-called 'lost territory'," from Taiwan to South China Sea islands to areas of the East China Sea and areas of the Himalayas contested with India. Jonathan Holslag, "The Smart Revisionist," 96.

[21] Michael J. Mazarr, *Mastering the Gray Zone: Understanding a Changing Era of Conflict* (Carlisle, PA: United States Army War College Press, December 2015), 57.

[22] Michael J. Mazarr, ibid., 38.

[23] Ibid.

objectives by incremental steps."[24] These steps, however, could be coercive or cooperative. Coercive gradualism therefore different of its cooperative counterpart in the balance of interests between the "aggressor" and the targeted states: It turns the struggle into a zero-sum game where the pursuit of the aggressor's interests will permanently erode other nation's interests.[25]

Beijing has employed a wide range of tools and techniques which falls into the categories of coercive gradualism: from the announcement of the "nine-dashed line", which in turn has been supported by a campaign of promoting China's own historical narrative and documentation in support of its claims both domestically and internationally; the deployment of a mixture of civil law enforcement, maritime militia and even the Chinese navy in swarming and presence missions throughout the region in what is called by the Chinese as the "cabbage strategy"; or the land reclamation campaign that turning uninhabited shoals and reefs in the disputed South China Sea waters into strategic choke points. These kinds of technique help ensure that China can exert its influence and effective control over not only the South China Sea but also all over the First Island Chain, as similar tactics have been also executed elsewhere in the East China Sea (albeit with different scale and scope). At the same time, "gray zone strategy" prevents conflicts from spinning out of control, as it keeps those events under key escalatory thresholds to avoid outright warfare.

Of all the techniques, the deployment of nonmilitary or non-kinetic tools is the most recognizable tactic. At least one Chinese official has used the term "cabbage strategy" to refer to a strategy of consolidating control over disputed islands by wrapping those islands, like the leaves of a cabbage, in successive layers of occupation and protection formed by fishing boats, Chinese Coast Guard (CCG) ships and then finally the Chinese naval vessels.[26] The deployment of nonmilitary forces like the

[24] William G. Pierce, Douglas J. Douds, and Michael A. Marra, "Countering Gray Zone Wars: Understanding Coercive Gradualism," *Parameters* 45, no. 3 (2015): 51.

[25] William G. Pierce et al., ibid., 52.

[26] See Harry Kazianis, "China's Expanding Cabbage Strategy," *The Diplomat*, October 29, 2013; Bonnie S. Glaser and Alison Szalwinski, "Second Thomas Shoal Likely the Next Flashpoint in the South China Sea," China Brief, June 21, 2013, https://jamestown.org/program/second-thomas-shoal-likely-the-next-flashpoint-inthe-south-china-sea/. Accessed August 9, 2013; and Rafael M. Alunan III, "China's Cabbage Strategy," *Business World* (Manila), July 8, 2013. See also Loida Nicolas Lewis, Rodel Rodis, and Walden Bello, "China's 'Cabbage Strategy' in West PH Sea," *Philippine Daily Inquirer*, July 27, 2013; Huseyin Erdogan, "China Invokes 'Cabbage Tactics' in South China Sea," Anadolu Ajansi, March 25, 2015.

CCG and the maritime militia fits perfectly well within the objectives of gray zone strategy mentioned above and therefore poses a significant threat to Vietnam's maritime rights and interests.

The question is how Vietnam can counter this kind of gray zone tactics at sea? Gray zone tactics emphasize the use of coercive and incremental methods to achieve the desired objectives without igniting wars.[27] Regarding the use of force, by exploiting the same incremental trajectory but in an active-defense manner, Vietnamese forces could reduce the effectiveness of that coercive gradualism. In order to exert actual control over the disputed waters, China has deployed its paramilitary forces with the intention of overwhelming other regional forces, especially those of weaker countries. Vietnam has undoubtedly mimicked what China has been doing in the South China Sea: by upgrading the VCG, which has similar tasks and characteristics; by transforming its own maritime militia into a more organized and disciplined force equipped with better technologies; and by sending these forces amassed to the sea to counter Chinese movements. It is the defensive manner of the VCG in recent incidents that differentiate it with a more assertive CCG, evidenced through the HD-981 standoff between the VCG and the CCG.

The VCG was established first and foremost as a mean to alleviate the burden on the navy in peacetime. It can also facilitate a legal approach in enforcing maritime sovereignty and jurisdiction rights, as granted by the United Nations Convention on the Law of the Sea. However, the never-before-seen effort from Vietnamese government since 2010 to modernize its coast guard, alongside its navy, is a direct response to what China is doing in the South China Sea. Utilizing the VCG would also minimize the military and political cost of a direct confrontation with other stronger forces at sea should such incidents spiral up into a crisis. Take for instance the 2014 oil rig standoff between China and Vietnam; although the VCG itself was overwhelmed and outnumbered by the CCG, it was still able to fend off the aggressor. This opened the way for the government as well as the party to negotiate directly with China. The VCG also plays an essential role in defending Vietnamese fishermen against China's maritime militia forces disguised as fishing boats. This approach has proven to be quite successful in maintaining Vietnam's effective control in the disputed waters and dealing with unexpected incidents at sea under untold pressure of China's maritime forces.

[27] Green, Michael, eds., ibid.

Because of that reason, the VCG now holds an important position in the overall Vietnam's maritime strategy, alongside the VPN. Vietnam could possibly come up with the idea of a three-layer defense strategy where the VCG stands at the middle of this spectrum. In peacetime scenario, the VCG becomes the cornerstone in the country's effort of keeping tight control over its sovereign waters. The VPN, at the same time, keeps its defensive and deterrent position against any potential adversaries. VCG's vessels and airplanes could also be helpful in reconnaissance and other intelligence activities. This role will be changed quickly when war breaks out, as the VPN would become spearhead in defending the country's maritime sovereignty and the VCG, alongside Vietnam's own maritime militia, which turns to be a supportive force.

Vietnamese strategists are confident that Vietnam could pursue that countermeasure, because investing in paramilitary forces is much more affordable, and cheaper, than investing in the navy. It is truly a remarkable transformation for the VCG, in just 20 years, to develop into one of the most capable coast guards in Southeast Asia. Paramilitary vessels do not require a huge amount of technological inputs. With enough shipbuilding skills and basic weapon technologies, a country with limited resources like Vietnam could possibly call up new vessels into service with a much faster pace than naval vessels (taking consideration the contract of purchasing two *Gepard*-class frigates of the VPN as an example, which took almost four years to be completed, as a comparison).

Another element that is unique to Vietnam's overall maritime security strategy is its own cooperative defense network, illustrated by various Joint Visions for defense cooperation with numerous regional powers (with the US, China, India and Indonesia, definitely with Japan and South Korea in the future). This kind of network strategy, with Vietnam as the core, serves several purposes: (1) increase Vietnam's prestige as an important element in maintaining peace and stability; (2) play a role of hedging against China and modernizing its armed forces (with also including the VCG); and (3) connect like-minded countries for a common goal, in turn strengthening regional cooperation. It is also because of this unique element that helps quicken the modernization and reorganization process of the VCG in an unimaginable pace. The service has hugely benefited from Vietnam's vast network of security and defense partnerships, especially from those with regional powers regarded as rivalries of China. As mentioned above, Japan, South Korea, India and the US have until recently supported, donated and aided the VCG with dozens of second-handed and even brand-new vessels.

The Vietnam Coast Guard's Challenges and Future Prospects

This kind of Coast Guard-Navy nexus is a rising phenomenon, not only applied by Vietnam but by other regional coast guards as well. Greater integration between the two services is considered a response to constant and changing maritime challenges and requirements. For Vietnam, a close cooperation between the coast guard and the navy could strengthen the effectiveness of the government effort in safeguarding the country's maritime rights and interests, especially when China is currently executing its version of "gray zone" tactics within the First Island Chain, and in the South China Sea in particular. Nevertheless, this trend also encounters several unique problems due to specific disparities between the two maritime agencies.

For Vietnam, the first obstacle could be the lack of a comprehensive cooperation framework between the VCG and the VPN, especially when contingencies appear requiring immediate coordination. At the moment, both of the two services have their own command and control structures under different lines of communication. Although Vietnam has its own maritime strategy pointing out some orientations for developing the country's maritime future, more details had been accorded to how best to fully integrate economic and maritime national defense measures than to how an inadequate navy is developed.

It is also confusing where it concerns the exact maritime obligations both agencies have, in times of war and peace. Competitive interactions or overlapped obligations could reduce the overall capabilities of the two and therefore can result in "gray zone" conflicts involving political and legal issues. A comprehensive cooperation framework between the VCG and the VPN has to be developed and broadly discussed in the context of the award issued by the Arbitral Tribunal in The Hague on July 12, 2016. This award has borne multiple legal implications in the South China Sea, which opened more room for the role of coast guards and a coast guard cooperative mechanism in the region.[28] Nevertheless, it would be easier

---

[28] For example, a clarification on the legal regime of the features may also contribute to defusing the tension over territorial sovereignty disputes. Sovereignty claims over the tiny insular features are usually aimed not at gaining control over the landmass of the features but at the vast maritime zones that are generated from these features up to, or in some cases beyond, 200 nm. Such control over the waters translates to possession of exclusive rights to explore and exploit fisheries resources and oil and gas reserves. This is, however,

for Vietnam to initiate this kind of close cooperation between the VCG and the VPN, because the VCG Command was actually put under the authority of the MoND, which is in turn controlled by the Communist Party's Central Military Commission.

So far, no truly maritime security strategy or doctrine has been publicized, and the public seems highly unlikely to get any knowledge of such strategy due to its secrecy. Experts and analysts, even inside Vietnam, have been able to gather no more than fragmented information. Therefore, incomplete analyses are made only by observing the VCG's modernization process and through several of statements from its leader. This thick fog of secrecy and lack of transparency surrounding the making maritime security strategy limits the participation in the policy-making process of other intellectuals outside the military realm, thus creating unnecessary restrictions on how to make comprehensive and effective comments or providing feedback. It is noteworthy that maintaining secrecy and confusion in how the military is operating has always been one of the traditional elements in the mindset of Vietnamese military strategists from a very long time. Changing this mindset, in our opinion, is essential in order to build more modern and efficient military forces and to contribute to a more transparent process of procurement and strategy building.

Second, budget constraints have always been one of the most enduring challenges to the efforts of the VPN as well as VCG in modernizing their outdated arsenal. According to SIPRI statistics, Vietnam's defense budget has increased dramatically since 1988–2015. Between 2005 and 2015, the country's military spending went up 115 percent, considered the largest among Southeast Asian states, but the percentage of this budget accounted for just around two percent of total GDP at the same period. The latest figure in 2016 shows that total spending could reach nearly US$5 billion.[29] Unfortunately, the exact amount of money

---

only possible if these insular features meet the criteria to be considered as islands under Article 121(1) UNCLOS. The arbitral tribunal finds that these insular features are merely rocks under Article 121(3) or low-tide elevations under Article 13, and this means they are not entitled to such vast area of waters surrounding them.

[29] Zachary Abuza and Nguyen Nhat Anh, "Vietnam's Military Modernization," *The Diplomat*, 2016, http://thediplomat.com/2016/10/vietnams-military-modernization/. Accessed February 23, 2017.

allocated to the VCG has always been shrouded in mystery, as well as those budgets for other military branches. Analysts and experts, even inside Vietnam, are facing immense difficulties in trying to figure out those data. It is not clear at the moment whether or not there is competition between different military branches for budget allocation, but one thing for sure: the VPN and the VCG are not the only branches of the armed forces that will "proceed directly to modernization." More guests joining the party means less resources for all, and it is very likely that the VPN and especially VCG has to compete with others such as the air force to gain its necessary funds. Additionally, Vietnam's economy after the 2007/2008 global financial crisis has not been fully recovered. The Vietnamese government is still struggling with mountainous tasks to restructure the economy; thus, any large-scale military buildup will require careful consideration, as to how it can be balanced in given account sheets.[30] As a consequence, the future modernization scenario of the VCG is dependent not only on China's ongoing assertiveness in the South China Sea, but also on how strong the economy will become and how much budget it would possibly get.

Less budget means less vessels and other infrastructure coming into service, which in turn slows down the modernization efforts. The VCG has in its service mostly small and less capable vessels than its naval counterpart, which in turn reduces the former's effectiveness and the latter's desire to cooperate with the VCG. Most of the vessels in service of the VCG are small and, as showed in the 2014 oilrig incident, could not effectively engage bigger Chinese vessels which have greater endurance.

---

[30] In most of the years, the current account balance in Vietnam showed negative values; however, the last year 2015–2016 was more or less balanced. In some of the years, the current account deficit was very high with values of more than 5% or even 10% of GDP. Current account deficits have several negative repercussions. They can lead to a lack of domestic demand. They also lead to foreign debt, which in the case of Vietnam is debt in foreign currency. Foreign debt implies a dangerous currency mismatch and the possibility of currency crises. With an actual foreign debt level of 45.2% of GDP in early 2016 (IMF 2016), Vietnamese foreign debt is high. In case of a strong depreciation of the dong, the foreign debt can become a high burden. Most of the debt is public debt. While official loans to Vietnam are shrinking, Vietnam might gradually seek ways to get more risky commercial loans with floating interest rates. Therefore, the risk of changing interest rates and exchange rates might substantially increase. See more: Hansjörg Herr, Erwin Schweisshelm and Truong-Minh Vu, "Vietnam in the Global Economy: Development Through Integration or Middle-Income Trap?" Global Labour University Working Paper No. 44, 2016.

The VCG also lacks experienced seamen, especially when it is commissioning more and bigger vessels. There is also a lack of necessary infrastructure such as shipyards, ports in remote islands, logistics capabilities, etc., which reduce the effectiveness of VCG operations.

Although the VCG does not require huge amount of funding to operate compared to that of the VPN, the service also needs a lot of investment in order to fit with the overall doctrine emphasizing a joint operation concept, especially in wartime. For peacetime missions, the service needs to invest more to develop sufficient code of conduct as well as new vessels and equipment to cope with the rise of various non-traditional challenges at sea, from protecting Vietnamese fishing vessels to search-and-rescue missions to fighting against terrorists or sea robberies/pirates. The VCG could also invest more in the high-end combat capability for its vessels and coordinate more with the VPN in terms of training and technical transfer. Training is another important aspect through which the two services could improve tactical and strategic cooperation. VCG's personnel, seamen and officials could definitely make use of their naval counterpart's training facilities in order to improve their own skills and seafaring capabilities. For a nation with limited resources like Vietnam, an effective nexus and close cooperation between the navy and the coast guard would become a tool for both defense and deterrence, a guarantee for security and prosperity in a new century where most of the country's wealth will be deprived of maritime trade and resources. The VCG, a new member of Vietnam's military structure, obviously requires a comprehensive and effective doctrine to deal with numerous challenges in a constantly changing maritime environment. This strategy has to include both operational and tactical issues as well as administration and coordination tasks with other maritime agencies in order to increase the overall constabulary capabilities. Those are all essential questions that need careful considerations by Vietnamese maritime strategists.

In conclusion, for a more effective nexus between the VPN and the VCG, it is important for the two services in the future to expand cooperation, not only to safeguard the country's maritime rights and interests along its own coast, but also on the high seas. The MoND could optimize this by developing the concept of "the national fleet" to provide a common concept of operation for meeting a wide spectrum of maritime needs and for the employment of the nation's maritime forces. We list out several initiatives that could be implemented in the short term in order to improve the engagement between the two services:

- First and foremost, a transparent and coherent national maritime security strategy/doctrine should be carefully created through which missions and objectives of the VPN and the VCG are clearly defined.
- Through that strategy/doctrine, maritime defense operations of the two services are integrated into ways that the two services could exploit their advantages in both peacetime and wartime scenarios.
- The simplest way to promote cooperation could be the establishment of joint command, control and communication (C3) centers. This is easy said and done because the VPN Command and VCG Command are all put under the authority of the CCP's Central Military Commission. C3 centers are important not just for creating nexus within Vietnam's own maritime forces, but could even play a role in future regional nexus of maritime cooperation and coordination among regional players.
- The VCG and to some extent the VPN have benefited a lot through Vietnam's own defense and security networks with numerous regional players, especially those with strong maritime capabilities. Fighting against coercive gradualism is not a simple task. Building a vibrant web of defense cooperation would give strength to Vietnam's overall balancing capabilities and more momentum to the current modernization process of Vietnam's maritime forces. The priority in the future could be to initiate joint operation mechanism among ASEAN's coast guards.
- Training, manning and quipping with enough manpower and vessels are the priorities in modernization that the VCG is currently trying to achieve. With vast sovereign waters under its jurisdiction, the service has to be equipped with modern and capable officers, seamen and vessels. In the next five years, it is estimated that at least two 4000-ton and several 3000-ton vessels will be commissioned. With sufficient training, the VCG could have the potential to become a powerful coast guard in the region having enough tools to counter against any tactics and strategies that aim to undermine Vietnam's sovereignty over the South China Sea.

CHAPTER 6

Singapore's Maritime Security Approach

Swee Lean Collin Koh

Singapore's geostrategic circumstances are well known—a small island surrounded by congested waterways and the lack of strategic depth. Its sense of vulnerabilities stems in large from dependence on seaborne commerce and trade for national survival and prosperity, thereby necessitating secure access to the vital sea lines of communications. It also does not help that not only Singapore is a well-positioned transhipment port and petrochemical hub, but it overlooks the strategic Straits of Malacca and Singapore. Taking altogether these factors, one should not overlook that having a constrained water-space to manage can be a virtue: compared to its neighbours which are almost perpetually plagued by maritime security capacity shortfalls, Singapore does have a much smaller maritime zone to police—the country does not enjoy the full 12 nautical miles of territorial sea due to the tightly confined nature of the surrounding waters and proximity with neighbours—and the capacity available appears sizeable by proportion. To illustrate, Indonesia has a maritime zone spanning about 5,409,981 square kilometres which is policed by 254 combat and patrol vessels and 32 maritime patrol aircraft mustered

S. L. C. Koh (✉)
S. Rajaratnam School of International Studies,
Nanyang Technological University, Singapore
e-mail: iscollinkoh@ntu.edu.sg

© The Author(s) 2019
I. Bowers and S. L. C. Koh (eds.), *Grey and White Hulls*,
https://doi.org/10.1007/978-981-13-9242-9_6

by both the navy and diverse MLE agencies as of 2018, whereas Singapore has 130 equivalent vessels and 5 aircraft to police approximately 343 square kilometres of sea space.[1]

But this is not to underestimate the complexity of maritime security operations the Republic of Singapore Navy (RSN) and the Police Coast Guard (PCG) undertake daily alongside with the other national agencies. This chapter argues that Singapore's navy-coastguard nexus is facilitated by the institutionalized habits of cooperation between the various actors within the country's maritime security architecture, as represented by the National Maritime Security Strategy (NMSS) framework. Within this architecture, inter-agency collaboration is also enabled by the minimized tendencies of rivalries between those actors due to the fact that the RSN has always been the lead actor and that the architecture has been shaped not only by the evolving security landscape but also clear policy directions from the top. The various actors are able to leverage on their respective specialized competencies to contribute as equal partners to the NMSS.

Inter-Agency Approach by Default?

Singapore's maritime security approaches were shaped in no small measure by the evolving security landscape. Because of the colossal economic and strategic stakes involved, it becomes imperative to deter, detect, pre-empt, defeat and mitigate the consequences of any conceivable maritime security threat in as efficient and effective manner possible. For this reason, inter-agency collaboration between Singapore's maritime security agencies is not a new phenomenon. Exercise Apex, conceived of in 1983 and led by the RSN, has been held annually to test inter-agency maritime security response covering a range of non-conventional and conventional security threats at sea, including those posed by naval mines.[2] The systems of the various agencies' operations centres are integrated, and their duty officers not only work closely but also communicate with each other on a day-to-day basis. Since the very beginning, the RSN has been the leading maritime security agency.

---

[1] International Institute of Strategic Studies, *The Military Balance 2019* (Oxford: Oxford University Press, 2019).

[2] These agencies, along with others, also conducted maritime security-related response drills, such as Exercise Northstar since 1997.

The RSN Coastal Command (COSCOM) served as the coordinating authority of national maritime security since 1988, which in no small part was influenced by those experiences in tackling the Vietnamese boat refugee inflows back in the 1970s and 1980s.[3]

The RSN and PCG, each respectively the primary maritime security actor from the Ministry of Defence (MINDEF) and Ministry of Home Affairs (MHA), are no stranger towards inter-agency cooperation. Then PCG's Head of Operations and Security, Superintendent Ang Eng Seng said: "Multi-agency collaboration is not something new. At the planning and operational levels, we have always worked together".[4] In the early 1990s till the early 2000s, this integrated approach was targeted at piracy and sea robbery, the occasional seaborne smuggling attempts, the anticipated threat of illegal immigrant inflows following the Asian financial crisis in 1997–1998, and to a lesser extent the dispute over Pedra Branca with Malaysia. The epochal events of 11 September 2001, and around the same time, the surge in piracy and sea robbery attacks in the Straits of Malacca and Singapore (SOMS) complicated Singapore's maritime security landscape. The potential nexus between piracy and maritime terrorism had been highlighted as the "greatest concern to maritime security".[5] The terror attacks on the USS *Cole* and MV *Limburg* sharpened Singapore's focus on maritime terrorism, a concept which was no longer confined to such acts at sea but also emanating from the sea, following the Mumbai attacks of 2008. These developments spurred a major change in how Singapore approaches maritime security. While the RSN and PCG remain key actors, other national maritime agencies are also drawn into a more formalized, inter-agency framework.

In 2009, COSCOM was restructured into the Maritime Security Task Force (MSTF) by pulling together both the armed forces and other national maritime agencies—PCG, Immigration and Checkpoints

---

[3] COSCOM, amongst various missions, is generally to safeguard the security of Singapore's coastal waters in peacetime and provide seaward defence in times of tension and war. It conducts maritime surveillance of the Singapore Straits, provides assistance to civil authorities in times of contingencies, and assists PCG in its operations. Factsheet: Coastal Command (COSCOM), Ministry of Defence, Singapore, 29 August 2006.

[4] Ong Hong Tat, "*Swift Multi-Agency Takedown at Exercise Highcrest*", Ministry of Defence, Singapore, 5 November 2015.

[5] Speech by Dr. Tony Tan Keng Yam, Deputy Prime Minister and Coordinating Minister for Security and Defence at the 2004 IDSS Maritime Security Conference Held on Thursday, 20 May 2004 at 9.00 am at Marina Mandarin Hotel.

Authority (ICA), Maritime and Port Authority of Singapore (MPA) and Singapore Customs (SC). Point to note is that prior to this change, COSCOM had been essentially a navy-level formation which hitherto could muster only RSN organic assets. As an armed forces-level body, MSTF answers directly to the Chief of Defence Force and is designed to promote and streamline cross-domain responses by coordinating deployment of assets across the Singapore Armed Forces (SAF), not just RSN, and muster assets of MHA agencies in order to conduct calibrated and flexible maritime security operations.[6] This further integration of effort also makes more practical sense, not least owing to the fact that the SAF possesses certain requisite assets which other agencies may not have to duplicate. The Republic of Singapore Air Force (RSAF) in particular could provide critical aerial assets since other agencies do not possess such resources. Forming MSTF thus formalizes this integration and sharing of assets that have been in place for some time. The MSTF comprises the following subordinate elements:

- *Comprehensive Maritime Awareness Group (CMAG)*: pieces together a comprehensive operational picture by collating information gathered by national agencies, international partners and the shipping community.
- *Operations Group*: comprises operations planners from Army, Navy and Air Force and plans and executes operations using an integrated approach that makes the best allocation of available resources.
- *Inter-Agency Coordination Group*: comprises PCG, MPA, ICA and SC representatives to ensure seamless coordination in the execution of national-level operations.

The RSN under this expanded maritime security approach remains the lead agency, "primarily responsible to coordinate all… efforts with various agencies".[7]

---

[6] "SAF Sets Up Integrated Maritime Security Task Force", *CyberPioneer*, publication of the Ministry of Defence, Singapore, 23 February 2009. *Fact Sheet: Maritime Security Task Force*, Ministry of Defence, Singapore, 23 February 2009.

[7] "*Minister for Defence Visits Maritime Security Task Force*", Ministry of Defence, Singapore, 10 November 2011.

Evolving and Adapting

Further integration of efforts was placed into motion as the threat environment continues to evolve. Singapore's congested waterways around SOMS do not offer any berth of comfort—a problem that has been perennially faced by the island city state that has never enjoyed any natural geostrategic depth for its national defence and security. As Rear-Admiral Frederick Chew, then MSTF commander, pointed out[8]:

> Singapore's maritime environment is getting increasingly congested, and also increasingly complex. We have various developments ashore, and the number of shipping has been increasing steadily over the years. In fact by 2025, it's projected that shipping in Singapore will increase by about 30 per cent. And so against that backdrop, there are challenges posed for security agencies because we have a lot of legitimate shipping in the Singapore Straits. It's not so easy now to differentiate between bona fide threats and legitimate shipping.

In 2011, Singapore unveiled the National Maritime Security System (NMSS) which constitutes a Whole-of-Government (WoG)-based strategy framework. Figure 6.1 shows Singapore's current postulated maritime security architecture, comprising in large part the NMSS framework and operational forces.

Before one gets lost in the clutter of acronyms, it is important to observe from Fig. 6.1 how the architecture that promotes the nexus between Singapore's maritime security actors can be broken down into various strategic and operational strata. Under NMSS, permanent secretaries of MINDEF and MHA co-chair the Homefront Crisis Executive Group (HCEG) (maritime security) for wider coordination at national level. HCEG (MARSEC) is supported by the Crisis Management Group (CMG) (MARSEC) which the Chief of Navy leads as Crisis Manager to ensure unified command and control. The Crisis Manager recommends maritime operational strategies and courses of action to HCEG (MARSEC) including coordinating information management efforts, managing consequences and ensuring coherence and unity of response

---

[8] "15 Govt Agencies Hold Maritime Security Drill in Singapore Waters", *Channel NewsAsia*, 5 November 2015.

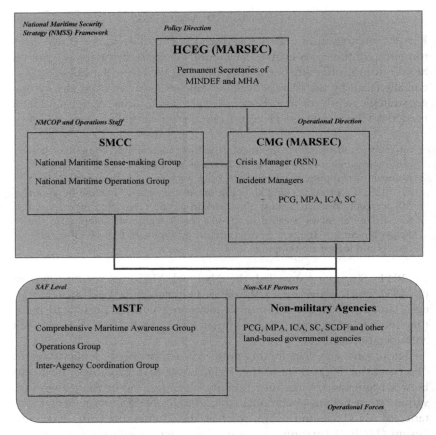

Fig. 6.1 Singapore's Maritime Security Architecture (*Source* By author based on available official information)

across the various Incident Managers (IMs) who are the commanders of the other four maritime agencies. In sum, the HCEG (MARSEC) provides policy direction, whereas CMG (MARSEC) provides operational direction and implements those policies under NMSS.

CMG (MARSEC) as the policy implementation entity of NMSS is housed within the Singapore Maritime Crisis Centre (SMCC) which was established in 2013 within Changi Command and Control Centre (CC2C) at Changi Naval Base and coordinates MSTF.[9] SMCC is not a tactical formation, but essentially a full-time facility staffed by senior officers from the RSN, PCG, MPA, ICA and SC. It presides over the formation of the National Maritime Common Operating Picture (NMCOP) and provides planning for operations. The centre comprises the following subordinate groups: (1) National Maritime Sense-making Group (NMSG) and (2) National Maritime Operations Group (NMOG). It is interesting to note that CC2C is not only home to SMCC but also CMAG of MSTF, as well as the Information Fusion Centre (IFC) and Regional Humanitarian Assistance and Disaster Relief Coordination Centre (RHCC). The co-location of these diverse bodies under one roof helps to foster cross-domain collaboration. NMSG should not be confused with the CMAG under MSTF. While CMAG collates and fuses information gathered by national agencies, international partners and the shipping community, and not least MSTF's organic ship-based and shore-based, as well as RSAF's aerial platform-based maritime surveillance assets, NMSG does more than that. It identifies anomalies and analyses the situation for any possible threats and shares information amongst the operations centres of other national maritime agencies to ensure a uniform understanding of the situation. It is also focused on building shared maritime awareness amongst national agencies by acting as 24/7 focal point for information-sharing, cross-domain threat assessment and establishment of NMCOP. As part of the WoG, MSTF feeds information to NMSG. NMOG commences planning across the maritime agencies upon NMSG establishing an early warning of a threat.[10] But unlike MSTF, NMOG is a planning body that possesses no organic assets of its own.

Overall, SMCC is the one-stop body that does sense-making and horizon-scanning, through maintaining a comprehensive maritime situation picture, analysing and sharing information between agencies, detecting suspicious patterns or anomalies, and then cues as well as coordinates responses

---

[9] *"Factsheet: Safeguarding Singapore's Maritime Security"*, Ministry of Defence, Singapore, 30 June 2017.

[10] Speech by Minister of State for Defence Associate Professor Koo Tsai Kee, at the Opening Ceremony of the 2nd International Maritime Security Conference, on Thursday, 19 May 2011, 0830 Hrs, Changi Exhibition Centre, Ministry of Defence, Singapore. Downloaded from the National Archives of Singapore. *"Factsheet: Singapore Maritime Crisis Centre"*, Ministry of Defence, Singapore, 5 November 2015.

to deal with potential threats. Exercise Northstar VIII in 2011 debuted, tested and validated NMSS and also robustness of consequence management plans for various emergency scenarios. It also validated the initial operational capability of SMCC. Since then, the various agencies within NMSS have gone about formalizing the linkages.[11] Exercise Highcrest tests the SMCC's ability to plan and manage WoG maritime security sense-making and operational responses and help tie down procedures and firm up the communication protocols. It is supposed to be the most comprehensive inter-agency maritime security exercise that involves multiple agencies beyond just those "big five" that constitute CMG (MARSEC). This does not obviate the need to continually build inter-agency nexus. During Exercise Highcrest 2013 which validated the full operational capability of SMCC, Singapore Prime Minister Lee Hsien Loong highlighted the importance of national-level coordinated response: "This exercise is the culmination of several years of work to prepare our National Maritime Security System… so you just look at all the logos which are involved in today's exercise—so many ministries, so many stat boards, the uniformed forces—they have to work seamlessly together. Otherwise, there will be some miscommunications, some clash in the plans or in the execution and then we will be in trouble".[12]

The long-standing habits of inter-agency collaboration would see opportunities to reap benefits. Amongst those reported instances, SMCC validated its utility by foiling terrorists' plot to fire a rocket at Marina Bay from Indonesia's Batam Island in August 2016, shortly before Singapore's National Day. Upon receiving information which indicated the potential plot, SMCC used analytics in the social media domain to pick up linkages between the syndicate of six plotters who were later arrested and another accomplice who was involved in the maritime domain.[13] Despite this success, there is no room for complacency. Exercise Highcrest in 2017 for the first time incorporated a land demonstration to simulate how scenarios that happen on land can impact sea

---

[11] Charissa Tan and Win Soon, "Home Team Agencies Participate in Sea-Land National Security Exercise", Singapore Home Team, 7 November 2013.

[12] "*Whole-of-Government Response to Simulated Terrorist Threats at Exercise Highcrest 2013*", Ministry of Defence, Singapore, 6 November 2013.

[13] "Keeping Singapore's Coastline Secure Amid Changing Threats", *Channel NewsAsia*, 27 March 2017.

operations and vice versa in view of the interconnectedness of land and sea activities. Senior Minister of State for Defence and Foreign Affairs Maliki Osman, who witnessed the exercise, stressed upon the importance of promoting inter-agency cooperation: "If we are all in our own domains and we're not talking to each other, then there will be gaps between us and that's where the vulnerabilities are. That's where the terrorist may enter, through those gaps. We must make sure those gaps are filled". He added that more of such inter-agency exercises are set to take place, involving more personnel on land and even in the air. "They need to be able to talk the same language, use the same systems, see the same feeds and analyse the same things… I think this is a continued work in progress… Moving forward, we'll see a lot more of such integration (including) the land and air domains and… different agencies".[14]

Former RSN Rear-Admiral Bernard Miranda pointed out that the SMCC's successes could be attributed to: (1) team forming and building to overcome inter-agency stovepipes; (2) commitment from agencies to fund and staff the posts from those five different agencies; (3) establishment of the SMCC at the CC2C and its sense-making and operations systems; (4) unifying management and leadership; (5) having a national-level training and exercises framework that validates capabilities and renews inter-agency commitment with the WOG approach; and (6) coherent public communications plan to emphasize the need for vigilance against would-be perpetrators.[15] Yet it also needs pointing out that this level of integration, while unprecedented in terms of the extent and scope, is basically a step up from has been practised in the past and enabled in so doing by technological advances. While such complex inter-agency exercises were carried out, diverse agencies also congregate for their pre-existing inter-agency drills too. Besides Exercise Apex, for instance, Exercise Blue Dolphin included such diverse agencies as the MPA, SAF, PCG, the Singapore Civil Defence Force and the People's Association in assessing emergency preparedness and post-incident consequence management; the 2014

---

[14] "Exercise Highcrest: Maritime, Land-Based Agencies Keep 'Terrorists' from Reaching Shore", *Channel NewsAsia*, 26 October 2017.

[15] Bernard Miranda, "Maritime Security Threats in Southeast Asia: A Collective Approach", *RSIS Commentary*, No. 268, S. Rajaratnam School of International Studies, 17 October 2016.

iteration simulated a rescue of over 700 people from a "burning" cruise ship about 4.5 km from Marina South Pier—clearly a plausible scenario in times of a terror attack, not merely a matter of maritime safety. While these exercises continue to be conducted from time to time, dealing with specific subject matter, they helped build on this WoG approach and this transcends the typical navy-coastguard nexus represented by integration between the RSN and PCG.

Navy as the First Amongst Equals?

Throughout the evolution of Singapore's maritime security architecture, it is clear that inter-agency collaboration has been a normative approach adopted by the country's maritime security actors since the start. And the RSN remains the lead agency. Yet despite this, it would be misleading to think of the navy as the domineering agency. It has been a more nuanced relationship between the navy and its non-military counterparts—in fact, the RSN appears to be more a first amongst equals. In the execution of operational responses, the RSN works alongside the PCG especially, and based on a first-responder basis, i.e. the asset closest to the scene of action would bear the responsibility to respond first to the contingency. Prior to 2007, the SAF possessed no powers of detention and seizure—this has been left to the Singapore Police Force (and its maritime arm PCG). To enhance response to crises in a more efficient and effective manner, the original SAF Act of 1972 was amended in 2007 with provisions specifying more clearly the SAF's role in support of civilian authorities.[16] Most crucially, the amended Act allows any SAF serviceman deployed to not only intercept and expel but also to pursue, stop, employ weapons to disable and compel compliance, board, as well as capture or recapture offending aerial and maritime vessels. And the actions enabled under this amended Act also include search and detention of the vessel or facility, its cargo and personnel on board.[17] Then Singapore's defence minister Teo Chee Hean explained the rationale behind the proposed amendments, which was primarily a response to the

---

[16] These operations include counter-piracy; detection and prevention of any aerial or maritime threat to the defence or security of Singapore; rescue of hijacked aerial and maritime vessels or other fixed or floating facility. *SAF Act*, pp. 143–144.

[17] *SAF Act*, pp. 145–146.

evolving security landscape and recognized weaknesses in the pre-existing legislation. He also clearly outlined the limitations of such powers bestowed upon SAF personnel under the amended Act[18]:

> Sections 201B and 201C also set out the selected legal powers that may be lawfully exercised by servicemen involved in the security operations. These include powers to stop, detain, search, and use reasonable force against suspect vehicles, vessels and persons. The SAF will not be given investigation or prosecution powers against civilians. Under Section 201G, any person arrested or thing seized, whether in a land, sea or air operation, must be handed over, as soon as practicable, to the police.

That said, the SAF would continue to serve as a backup for the police that takes the forefront of carrying out internal security duties, only intervening in more forceful actions such as detention and seizures under extreme conditions.[19] The navy also does not claim all maritime surveillance responsibilities under its purview since the division of labour has been clearly drawn. For example, in the wake of the spate of ship collisions off Singapore—including the high-profile incident involving the US Navy destroyer USS *John S. McCain* in August 2017 in the Singapore Strait—later that year, in response to a parliamentary question about role of the country's maritime security agencies in monitoring safety of the waterways Singapore's defence minister Dr. Ng Eng Hen elaborated on the division of responsibilities between these bodies: "The MSTF's key focus is on potential threats to Singapore… while the MPA watches over the navigation of ships in our waters".[20]

Fortuitously, it needs to be pointed out that various actors within Singapore's maritime security architecture would find little incentive or reason to engage in inter-service rivalries because they are each entitled to and received their fair share of resources. Both MINDEF and MHA, which are essentially custodians of Singapore's external and internal security respectively, have been able to avail themselves to necessary

---

[18] "*Speech by Mr. Teo Chee Hean, Minister for Defence, at Second Reading of the SAF (Amendment) Bill*", Ministry of Defence, Singapore, 21 May 2007.

[19] Author's discussion with a senior RSN officer, April 2019.

[20] "*Oral Reply by Minister for Defence, Dr. Ng Eng Hen, to Parliamentary Question on the Republic of Singapore Navy's Capabilities to Survey Maritime Traffic*", Ministry of Defence, Singapore, 2 October 2017.

funding opportunities, which is enabled by the fact that the Singapore Government has always placed a premium on national security investments. Notably, while the RSN does get considerable funding for its acquisition programmes, its civilian counterpart the PCG does not lag either. For example, in recent years the PCG reaps further dividends from the Singapore Government's increased attention on enhancing maritime security, thus being able to tap on funding to further recapitalize its assets and enhance capabilities. The RSN has relinquished some of its policing duties around Pedra Branca after PCG received new offshore patrol vessels built by the Netherlands. In April 2017, the PCG established a new Emergency Response Forces (ERF)—a maritime counterpart to those that already pre-exist in the land division—to be part of the first response wave against heavily armed threats in Singapore's waters and offshore islands.[21] In December the same year, PCG inaugurates its first unmanned surface vessels—Venus 9 and Venus 16—not too long after RSN began to mainstream such operations. Overall, it has been a happy family between the RSN and its civilian counterpart, even if there are some occasional issues with inter-agency information-sharing—which would not have been too alien to government institutions worldwide.[22]

Conclusions: The Right Formula?

Singapore views maritime security as an extremely complex issue that transcends boundaries, thus requiring diverse actors within its maritime security architecture to act in concert against a myriad of challenges at sea. The country's geostrategic circumstances are both fortuitous and otherwise. From the negative perspective, they present a complex maritime security environment for the country that leaves very little margin for error. Yet positively seen, it allows Singapore to focus on more immediate threats without having to be distracted by so many other priorities that require overstretching forces thinly over a broad geographical region

---

[21] ERF training started in December 2016, and all PCG frontline officers will be trained to become ERF officers. Every PCG patrol boat will have ERF-trained officers on board by June 2017. "Police Launch Marine Counter-Terrorism Team", *Channel NewsAsia*, 7 April 2017.

[22] Discussion with former senior official from MPA, May 2018.

like what its larger neighbours are long confronted with. Singapore has been obliged by the evolving security landscape to adopt a WoG approach, using technology as a key enabler.

This WoG approach, borne out of geostrategic, domestic, fiscal, operational and technical necessity, looks set to be a "right formula" forward. But Singapore's success story, albeit one with its own inherent limitations—especially the effectiveness of its maritime security architecture in times of real, major crisis,[23] which should never be prayed for to come—cannot be necessarily replicated by other countries with different contexts.

---

[23] Various conceivable scenarios had been played out by SMCC over the years to build competency, but Singapore's defence and security planners are far from complacent, also acknowledging the limitations of peacetime training. Read for example, "*Oral Reply by Minister for Defence, Dr. Ng Eng Hen, to Parliamentary Question on the Republic of Singapore Navy's Capabilities to Survey Maritime Traffic*", Ministry of Defence, Singapore, 2 October 2017.

CHAPTER 7

The Navy-Coast Guard Nexus and the Nature of Indonesian Maritime Security Governance

Muhamad Arif

Security and safety in Indonesia's waters and maritime jurisdiction has long been a critical interest of not only the world's biggest archipelagic country but also the international community. Choke points and sea lines of communication within Indonesia's jurisdiction have long served as critical veins of global seaborne trade. Moreover, as the world's geoeconomic and geopolitical centre of gravity is shifting from the Western Hemisphere to Asia, the importance of the security of Indonesian waters has become more evident. Uninterrupted flows of goods and services through Indonesian waters are necessary to ensure economic growth in the region. In recent years, the Indonesian government, realising the untapped potential of its maritime domain, has stepped up its efforts to manage this abundant maritime resource to support its vision to transform the country into a maritime power amid increasingly volatile geostrategic circumstances.

For a country that relies heavily on the effective maintenance of order and security of its waters, Indonesian maritime security governance is

M. Arif (✉)
Department of International Relations, Universitas Indonesia,
Depok, Indonesia

© The Author(s) 2019
I. Bowers and S. L. C. Koh (eds.), *Grey and White Hulls*,
https://doi.org/10.1007/978-981-13-9242-9_7

a tangled mess. A number of analyses argue that Indonesian maritime security governance is characterised by the overlapping roles and authority of its various maritime security-related institutions, sectoral egoism as well as inter-agency competition for resources.[1] There are currently no less than thirteen agencies directly involved with maritime law enforcement in Indonesia's waters and jurisdiction. The establishment of BAKAMLA (*Badan Keamanan Laut*/Maritime Security Agency), which was initially envisioned to assume the role as the leading civilian maritime law enforcement agency, has proven to be unsuccessful as far as the agenda to streamline Indonesian multi-agency maritime security governance is concerned. The Navy (*Tentara Nasional Indonesia Angkatan Laut*/TNI-AL), meanwhile, appears to be reluctant to relinquish its dominance of maritime law enforcement to its civilian counterparts.

This chapter explains why Indonesian maritime security governance is structured as it is. It seeks to understand the determinants that shape Indonesia's response towards maritime security challenges across the spectrum of traditional/military and non-traditional maritime law enforcement missions. This understanding will in turn be helpful as a framework to explain how Indonesia has been trying to balance military and law enforcement roles at sea in the contemporary period as well as to identify the benefit and drawbacks of such an approach.

As the following analysis shows, the nature of Indonesian maritime security governance throughout its period of development is typified by the blurred distinction between "defence" or "military" and "security" or "law enforcement" roles. This paradigm is embodied in the persistent attempts by the Navy (*Tentara Nasional Indonesia Angkatan Laut*/TNI-AL) to sustain its dominance in Indonesian maritime security

---

[1] See Dirham Dirhamsyah, "Maritime Law Enforcement and Compliance in Indonesia: Problems and Recommendations," *Maritime Studies*, no. 144 (2005): 1–16; Jun Honna, "Instrumentalizing Pressures, Reinventing Mission: Indonesian Navy Battles for Turf in the Age of Reformasi," *Indonesia*, no. 86 (2008): 63–79; Ristian Atriandi Supriyanto and Siswanto Rusdi, "Maritime Security Agencies in Indonesia: More Not Merrier," RSIS Commentaries (Singapore, 2013); Evan A. Laksmana, "Rebalancing Indonesia's Naval Force: Trends, Nature, and Drivers," in *Naval Modernisation in South-East Asia: Nature, Causes and Consequences*, ed. Geoffrey Till and Jane Chan (New York: Routledge, 2014), 175–203; Ristian Atriandi Supriyanto, "Naval Counter-Piracy in Indonesia," in *Piracy in Southeast Asia: Trends, Hot Spots and Responses*, ed. Carolin Liss and Ted Biggs (New York: Routledge, 2017), 97–119; and Muhamad Arif and Yandry Kurniawan, "Strategic Culture and Indonesian Maritime Security," *Asia & the Pacific Policy Studies* 5, no. 1 (2018): 77–89.

governance. As the *primus inter pares* among various maritime security agencies in Indonesia, the institutional behaviour of TNI-AL to a significant extent also determines the actual structure of Indonesian maritime security governance. Finally, the evolving maritime security governance architecture is also susceptible to the ever-changing domestic political context. Domestic political priorities and leaders' threat assessments play a significant role in shaping the state's response towards its maritime security challenges.[2]

After a brief overview of the current approach of Indonesia towards maritime security governance, highlighting the unfamiliarity of Indonesia towards the concept of a coast guard as a single civilian maritime security agency, the chapter will provide a structured historical analysis on the nature and determinants that shape Indonesian maritime security governance. After a brief analysis of Indonesian maritime security governance in the context of the Global Maritime Fulcrum (GMF) vision under President Joko Widodo's administration, this chapter will conclude with a number of observations with regard to the drawbacks and benefits of Indonesia's approach to maritime security amid contemporary maritime security challenges.

THE NAVY AND COAST GUARD IN INDONESIAN MARITIME SECURITY GOVERNANCE

It is fair to say that Indonesia has never fully embraced the concept of a coast guard as a dedicated civilian maritime law enforcement institution with a clear delineation of responsibilities vis-à-vis other agencies. This

---

[2] This line of logic is influenced by the neoclassical realism school of thought in International Relations. The theories are built upon the premise that the actual behaviour of states, i.e. foreign and security policy, is not a deterministic result of external systemic pressure. The systemic pressure is rather translated through intervening variables at states' domestic level. These intervening variables include leaders' threat assessment, identity, interests of domestic actors and states' power to mobilise resources. See Gideon Rose, "Review Article: Neoclassical Realism and Theories of Foreign Policy," *World Politics*, no. 51 (1998): 144–172; Brian Rathbun, "A Rose by Any Other Name: Neoclassical Realism as the Logical and Necessary Extension of Structural Realism," *Security Studies* 17, no. 2 (2008): 294–321; Steven E. Lobell, Norrin M. Ripsman, and Jeffrey W. Taliaferro, eds., *Neoclassical Realism, the State, and Foreign Policy* (Cambridge: Cambridge University Press, 2009); and Norrin M. Ripsman, Jeffrey W. Taliaferro, and Steven E. Lobell, *Neoclassical Realist Theory of International Politics* (New York: Oxford University Press, 2016).

is partly due to the geography of the country. Unlike non-archipelagic states that "only" need to worry about the territorial waters, exclusive economic zones (EEZ) and the adjacent seas, Indonesia also needs to maintain a maritime presence in multiple directions due to the existence of archipelagic waters. The Navy, for instance, while in theory is first and foremost responsible for the protection of EEZ, also needs to monitor the archipelagic sea lanes through which even foreign warships are allowed to pass.

There are currently thirteen institutions responsible for maritime security-related functions. These agencies are BAKAMLA, the Ministry of Foreign Affairs, the Ministry of Home Affairs, the Ministry of Transportation, the Ministry of Marine Affairs and Fisheries, the Ministry of Law and Human Rights, the Ministry of Finance, the Ministry of Defence, the Office of Attorney General, the Military (*Tentara Nasional Indonesia*/TNI), the National Police, TNI-AL and the State Intelligence Agency. The evolution of this structure will be explored in the next section. It is sufficient to note here that synergising capabilities and harmonising the roles and responsibilities of these agencies has been a challenging task for the Indonesian government.

The TNI-AL is primarily responsible for the protection of maritime sovereignty, particularly in the EEZ while the police's Directorate of Marine Police is in charge of law enforcement in territorial seas.[3] However, as will be explained in the next section, the Navy's warships also conduct law enforcement operations in Indonesia's territorial and archipelagic waters. The Ministry of Marine Affairs and Fisheries' Directorate General of Marine Resources and Fisheries Surveillance, Ministry of Transportation's Directorate of Sea and Coast Guard, and the Ministry of Finance's Directorate General of Customs are tasked with marine environmental protection, navigational safety, and port security and tax revenue, respectively.[4] The rest of the agencies maintain policy and information coordination without committing patrol assets at sea.[5] In addition to these thirteen agencies, there are a number

---

[3] Ristian Atriandi Supriyanto and Siswanto Rusdi, "Maritime Security Agencies in Indonesia: More Not Merrier," RSIS Commentaries (Singapore, 2013).
[4] Ibid.
[5] Ibid.

of agencies dealing indirectly with maritime-related issues including the Ministry of Forestry, the Ministry of Tourism, the Ministry of Energy and Mineral Resources, the Ministry of Trade, the National Agency of Search and Rescue and the National Agency of Border Areas Development.[6]

On paper, BAKAMLA is supposed to be the leading actor for Indonesian maritime security. In fact, its proponents consider BAKAMLA as the answer to the long-standing problems of ineffective maritime policing in Indonesian waters and jurisdiction due to the lack of coordination between the related agencies. Indeed, Presidential Regulation No. 178/2014 on the establishment of BAKAMLA mandates BAKAMLA to synergise and monitor patrols conducted by other maritime security-related agencies; formulate national maritime security and safety policy; operate early warning systems; carry out protection, surveillance, prevention and law enforcement; provide technical assistance to other maritime security-related agencies; search and rescue; and assist in the national defence system. It is also envisioned to be the sole civilian maritime law enforcement agency to conduct coast guard tasks along with the TNI-AL which, as the vision goes, would focus more on the protection of sovereignty against military threats.[7]

A study endorsed by BAKAMLA in 2015 argues for shifting the paradigm from "multiple agencies, single function" to "single agency, multiple functions". This would involve establishing a dedicated civilian maritime law enforcement agency and BAKAMLA, the authors conclude, is well placed to take up that responsibility.[8] Today, however, it seems like the notion of BAKAMLA becoming the single agency with multiple functions has lost out to persisting orthodoxy.[9] No one seems to be quite happy to be told what to do by a newly established agency, least of all established institutions such as the Navy or the Ministry of Fisheries and Marine Affairs.[10] Consequently, there has been hardly any

[6] Sulistyaningtyas, Susanto, and Munaf, *Sinergitas Paradigma Lintas Sektor Di Bidang Keamanan Dan Keselamatan Laut* [Cross-Sectoral Synergy Between Maritime Security and Safety Paradigms] (Jakarta: PT. Gramedia Pustaka Utama, 2015), 23–24.
[7] See ibid.
[8] See ibid.; Muhamad Arif, "Power Plays in Indonesian Waters," *APPS Policy Forum*, 2018, https://www.policyforum.net/power-plays-indonesian-waters/.
[9] Ibid.
[10] Ibid.

significant alteration in the legal framework, budgeting mechanism or operations.[11]

The establishment of BAKAMLA also took up the momentum of the call for greater coast guard cooperation in the region. The expansion of coast guards and the opportunities and challenges this poses to regional countries have indeed highlighted the necessity to strengthen cooperation in the areas such as capacity building and the designing of common operating principles.[12] In many previous instances, the absence of a single Indonesian coast guard had also complicated law enforcement especially when it involved foreign vessels or citizens as the governments in question often found it difficult to reach out to a designated contact point in Indonesia.[13] It is perhaps only in this domain of maritime diplomacy that BAKAMLA is able to exclusively claim the title as the Indonesian coast guard.

Moreover, the establishment of BAKAMLA took place amid the ongoing deliberation for the establishment of the Sea and Coast Guard Indonesia (*Penjagaan Laut dan Pantai Indonesia*/SCGI) built upon the existing unit under the Ministry of Transportation. The proponents of this initiative argue that the 2008 law on shipping which mandates the establishment of the Sea and Coast Guard preceded the 2014 law on maritime affairs which rules the establishment of BAKAMLA.[14] It is more limited in terms of the scope of responsibilities as it would mainly deal with the safety of navigation and search and rescue in the territorial sea. However, unlike BAKAMLA which is headed by a senior official under the coordination of the Coordinating Minister for Politics, Law, and Security, the Ministry of Transportation's sea and coast guard unit would be responsible directly to the president which could potentially make it superior. This has resulted in a tension between the two institutions, both claiming the right to bear the title of Indonesian coast guard.

---

[11] Ibid.

[12] See, for instance, Swee Lean Collin Koh, "The South China Sea's 'White-Hull' Warfare," *The National Interest*, 2016, http://nationalinterest.org/feature/the-south-china-seas-"white-hull"-warfare-15604.

[13] "Interview with a Mid-Ranking BAKAMLA Officer" (Jakarta, 2017).

[14] The law mandates the government to establish the Sea and Coast Guard (*Penjagaan Laut dan Pantai*) in three years after the legalisation of the law. The initiative momentarily lost its traction after the establishment of BAKAMLA.

Amid the confusion regarding the rightful bearer of coast guard title, the TNI-AL retains its predominant role in not only safeguarding the country's territorial sovereignty against military threats but also enforcing laws against illegal activities at sea including in territorial and archipelagic waters. As one scholar notes, naval defence and maritime security, along with naval diplomacy, form a core task for the TNI-AL.[15] The 2004 law on armed forces, for instance, rules that the missions of the TNI-AL include law and security enforcement in the national jurisdictions on the sea. The law enforcement roles are enshrined in the Navy's doctrine and institutionalised in its organisational structure and operational missions.[16] Maritime security task forces, in addition to combat task forces, are thus attached to the two fleets under the Navy command.

The TNI-AL's prominence and influence is at such a level that other actors recognise its centrality.[17] The push to establish the aforementioned SCGI, for instance, only gained traction after it received favourable support from the TNI-AL leadership who felt that their institutional interests would not be hampered by the establishment of the new agency.[18] Similarly, it can also be argued that the ascendancy of the Ministry of Marine Affairs and Fisheries in recent years can be partly attributed to the favourable stance of the TNI-AL towards it. The task force to combat illegal fishing that was established under the Ministry of Marine Affairs and Fisheries in 2015 relied heavily on intelligence and logistical support from the Navy. The Navy Deputy Chief of Staff also acts as the Chief Executive of the task force. In BAKAMLA itself, TNI-AL officers fill up most of the high-ranking positions. As the most capable maritime security agency compared to its mission-tailored counterparts, TNI-AL has succeeded in selling itself as the most

---

[15] Evan A. Laksmana, "Rebalancing Indonesia's Naval Force: Trends, Nature, and Drivers," in *Naval Modernisation in South-East Asia: Nature, Causes and Consequences*, ed. Geoffrey Till and Jane Chan (New York: Routledge, 2014), 188.
[16] Ibid.
[17] Ioannis Chapsos and James A. Malcolm, "Maritime Security in Indonesia: Towards a Comprehensive Agenda?" *Marine Policy* 76 (2017): 182.
[18] Honna, "Instrumentalizing Pressures, Reinventing Mission: Indonesian Navy Battles for Turf in the Age of Reformasi," 75.

multifunctional agency amid changing domestic political priorities, budgetary constraints and inter-agency competition.[19]

THE HISTORICAL DEVELOPMENT OF INDONESIAN MARITIME SECURITY GOVERNANCE

The difficulty Indonesia is facing in delineating the roles and responsibilities of its overlapping maritime security agencies, and the predominant role of the Navy in enforcing laws at sea is rooted in history. This section provides a brief overview of the historical development of Indonesian maritime security governance. As the following analysis shows, some of the major institutional developments in Indonesian maritime security governance took place during the so-called New Order (*Orde Baru*), the 32 years (1966–1998) regime led by Suharto. The following historical analysis is thus structured into three periods: pre-*Orde Baru*, *Orde Baru* and post-*Orde Baru*.

Pre-Orde Baru

Soon after Indonesia's self-declared independence in 1945, the country's founding fathers realised the necessity to secure vulnerable Indonesian waters. Prior to the Second World War, for instance, Japanese fishing boats were often found approaching the coasts of Indonesian islands in an effort to map the Indonesian coast as part of the preparation for the incoming war.[20] The territorial waters as determined by the colonial-era ordinance were considered insufficient in regard to national security as their three-mile limit exposed Indonesia to threatening manoeuvres of foreign warships close to its coast. Moreover, effective control of the sea around and between Indonesian islands was necessary to protect resource extraction that had so far been undermined by extensive

---

[19] Jo Inge Bekkevold, Ian Bowers, and Michael Raska, "Conclusion: Security, Strategy and Military Change in the 21st Century," in *Security, Strategy and Military Change in the 21st Century: Cross Regional Perspectives*, ed. Jo Inge Bekkevold, Ian Bowers, and Michael Raska (London: Routledge, 2015). Cited in Jo Inge Bekkevold and Ian Bowers, "A Question of Balance: Warfighting and Naval Operations Other Than War," in *International Order at Sea: How It Is Challenged. How It Is Maintained*, ed. Jo Inge Bekkevold and Geoffrey Till (London: Palgrave Macmillan, 2016), 243.

[20] Hasjim Djalal, *Indonesia and the Law of the Sea* (Jakarta: Centre for Strategic and International Studies, 1995), 298.

smuggling.[21] The military and diplomatic campaign to defend independence against the returning Dutch consumed all of the government's attention and resources and left hardly any space to seriously think about the peacetime administration of maritime security.

In response to those challenges, the People's Security Forces-Navy (*Tentara Keamanan Rakyat Angkatan Laut*/TKR-Laut) was established in October 1945.[22] Due to the lack of capacity, this embryo of Indonesia's modern Navy only played a minor role in the war of independence (1945–1949), focusing on maintaining security around ports and naval facilities and supporting the land-based guerrilla campaign.[23] The lack of capacity and the nature of threat during this period also restricted the Indonesian government from moving beyond the minimal institutional arrangement required for law enforcement at sea. The colonial-era customs agency, for instance, was nationalised and put under the Department of Finance. A Sea and Coast Guard Unit was also established under the Department of Transportation and a Water Police Unit (*Polisi Air*/Polair) under the National Police.

After Indonesia gained its full independence from the Dutch in 1949, the government started to think seriously about administering its waters in order to secure them from threats and exploit their full economic potential. The experience during the war of independence demonstrated the vulnerability of Indonesian archipelagic waterways being used by external powers and thus threatening Indonesian security. During the war, Dutch Naval forces imposed blockades at some of the most crucial Indonesian SLOC in the Java Sea and the Strait of Malacca. This complicated the Indonesian war effort as weapons and munitions had to be smuggled through the blockade.[24] Meanwhile, illegal activities on the archipelagic waterways continued to damage the Indonesian economy.

[21] Ibid., 299.

[22] TKR was actually preceded by the People's Security Body (*Badan Keamanan Rakyat*/BKR) and the People's Security Body-Navy (BKR-Laut) which were established on August 22, 1945. As the name suggests, the BKR was not intended to be a state military. A military organisation, it was thought, would provoke the Japanese and the incoming allied forces and undermine the objective of diplomatic campaign to secure international recognition of Indonesian independence. See Pusat Sejarah dan Tradisi TNI, *Sejarah TNI Jilid I (1945–1949)* (Jakarta: Pusat Sejarah dan Tradisi TNI, 2000), 1–9.

[23] Robert Lowry, *The Armed Forces of Indonesia* (Sidney: Allen & Unwin, 1996), 95.

[24] Alfred Daniel Matthews, "Indonesian Maritime Security Cooperation in the Malacca Straits" (Naval Postgraduate School, 2015), 12.

Indonesia then decided to revitalise the role of its Navy. The TKR-Laut which had been renamed the Navy of the Republic of Indonesia (*Angkatan Laut Republik Indonesia*/ALRI) was given the responsibility to: (1) defend the country against enemy's offensive at and from the sea and secure inter-islands exchanges and access to ports and (2) to carry out policing tasks to enforce the government's laws and pacify the regions.[25] The Indonesian government also started to give attention to multi-agency governance at sea. In what was perhaps the first attempt to organise Indonesian maritime security agencies, an ordinance was then issued by the central government that identified the government agencies involved in maritime management. These agencies included the Navy, the Water Police, Customs, the Department of Maritime Affairs and Fisheries and the Directorate of Sea Communication in the Department of Transportation.[26] Maritime management during this period was, as one scholar notes, chaotic as competition among stakeholders encouraged a "go your own way" mentality which undermined efforts to coordinate missions and visions.[27]

Throughout much of the 1950s until early the 1960s, a series of armed movements, some of which evidently supported by foreign powers, emerged across the country and challenged the authority of the central government in Jakarta. These separatist movements included the Darul Islam/Islamic Armed Forces of Indonesia (Darul Islam/*Tentara Islam Indonesia* or DI/TII) in western and central Java, Aceh, southern Sulawesi and southern Borneo; the Republic of South Moluccas (*Republik Maluku Selatan*/RMS) in the Moluccas islands; and the Revolutionary Government of Republic of Indonesia/People's Total Struggle (*Pemerintahan Revolusioner Republik Indonesia/Perjuangan Rakyat Semesta* or PRRI/Permesta) in some parts of Sumatera and Sulawesi. Marine forces and a number of warships were deployed to thwart the DI/TII resistance.[28] In the more distant Moluccas islands, the Indonesian Navy played a bigger role with the deployment of a

---

[25] Pusat Sejarah dan Tradisi TNI, *Sejarah TNI Jilid II (1950–1959)* (Jakarta: Pusat Sejarah dan Tradisi TNI, 2000), 11.

[26] Honna, "Instrumentalizing Pressures, Reinventing Mission: Indonesian Navy Battles for Turf in the Age of Reformasi," 65.

[27] Ibid., 65–66.

[28] See Pusat Sejarah dan Tradisi TNI, *Sejarah TNI Jilid II (1950–1959)* (Jakarta: Pusat Sejarah dan Tradisi TNI, 2000), 81–110.

number of corvettes to control the seas surrounding the islands, provide fire support and land ground forces. The Netherlands were believed to have provided political support for the RMS. In countering PRRI/Permesta, which was believed to have been provided with extensive military aid by the US military, the TNI-AL deployed quite a substantial fleet consisting of 17 warships and 19 transport ships in what was its first experience operating in a large formation. Despite the overall limited capacity, these internal security operations had nevertheless allowed the Indonesian Navy to secure its presence in many parts of the archipelago. Moreover, the potential re-emergence of separatist movements which, given the geographical nature of Indonesia, could get clandestine support from external powers, continued to form a major part of the Navy's strategic narrative.[29]

The radical change in domestic political structure and foreign policy direction in the early 1960s enabled the Navy to significantly increase its capacity. Despite an economic crisis, President Sukarno, who had secured his position as nominally the sole political authority in the country, mobilised the national resources to support his vision of anti-colonialism. Consequently, the country began to lean towards the Eastern Bloc. Indonesia received a large amount of aid from the Soviet Union with the Navy, along with the Air Force, among the biggest beneficiaries. Between 1959 and 1965, Indonesia received 12 submarines, seven destroyers, one cruiser, seven frigates, 26 fast attack craft, seven minesweepers, 26 patrol craft and two support ships.[30] The much-improved capabilities allowed the Indonesian Navy to contest the command of the sea during the campaign to retake Papua from the Dutch.[31]

---

[29] Djalal, *Indonesia and the Law of the Sea*, 299. For the role of the interpretation of the historically shaped strategic culture, and subjective interpretation of its geographical nature, on the contemporary behaviour of the Navy see Arif and Kurniawan, "Strategic Culture and Indonesian Maritime Security".

[30] Data generated from the SIPRI Arms Transfer Database. See also Pusat Sejarah dan Tradisi TNI, *Sejarah TNI 1960 Jilid III (1960–1965)* (Jakarta: Pusat Sejarah dan Tradisi TNI, 2000).

[31] The Netherlands retained its control over Papua or Western New Guinea after the official recognition of Indonesia's independence in 1949. Since the mid-1950s Indonesian government, considering itself as the rightful authority over Papua, had launched a diplomatic campaign to retake the region. In 1962, after protracted negotiations, the region was placed under United Nations administration, and in 1963, it was transferred to Indonesia.

The nature of maritime security challenges and certain domestic political priorities during the pre-*Orde Baru* period forced the Indonesian government to come up with a particular response in which the Navy, exploiting the country's sense of maritime vulnerability, was able to lay the groundwork for its future dominance of the country's maritime security architecture. As noted by Liow and Shekhar,

> Acutely aware of how the Dutch sought to reimpose colonialism after the Second World War by using Indonesia's vast waterways, how Sumatran rebels engaged in seaborne political subversion during the 1957 PRRI/Permesta Rebellion, and the deployment of a Dutch aircraft carrier in the vicinity during the 1960 crisis over Irian Jaya, Indonesian leaders have struggled to come to terms with the insecurity of its proximate waterways.[32]

The aforementioned military campaigns had thus allowed the Navy to gain ascendancy over other maritime security agencies to dominate maritime administration in the territorial waters.[33] This dominant position has not been relinquished by the Navy since.

Orde Baru

The rise to power of Suharto and his New Order (*Orde Baru*) regime brought a further momentum for the militarisation of Indonesian security governance as the blurred distinction between "defence" or the protection of sovereignty against military threats and "security" which mostly covered law enforcement tasks was institutionalised. A regime founded by the Army, *Orde Baru* basically turned Indonesia into a "national security state" in which the military played an extensive role.[34] Under the banner of Dual Function (*Dwi Fungsi*) doctrine, the military

---

[32] Vibhanshu Shekhar and Joseph Chinyong Liow, "Indonesia as a Maritime Power: Jokowi's Vision, Strategies, and Obstacles Ahead," *The Brookings Institution*, 2014, http://www.brookings.edu/research/articles/2014/11/indonesia-maritime-liow-shekhar.

[33] Ibid.

[34] See Salim Said, *Tumbuh Dan Kembangnya Dwifungsi: Perkembangan Pemikiran Politik Militer Indonesia 1958–2002* (Jakarta: Aksara Karunia, 2002); Leonard C. Sebastian, *Realpolitik Ideology: Indonesia's Use of Military Force* (Singapore: Institute of Southeast Asian Studies [ISEAS], 2006).

considered itself as not only a "military power" but also a "political power" which enabled the Army to engage in non-military areas.[35]

The blurred distinction between defence and internal security roles of the military, which consequently gave more flexibility for the Navy to engage in law enforcement tasks, was also codified in their operational doctrines. The "*Tjatur Darma Eka Karma*" doctrine that was released in the early days of *Orde Baru* defined "total people warfare" (*Perang Rakyat Semesta*/Perata), operationalised in defence as well as internal security operations, as the core concept of national defence.[36]

Despite its rather awkward position during the transitional period, the Navy still managed to take up the momentum and expand its influence vis-à-vis other maritime security agencies.[37] *Dwi Fungsi*, for instance, enabled the military to expand its roles and responsibilities to areas beyond defence against military threats. Military officers, including from the Navy, were seconded to high-ranking posts in civilian maritime security-related agencies.[38] By 1977, for instance, there were 926 Navy officers seconded to such posts.[39] The policy had allowed the Navy leadership to control the respective agencies and promote the Navy's institutional interests within the broader maritime security governance structure.

In 1982, a new law on national defence and security was signed by the government. The law codified the "national defence and security" (*Pertahanan dan Keamanan Negara*/Hankamneg) which mandated military professionalism in the management of internal security. At the

---

[35] As quoted in Harold Crouch, *The Army and Politics in Indonesia* (Ithaca: Cornell University Press, 1978), 345.

[36] Andi Widjajanto, "Evolusi Doktrin Pertahanan Indonesia," *Prisma* 29, no. 1 (2010): 12.

[37] The Navy, and the Air Force, was not considered as the main supporters of Suharto when he rose to power in the middle of 1960s. This was famously captured in the relations between *Orde Baru* and Lieutenant General Hartono, then Marine Corps Commandant. Hartono was well known as a strong loyalist of Sukarno, Indonesia's founding father and Suharto's predecessor. Hartono was immediately sidelined after the rise of *Orde Baru* and later was found dead in his house in 1971.

[38] Honna, "Instrumentalizing Pressures, Reinventing Mission: Indonesian Navy Battles for Turf in the Age of Reformasi," 67.

[39] Nugroho Notosusanto, ed., *Pejuang Dan Prajurit: Konsepsi Dan Implementasi Dwifungsi ABRI* (Jakarta: Penerbit Sinar Harapan, 1984), 379. As cited in Honna, "Instrumentalizing Pressures, Reinventing Mission: Indonesian Navy Battles for Turf in the Age of Reformasi," 67.

service level, the Navy leadership developed the concept of "*Hankamneg at Sea*" (*Hankamneg di Laut*) and started to conduct routine maritime policing under the flag of Operasi Keamanan Laut (Kamla), or Maritime Security Operations.[40] Furthermore, in 1991 the Department of Defence and Security released a new military operational doctrine. The new doctrine contained the concept of "defence zones preparation" in which defence zones were divided into three layers: a buffer zone outside of the EEZ and air space above it; a main defence zone covering the EEZ and the territorial seas and the air space above it; and finally, a resistance zone covering strategic land compartments, archipelagic waters and the air space above them.[41] The doctrine underlines the land-based defence strategy which had been adopted by the military and was based on a worst-case scenario where an invading force managed to land on Indonesian shores. Nevertheless, the doctrine also provided further justification for the Navy to maintain its presence in the territorial and archipelagic waters as part of the missions to prepare the defence zones.

Suharto's choice to base his political legitimacy on economic development, which was left untouched by his predecessor, as well as internal stability and order also drove the military to focus most of its attention and resources on internal security tasks. In this regard, the intervention of the military in guarding internal security and order was deemed necessary for the uninterrupted implementation of economic development programs. The TNI assumed the title of the "stabiliser" and "dynamist" of national development.[42]

In 1972, a joint decision letter was signed by the then Minister of Defence and Security/Commander of the Armed Forces, the Minister of Transportation, the Minister of Finance, the Minister of Justice, and the Attorney General to establish the Maritime Security Coordinating Agency (*Badan Koordinasi Keamanan Laut*/BAKORKAMLA). As the name suggests, BAKORKAMLA was meant to be the national body responsible to coordinate policies and activities of different maritime-related agencies.[43] The signatories of the letter, however, reflected the

---

[40] Ibid., 67.

[41] Widjajanto, "Evolusi Doktrin Pertahanan Indonesia," 17–18.

[42] Ahmad Yani Basuki, *Reformasi TNI: Pola, Profesionalitas Dan Refungsionalisasi Militer Dalam Masyarakat* (Jakarta: Yayasan Pustaka Obor Indonesia, 2013), 71.

[43] Evan A. Laksmana, "Rebalancing Indonesia's Naval Force: Trends, Nature, and Drivers," in *Naval Modernisation in South-East Asia: Nature, Causes and Consequences*, ed. Geoffrey Till and Jane Chan (New York: Routledge, 2014), 181.

then rather narrow concerns of Indonesian maritime security; it hardly went beyond defence, safety of navigation and customs enforcement. Thus, in terms of the actual patrol operations, the TNI-AL carried out most of the maritime law enforcement tasks under the rubric of the Navy's constabulary functions.[44] In fact, in terms of the institutional arrangement BAKORKAMLA was operating directly under the supervision of the commander of the armed forces with its regional divisions were headed by the Navy's Eastern and Western fleet commanders.[45]

The expansion of the maritime security landscape, with increased attention given to issues previously considered marginal to national security, has resulted in the subsequent proliferation of maritime security agencies both horizontally in terms of the number of the agencies and vertically in terms of the perceived responsibilities and capabilities of some, if not all of the agencies. In the last couple of decades, for instance, issues like illegal fishing and environmental protection have come to the fore. As a result, though it remained the most capable organisation, the TNI-AL's dominance in Indonesian maritime security governance started to come under pressure.

Moreover, there was a substantial expansion of international regulation and corresponding domestic laws with the United Nations Convention on the Law of the Sea (UNCLOS) which contains provisions on legal principles and regime of archipelagic state which came into force in 1994 and the new law concerning Indonesian waters signed in 1996. UNCLOS, therefore, extended Indonesia's marine resources base to the extent that it is now larger than the land resources base.[46]

> The application of the archipelagic principles in Indonesia requires substantial expansion of law enforcement at sea which could not be easily or quickly met because of the emphasis given in the national development plan on economic sectors especially on agriculture. Moreover, cooperation and more effective coordination between the various enforcement agencies at sea need a lot of improvement and constant attention. The problems of

---

[44] Sulistyaningtyas, Susanto, and Munaf, *Sinergitas Paradigma Lintas Sektor Di Bidang Keamanan Dan Keselamatan Laut*, 22.

[45] Honna, "Instrumentalizing Pressures, Reinventing Mission: Indonesian Navy Battles for Turf in the Age of Reformasi," 67.

[46] Ibid., 207.

enforcement and coordination of the various enforcement agencies would be greater and much more complicated if the establishment of Exclusive Economic Zone there added to the already extensive problems of enforcing and implementing the archipelagic principles and continental shelf.[47]

All of these factors have contributed to shape the Indonesian contemporary strategic environment and thus the need to rethink Indonesian maritime security governance.[48]

Post-Orde Baru

The collapse of *Orde Baru* in 1998 was a turning point for the Indonesian military. The *Dwi Fungsi* doctrine was scrapped, and a number of organisational adjustments were implemented. The military, for instance, decided to reduce the practice of seconding active personnel to civilian posts.[49] This led to the gradual withdrawal of uniformed Navy personnel from other maritime security agencies, and it contributed to the process of civilianising and demilitarising Indonesia's maritime security administration.[50] In 1999, the police was separated from the armed forces with a subsequent delineation of responsibilities between the two institutions. The TNI was assigned responsibility for national "defence", and the police was given the role of maintaining domestic "security" and "order".[51]

---

[47] Djalal, *Indonesia and the Law of the Sea*, 19–20.

[48] On the role of law on maritime strategy and operations see Steven Haines, "The Influence of Law on Maritime Strategy," in *Maritime Strategy and Global Order: Markets, Resources, Security*, ed. Daniel Moran and James A. Russell (Washington, DC: Georgetown University Press, 2016), 239–260.

[49] Honna, "Instrumentalizing Pressures, Reinventing Mission: Indonesian Navy Battles for Turf in the Age of Reformasi," 2008, 69. The 2004 law on armed forces rules that active military personnel may only be posted in civilian posts in the following government agencies: Coordinating Ministry for Politics and Security, Ministry of Defence, Military Secretary to the President, State Intelligence Agency, State Cryptography Agency, National Resilience Institute, National Defence Council, National Search and Rescue Agency, National Narcotics Agency and the Supreme Court.

[50] Ibid.

[51] Ibid.

The separation of the police from the military and the delineation of responsibilities between the two institutions have arguably had the greatest impact on the Army. While law enforcement and domestic security were almost entirely omitted from the list of tasks of the Army, the TNI-AL, under the banner of Naval constabulary roles, still retained such missions.[52] Although there is nothing unique in itself about the TNI-AL being tasked with law and security enforcement, it is worth noting that the reaffirmation of this task in the 2004 law on armed forces stands in contrast to the omission of such task from the Army. The 2004 law on armed forces was indeed formulated in the political context of military reform during which the Army, which had previously played extensive role in internal security matters during the *Orde Baru* period, faced enormous pressure to relinquish its roles and responsibilities in internal security. Nevertheless, with the maintenance of domestic security no longer to be used as justification, the Navy has now more limited space in terms of non-defence-related roles. Moreover, the separation of the police from the armed forces has also allowed the *Polair* to expand its presence and capabilities vis-à-vis the Navy.

The TNI-AL leadership, however, did not stand idle in facing the unfavourable post-*Dwi Fungsi* institutional environment. As it began to be clear that the TNI-AL was losing its ground, the Navy leadership immediately invoked the old mantra: Indonesian geostrategic vulnerabilities against the interference of external powers. In a TNI seminar in 1999, Navy leadership presented their vision for strengthening the Navy's role and presence in maritime administration.[53] The vision stressed that, given its geographical strategic position, Indonesia is expected by the international community to improve security and safety in Indonesian waters and jurisdiction, a task that only the Navy was able to execute. Failure to do so, the Navy leadership argued, would provide foreign governments a pretext to intervene in the sovereign territory of Indonesia.[54]

---

[52] The 2004 law on armed forces stipulates that the Army is responsible for carrying out the following functions: defence, security of the land border areas, capability building-up and development, and land defence areas empowerment. In addition to the corresponding functions on the sea and air space, respectively, the Navy and Air Force are also tasked with carrying out law enforcement duties on the sea and national air space.

[53] Ibid., 70.

[54] Ibid.

Realising the need to streamline the maritime security governance, a presidential regulation was signed in 2005 to revitalise the BAKORKAMLA. According to the regulation, it was now headed by the Coordinating Minister for Politics, Law, and Security who was responsible directly to the president. Twelve ministerial-level officials whose agencies' tasks and responsibilities include maritime security sit in the BAKORKAMLA as members. These agencies are the Minister of Foreign Affairs, the Minister of Home Affairs, the Minister of Transportation, the Minister of Marine Affairs and Fisheries, the Minister of Law and Human Rights, the Minister of Finance, the Minister of Defence, the Attorney General, the military (TNI) commander, the Chief of Police, the Navy Chief of Staff (TNI-AL) and the Head of the State Intelligence Agency.

The idea of having effective maritime policing through BAKORKAMLA, however, has proven to be unrealistic.[55] Problems such as parochial institutional interests, competition for resource, slow legal enforcement as well as a lack of firm leadership continued to hinder inter-agency coordination.[56] In October 2014, the unprecedented law on maritime affairs was signed. The law, among others, mandates the government to establish the Maritime Security Agency (*Badan Keamanan Laut*/BAKAMLA) to carry out law enforcement activities in Indonesian waters and jurisdiction, particularly to conduct maritime security and safety patrol. With the signing of the Presidential Regulation No. 178/2014, BAKORKAMLA was officially transformed into BAKAMLA.

From this historical overview of Indonesian maritime security governance development, a number of observations can be made regarding the nature of Indonesian maritime security governance and how it approaches military and civilian roles at sea. First, Indonesian maritime security governance is generally typified by the blurred distinction between "defence" or protection of sovereignty and territorial integrity against military threat and "security" which in the case of Indonesia is understood in terms of internal security or law enforcement tasks. The embodiment of this paradigm has allowed the Navy to sustain its dominance in the country's maritime security governance, making clear delineation of roles more difficult. Second, it has been proven that

---

[55] Supriyanto and Rusdi, "Maritime Security Agencies in Indonesia: More Not Merrier".
[56] Ibid.

throughout its history, Indonesian maritime security governance is susceptible to the ever-changing domestic political priorities. The institutional arrangement and the balance of power among various maritime security-related agencies are to a significant extent shaped by the nature of maritime security challenges, as understood by the political leaders, as well as the development agenda's priority.

THE GLOBAL MARITIME FULCRUM AND MARITIME SECURITY GOVERNANCE

The election as president of Joko Widodo in 2014 gained wide domestic and international attention. In a country where foreign and security policy had never really taken part in public discussion, Jokowi came to power with a vision to transform Indonesia into a maritime power capable to "assert itself as a force between the two oceans: the Indian Ocean and the Pacific Ocean". The GMF vision rests on five pillars: rebuild maritime culture; maintain and manage maritime resources; develop maritime infrastructure and connectivity; promote maritime diplomacy; and develop maritime capabilities.[57] Underlying this vision is the renewed realisation of the natural dictate of Indonesian geography; it is an archipelagic state with abundant marine resources and other maritime economic potentials residing in between two increasingly strategic oceans, the Indian Ocean and the Pacific Ocean. Jokowi, in other words, had arguably managed to come up with a grand strategy that places Indonesian domestic economic development within the broader context of changing geostrategic circumstances.

In order to operationalise the aforementioned vision, Jokowi's administration prepared a five-year development programme, the 2015–2019 National Midterm Development Plan (*Rencana Pembangunan Jangka Menengah*/RPJMN). The missions included achieving a national security system capable of protecting territorial sovereignty, sustaining economic independence through maritime resources security and reflecting the Indonesian identity as an archipelagic state; realising a free and active foreign policy and Indonesian identity as a maritime nation; and realising Indonesia as an independent, developed, strong and national

[57] Rendi A. Witular, "Presenting Maritime Doctrine," *The Jakarta Post*, 2014, m.thejakartapost.com/news/2014/11/14/presenting-maritime-doctrine.htm.

interests-based maritime nation. Nine-point development priorities, called *Nawa Cita*, were also devised covering issues such as maritime border areas security; elimination of illegal fishing, illegal logging, human trafficking and other illegal activities at sea; security of maritime resources and EEZ; infrastructure, coverage and institutional arrangement of maritime law enforcement; and maritime law enforcement coordination. Thus, in terms of policy and development planning, the Jokowi administration's focus on maritime security, primarily to protect Indonesian territorial integrity and sustain economic development, was clear. The interlinked objectives of safeguarding Indonesian territorial integrity and increasing the utilisation of Indonesian marine resources potential largely governed these domestic political priorities.

Indonesia's domestic priority on maritime security under Jokowi and how it shaped the structure of the maritime security governance was perhaps most visible through its approach to illegal fishing. The presence of over 5000 fishing vessels operating illegally in its waters, violating Indonesian territorial integrity and food sovereignty has resulted in annual losses of over $20 billion.[58] A series of policies had been taken by the widely popular Minister of Marine Affairs and Fisheries Susi Pudjiastuti in order to free up Indonesian waters and jurisdictions from illegal foreign fishing vessels and increase the utilisation of Indonesian marine resources by Indonesian fishermen. Along with the moratorium on fishing licenses and law enforcement efforts against transhipment, Susi was publicly heralded for her harsh policy to sink vessels seized on allegations of conducting illegal activities in Indonesian waters. During the period of 2014–2016, 236 fishing vessels, 229 of which were foreign vessels, were sunk by the Indonesian authority.[59] In addition to that, a presidential regulation was also signed which gave a mandate to the Minister of Marine Affairs and Fisheries to head a new task force to combat illegal fishing. This task force, known as Task Force 115 (*Satuan Tugas 115*/Satgas 115), is an ad hoc team comprised of assets from the Navy, BAKAMLA and Polair. The priority the Indonesian government under Jokowi gave to the issue of illegal fishing had significantly

---

[58] Prashanth Parameswaran, "Explaining Indonesia's 'Sink the Vessels' Policy Under Jokowi," *The Diplomat*, 2015, https://thediplomat.com/2015/01/explaining-indonesias-sink-the-vessels-policy-under-jokowi/.

[59] See Biro Perencanaan Sekretariat Jenderal KKP RI, "Laporan Tahunan Kementerian Kelautan Dan Perikanan 2016" (Jakarta, 2017).

increased the visibility of the Ministry of Marine Affairs and Fisheries in the domain of maritime security governance when compared to other civilian maritime law enforcement agencies.

As far as maritime security governance is concerned, the renewed focus on the maritime domain had given a new momentum for further reorganisation of Indonesian maritime security agencies. This is best exemplified by the establishment of BAKAMLA in 2014. With more authority compared to its predecessor, BAKORKAMLA, BAKAMLA was thought to be the answer to the complicated management of Indonesian maritime security. This should mean that BAKAMLA would have a centralised authority which would enable it to assign and define the roles and tasks of other agencies.[60]

The vision, however, appears to have faltered due to long-standing sectoral egoism and inter-agency competition for resources. As mentioned before, no one seems to be quite happy to be told what to do by a newly established agency, least of all established institutions such as the Navy or the Ministry of Fisheries and Marine Affairs.[61] BAKAMLA itself, due to the lack of its organic capabilities, still needs to rely on the capabilities and capacities of other agencies in conducting joint operations. In some instances, these joint operations are compromised by the conflicting schedules and operational plans of the participating agencies.

The tension between BAKAMLA and the Ministry of Transportation's Directorate of Sea and Coast Guard also continues to hinder the optimal implementation of BAKAMLA's mandate. Throughout 2017, for instance, the Ministry of Transportation's Directorate of Sea and Coast Guard only contributed one vessel to the BAKAMLA's joint operations, compared to 92 and 29 vessels from the TNI-AL and the Ministry of Marine Affairs and Fisheries, respectively.

The substantial increase in terms of data, information and intelligence that needs to be gathered to create and maintain maritime domain awareness has resulted in the realisation that the comprehensive and effective understanding of maritime environment with its security, safety, economic and ecological implication is crucially needed. Despite continued discussion on the topic among security planners and policy-makers, the lack of

---

[60] Ristian Atriandi Supriyanto, "Naval Counter-Piracy in Indonesia," in *Piracy in Southeast Asia: Trends, Hot Spots and Responses*, ed. Carolin Liss and Ted Biggs (New York: Routledge, 2017), 101.

[61] Arif, "Power Plays in Indonesian Waters".

coordination and inter-agency competition has so far hindered the realisation of maritime domain awareness. The various maritime security agencies described above continue to maintain and develop their own intelligence gathering, surveillance and reconnaissance system and infrastructure without a clear mechanism of information sharing and centralised command and control. While such separated development might be justified by different needs and technical requirements of the respective agencies, it is fair to say that better coordination and a clear mechanism of information sharing would minimise the risk of redundancy and duplication of the scattered capabilities as well as information and intelligence collected.

Indonesian maritime security governance development under the Jokowi administration also continued to be characterised by the dominance of the TNI-AL. In the post-*Orde Baru* environment, where the military was pressured to focus on defence roles, the Indonesian Navy managed to find its way around and maintain its primacy and influence vis-à-vis other maritime security agencies. As noted before, the TNI-AL's institutional interests are guaranteed with the presence of its officers in other civilian agencies that are emerging including the BAKAMLA and the Ministry of Marine Affairs and Fisheries' Task Force 115. Moreover, the TNI-AL's support for the establishment of Sea and Coast Guard within the Ministry of Transportation has also not been withdrawn. In other words, the TNI-AL has managed to retain its relevance in Indonesian maritime security governance and ensure its dominance is not compromised by the rise of any single civilian maritime law enforcement agency by expanding the landscape of the governance itself. With more players and capabilities remaining scattered, the TNI-AL will most likely retain its position as the major player in Indonesian maritime security governance.

The aforementioned post-*Orde Baru* military reform notwithstanding the Navy leadership appears to be persistent in defending its role in maritime law enforcement. In a discussion concerning the role of the TNI-AL in law enforcement, a senior naval officer once said, "Do not consider sovereignty merely about external borders as it also entails security threats in the (internal) waters. The difference is that the Navy uses warships instead of civilian ships. When dealing with illegal practices, we cannot separate defence and civilian maritime (law enforcement)".[62]

---

[62] "Dicky Munaf, Sestama Badan Keamanan Laut: Pengamanan Dan Keselamatan Laut Seimbang," *Republika Online*, 2016, http://www.republika.co.id/berita/koran/wawasan/16/01/27/o1lt0h5-dicky-munaf-sestama-badan-keamanan-laut-pengamanan-dan-keselamatan-laut-seimbang.

Conclusion

Indonesia has never been familiar with the concept of a coast guard as a dedicated civilian maritime law enforcement institution with a clear delineation of responsibilities vis-à-vis other agencies. To be fair, the geographical nature of the country makes it challenging to delineate the roles and responsibilities as well as to divide the areas of operation of the various maritime security agencies. The Navy leadership, for instance, could argue that the presence of warships in territorial and archipelagic waters is necessary to protect Indonesian UNCLOS-designated archipelagic sea lanes through which not only commercial ships but also foreign warships pass. On the other hand, it is not easy for civilian agencies to call for the greater allocation of resources and expand their presence in the natural habitat of the Navy in the EEZ and high seas.

Moreover, the long experience of the blurred distinction between "defence" and "security" has made it almost impossible to make the military focus solely on defence roles and relinquish internal security or law enforcement tasks. If there is any lesson learned from the Indonesian case, therefore, is that the approach country takes with regard to its maritime security governance is very much a result of its unique geostrategic circumstances as well as its strategic history.

Meanwhile, the susceptibility of Indonesian maritime security governance to ever-changing domestic political priorities means that nothing can be taken for granted when it comes to Indonesia's structural approach towards administering its seas. Succession in the government and shift in threat assessment and development agenda could result in changes in the structure of Indonesian maritime security governance. In fact, at the time of writing, Indonesia was preparing for the presidential election with Jokowi's bid for a second term was still highly contested.

It is safe to argue, however, that the current approach that Indonesia takes with regard to maritime security governance is not ideal. Duplication of roles and responsibilities could or have undermined effective governance of Indonesian waters and jurisdictions. With capabilities scattered, it is also difficult for Indonesia to achieve maritime domain awareness which is extremely necessary to ensure the safety and security of its waters and jurisdictions.

PART III

Europe

CHAPTER 8

Arctic Coast Guards: Managing New Challenges?

Andreas Østhagen

Maritime activity in the Arctic is changing.[1] While the region's littoral states are actively encouraging new economic endeavours in the north, they are also forced to provide presence and capabilities to deal with incidents in Arctic waters. Debates concerning capabilities in the Arctic have developed over the last decade as increased activity has led to questions concerning the lack of public investment in the capacity to manage potential emergencies. Demands have thus been made for national governments to invest in and sustain relatively expensive Arctic capacities, such as coast guard vessels, long-range helicopters, and oil-spill response units.

The three small North East Atlantic and Arctic states Denmark, Norway, and Iceland are all grappling with these challenges. Yet their institutional set-ups concerning coast guards and navies seem to differ.

---

[1] Odd Jarl Borch et al., "Maritime Activity in the High North—Current and Estimated Level up to 2025," 2016, 1–130. MARPART-Report.

A. Østhagen (✉)
Fridtjof Nansen Institute, Oslo, Norway
e-mail: aosthagen@fni.no

© The Author(s) 2019
I. Bowers and S. L. C. Koh (eds.), *Grey and White Hulls*,
https://doi.org/10.1007/978-981-13-9242-9_8

This chapter identifies these differences and explores the consequences of this variance in structure and competence in the context of the new challenges arising in Arctic waters.

The chapter will first examine how the maritime domain in the North East Atlantic/Arctic has changed, with regard to maritime activity. What does this entail for the littoral states and their coast guards? It then explores how Denmark, Iceland, and Norway have chosen to set up their respective coast guards and navies, in tandem with other military and civilian institutions. Finally, it connects the role of these institutions with an increasing number of tasks and demand for presence in their maritime domains, aimed at understanding both why (1) each country has chosen its particular set-up and (2) what this means for the overall response to a changing maritime situation.[2]

An Arctic Paradox

The Arctic is changing. Although maritime conditions vary across this vast region, increased activity from state and non-state actors alike is challenging the littoral northern states. This section will look at the changes occurring in the Arctic parts of Denmark, Iceland, and Norway. Within these, there is a marked increase in maritime activity, and thus a consequent increase in coast guard tasks. This means that we must examine Greenland, as well as northern parts of Norway including Svalbard, and all of Iceland. Despite some climatic differences,[3] due to similarities concerning fish stocks, climate and economic activity across the North Atlantic, it is reasonable to compare and contrast all three regions. The strategic environment that these three countries face is thus changing, in turn leading to questions of capacity, resources, and the division of labour between respective navies and coast guards.

---

[2] This chapter is concerned with the northern parts of the North East Atlantic/Arctic, defined as Denmark (predominantly Greenland), Iceland, and North Norway (including Svalbard and Jan Mayen).

[3] Greenland has more multi-year and annual sea ice than Iceland and North Norway.

ACTIVITY PATTERNS

In the maritime areas in question, the overall trend has been a steady increase in the number of vessels since the 1990s. As with climatic conditions, the situation varies; the number of vessels farthest north drops when sea ice does not retract as expected or commercial ventures are postponed or cancelled altogether. Yet the trends all indicate an increased number of vessels or vessel activity becoming more complex, diverse, and spread-out.[4]

Waters around Greenland have experienced growing levels of maritime activity over the last decade. When seismic activity was conducted in tandem with exploratory petroleum drilling in 2010–2011, vessel numbers increased dramatically.[5] There has also been a steady increase in the number of cruise ships around the world's largest island.[6] In total, vessel activity is a combination of local transport, fisheries, cargo transport, and cruise ship tourism. The fishing fleet makes up a significant portion of this activity. In 2014, there were 530 vessels with licences in Greenland, while 1500–2000 smaller boats exist, used for small-scale hunting and fishing.[7] While the number might be far less, 60–100 vessels in Greenlandic waters annually, cruise ships account for the greatest number of passengers, between 20,000 and 30,000 per year.[8] It should also be noted that the traffic numbers vary depending on which part of Greenland is examined. Most activity takes place in the south or southwest, as this is where most Greenlanders reside, and ice conditions are less severe. Activity is far more limited in the waters to the north and north-east.

---

[4] Andreas Østhagen, "Coast Guards in the Arctic—Troubles Ahead?" *The Arctic Institute*, 2014, http://www.thearcticinstitute.org/2014/10/100914-Coast-Guard-Arctic.html.

[5] Andreas Østhagen and Munk-Gordon Arctic Security Program, *Coast Guard Collaboration in the Arctic: Canada and Greenland (Denmark)* (Toronto: Gordon Walter & Duncan Foundation, 2014), 6–7, http://gordonfoundation.ca/publication/731.

[6] Danish Ministry of Defence, *Rapport Vedrørende Placering Af Værnsfælles Arktisk Kommando* [Report Concerning the Location of Arctic Command] (Copenhagen: Danish Ministry of Defence, 2011), http://www.fmn.dk/nyheder/Documents/Rapport_vedr_placering_af_Værnsfaelles_Arktisk_Kommando.pdf.

[7] Valur Ingimundarson et al., "The Icelandic Sea Areas and Activity Level up to 2025," in *Maritime Activity in the High North—Current and Estimated Level up to 2025* (Bodø: MARPART Projects Reports, Vol. 1, 2016), 74–86.

[8] Ibid.

In contrast to waters around Greenland, the Icelandic Arctic waters are ice-free. A relatively large population (in the Arctic context) of 323,000 also means high local activity levels. As with the waters around Greenland, activity is predominantly made up of fisheries, local transport, cargo transport, and cruise ship tourism. Since the economic crash in 2008, however, the number of goods shipped to and from Iceland has decreased.[9] In sum, the number of vessels related to transport and cargo has slightly decreased in the last decade.

Nevertheless, as in the other Arctic maritime domains, cruise ship tourism and fisheries have increased. Ingmundarson and Gunnarsdóttir found that out of 2300 vessels registered in Iceland, 1700 are fisheries-related.[10] Warmer waters have resulted in fish stocks moving further north, which is advantageous for Iceland and the Faroe Islands.[11] Cruise ship tourism around Iceland has also changed, as numbers have steadily increased from around 9000 passengers in the 1970s and 1980s to around 90,000 passengers in 2013. Almost all vessels arrive in Reykjavik, but many also traverse further north to less-developed ports such as Akureyri and Isafjordur. Cruise ship tourism is expected to continue to increase, at least in terms of vessel size.[12]

With almost 500,000 inhabitants, North Norway (the mainland) is the most populated of the areas in question, and thus confer a higher basic level of maritime activity. As with Iceland, climatic conditions are less harsh than in the North American Arctic, and population density is higher. Along the coast of the mainland, there is considerable industry-related shipping going to and from industrial hubs in North Norway and Northwest Russia. Some of this activity is directly linked to the petroleum industry, operating in the Barents Sea and stretching northwards in the Norwegian Sea. Many of the vessels also come from, or are going to, Murmansk, which is a hub for much of the regional maritime transport in the Russian Arctic.[13]

---

[9] Ibid.

[10] Ibid.

[11] Clemens Bomsdorf, "Iceland to Set Own Mackerel-Fishing Quota," *The Wall Street Journal*, March 13, 2014, http://www.wsj.com/articles/SB10001424052702303546204579437291728713068.

[12] Ingimundarson et al., "The Icelandic Sea Areas and Activity Level up to 2025." MARPART-Report.

[13] Norwegian Government, *Norway's Arctic Strategy: Between Geopolitics and Social Development* (Oslo, 2017), https://www.regjeringen.no/contentassets/fad46f0404e-14b2a9b551ca7359c1000/arctic-strategy.pdf.

Table 8.1 Characteristics of Denmark, Iceland, and Norway

State	Region	Population total/ region (ca.)	Level of maritime activity	Location of northern coast guard headquarters
Denmark	Greenland	5,731,000/56,000	Intermediate (seasonal)	Nuuk (Greenland)
Iceland	Iceland	323,000	High	Reykjavik (Iceland)
Norway	North Norway (incl. Svalbard and Jan Mayen)	5,233,000/483,000	High	Sortland (North Norway)

Note that all regions experience seasonal variations in activity, although Greenland is more influenced by ice-conditions in winter time

Maritime traffic patterns are, however, divided between vessel activity along the mainland and the traffic surrounding the Svalbard Archipelago further north. Svalbard only has a population of 2600, with around 2100 residing in Longyearbyen. While the amount of local traffic is therefore limited, the number of cruise ships has been increasing slightly, the number of annual cruise ship passengers having almost tripled since 1997.[14] Svalbard is unique in the Arctic context, as it is the only place large cruise vessels can reach as far as 80 degrees north without ice-classification.[15] Fisheries around Svalbard have also been increasing and constitute roughly 70% of all traffic.[16] The movement of stocks has led to more complex fishing vessel patterns, especially when it comes to shrimp fisheries to the north and east of the archipelago.[17]

[14] Johan N. Vold et al., "Økt Skipsfart I Polhavet: Muligheter Og Utfordringer for Norge" [Increased Shipping in the Arctic Ocean: Opportunities and Challenges for Norway], Report, Norwegian Ministry of Foreign Affairs, April 2013 (Oslo, 2013), 32; Norwegian Ministry of Justice, "Meld. St. 32 (2015–2016): Svalbard" (Oslo, 2016), 90.

[15] Odd Jarl Borch, Natalia Andreassen, and Nataly Marchenko, "The Norwegian Waters and Svalbard Sea Areas and Activity Level up to 2025," in *Maritime Activity in the High North—Current and Estimated Level up to 2025* (Bodø: MARPART Projects Reports, Vol. 1, 2016), 63.

[16] Norwegian Ministry of Justice, "Meld. St. 32 (2015–2016): Svalbard," 104.

[17] This also entails snow crab fisheries, which have been increasing in recent years. The crabs have been moving westwards into the waters surrounding Svalbard and have started to constitute a considerable resource.

The three regions in question have somewhat different characteristics, as laid out in Table 8.1. The population is particularly spread out in Greenland and very low in Svalbard, albeit high in North Norway in general. Iceland is in relative terms densely populated. Shipping activity varies greatly, and the summer activity levels generally constitute the annual peak in all areas.

Challenges

As the number of ships in Arctic waters increases, there is a corresponding increase in the risk of accidents.[18] Similarly, a number of other tasks ranging from environmental protection to sovereignty enforcement are increasingly in demand. This new Arctic reality has spurred demand for presence and capabilities amongst the Arctic states. When fisheries grow in volume, so does the need for regular fisheries inspections. At the same time, public assets are needed to respond to immediate incidents, such as the search and rescue of sailors and passengers, or environmental protection due to a spill from a vessel or a platform. Less immediate, but still in response to specific demands, are tasks related to the assistance of navigation and passage.[19]

The factors that contribute to a heightened risk of emergencies in the Arctic can be categorised as (1) geographic factors, (2) the lack of infrastructure, and (3) limited information. Geographic factors include the ice conditions, which are increasingly difficult to predict as the ice thaws and areas previously covered by sea ice are opening. Related factors include low temperatures and the winter darkness. There is a limited amount of infrastructure in the region, given the few human settlements and the distances between them. For example, SAR aircraft can

---

[18] Allianz, *Safety and Shipping Review 2015* (Munich, 2015), http://www.agcs.allianz.com/assets/PDFs/Reports/Shipping-Review-2015.pdf; Ron Kroeker, Interview Concerning Emergency Preparedess in the Canadian North (Kitchener, ON: Interview by: Andreas Østhagen, 2016).

[19] Andreas Østhagen, "Coastguards in Peril: A Study of Arctic Defence Collaboration," *Defence Studies* 15, no. 2 (2015): 143–60; Andreas Østhagen and Vanessa Gestaldo, *Coast Guard Co-operation in a Changing Arctic* (Toronto: Munk-Gordon Arctic Security Program, 2015), http://gordonfoundation.ca/publication/749; and James R. Mitchell, "The Canadian Coast Guard in Perspective: A Paper Prepared for Action Canada," August (Ottawa: Action Canada, 2013), http://www.actioncanada.ca/en/wp-content/uploads/2013/08/Canadian-Coast-Guard-In-Perspective_EN.pdf.

take anywhere from 6–10 hours to travel from southern airbases before arriving to drop equipment in the Arctic.[20] Finally, lack of information relates to the understanding of the area in which you operate. There are issues with the use of satellites, making it difficult to perform missions with the precision needed for SAR. Related to this is the fact that great portions of the underwater Arctic geography have yet to be mapped sufficiently.[21]

In turn, the growth in traffic increases the number of incidents requiring the involvement of public assets as well the risk of a severe emergency. In their annual shipping report for 2015, the insurance company Allianz highlights how there were 55 shipping incidents (termed causalities) in Arctic waters in 2014 as compared to only three a mere decade earlier.[22] Similarly, the number of emergency response incidents in northern Norway rose by 10.5% from 2013 to 2014.[23] The Norwegian government reckons that responding to an oil spill from a vessel along the east coast of Svalbard might take as long as 1–2 days.[24]

Similarly, constabulary tasks under the prerogative of police authorities demand a constant presence in the maritime domain. In instances where vessels traverse maritime borders, control is required. Such tasks, in addition to military actions, are part of maintaining national sovereignty. Protecting sovereign rights in the respective maritime zones—through presence and inspections—have received increased attention in the countries in question. At the same time, focus on Russian investments in its Northern Fleet has led the other Arctic littoral states—in particular Norway—to emphasise on the need to be present in Arctic waters.

[20] Brynn Goegebeur, *Canadian Arctic Search and Rescue: An Assessment*, November (2014), http://www.ruor.uottawa.ca/handle/10393/31976.

[21] Tobi Cohen, "Canadian Rescue Capacity Questioned in the Wake of Arctic Ship Grounding," *Canada.com News*, August 29, 2010, http://www.canada.com/technology/Canadian+rescue+capacity+questioned+wake+Arctic+ship+grounding/3457291/story.html.

[22] Allianz, *Safety and Shipping Review 2015*.

[23] Norwegian Government and Norwegian Ministry of Foreign Affairs, "Nordkloden," ed. Norwegian Ministry of Foreign Affairs, *Nordområdene Statusrapport 2014* (Oslo, 2014).

[24] Norwegian Ministry of Justice, "St. Meld. Nr. 22 (2008–2009): Svalbard" (Oslo, 2009), 108.

Table 8.2 The different types of maritime tasks/challenges becoming more prevalent in the Arctic areas in question

Maritime task	Type of task	Mode of task
Constabulary tasks (*anti-terrorism, law enforcement, etc.*)	Legal	Constant and responding
Border controls	Legal	Constant
Fisheries inspection	Legal/environmental	Constant
Sovereignty protection (*involves constabulary tasks and border control, in addition to military actions*)	Legal/defence	Constant and responding
Search and rescue	Safety	Responding
Assisting passage and navigation (*including ice-breaking*)	Safety	Responding
Oil spill preparedness and response	Safety/environmental	Responding

Source Andreas Østhagen, *Nye utfordringer i nord: Kystvakten i nordområdene* [New Challenges in the North: The Coast Guard in the High North] (Institutt for forsvarsstudier, 2014)

In sum, we see a paradox in the Arctic concerning activity and maritime risk. The Arctic states—including those in focus here—have promoted their own northern regions in search of investments and regional development. But this increase in activity is leading to new challenges, or an increase in the number of incidents to manage, in Arctic waters (Table 8.2).

Three Ways of Managing a Changing Arctic

Coast guards and navies vary across the countries in question. Each set-up and division of labour are tailored to the national and historic circumstances in which they were developed, while they are also often a result of the size of both the country itself (geographically), its population and economy.[25] When an emergency incident in the maritime occurs, the first point of contact is usually the civilian Joint Rescue Coordination Centres (JRCCs) located in the various Arctic countries. After contacting a JRCC, how each country responds to a given incident depends on the national structure and the capabilities available. In most instances, the military provides additional capacities and information

[25] Østhagen, "Coast Guards in the Arctic—Troubles Ahead?"

relevant to the emergency response. After the initial coordination between the civilian and military structures, coast guards are often the first institution tasked with handling a maritime incident.

For Arctic waters around Greenland, Denmark does not have a specific coast guard entity, as the *Royal Danish Navy* (Søværnet) is responsible for providing the services that would normally fall to a coast guard. In the Danish Defence Agreement for the period 1995-1999, it was decided that the responsibility for maritime environmental monitoring and protection should be transferred from the Ministry of Environment and Energy to the navy for cost-efficiency purposes.[26] This was further consolidated with the agreement for 2000-2004, which also led to the transfer of icebreaker capacity to the navy.[27] The navy is thus used by various agencies to carry out search and rescue, navigation assistance, environmental protection, and fisheries inspections, in addition to sovereignty and maritime surveillance.

Today, the Danish Navy is divided into the first and second squadrons. While the second squadron is focused on foreign operations, the first squadron has responsibility for internal affairs, which includes the northern Atlantic (Greenland) and the North Sea (Faroe Islands). Responsibility for coast guard tasks therefore falls under the first squadron headquarters in Frederikshavn, as well as the newly established (2012) Arctic Command in Nuuk, Greenland.[28] The Arctic Command is responsible for overseeing all maritime activity in the waters around Greenland and the Faroe Islands, so that the Danish Navy and the local authorities are in close coordination in crisis situations in the High North. It was set up to enhance the presence of the Danish Defence on Greenland as the demand for this presence increased with the envisioned Arctic "boom".

In *Greenland*, local public resources are split between the police and defence forces. The various maritime tasks are divided between the Danish and Greenlandic governments, following increased autonomy

---

[26] Danish Ministry of Defence, *Aftale Om Forsvarets Ordning 1995–1999* [Agreement on the Defence 1995–1999] (Copenhagen, 1995).

[27] Danish Ministry of Defence, *Forsvarsforlig 2000–2004* [Agreement on Defence 2000–2004] (Copenhagen, 2000), http://www.fmn.dk/videnom/Pages/Tidligereforsvarsforlig.aspx.

[28] Danish Ministry of Defence, Rapport Vedrørende Placering Af Værnsfælles Arktisk Kommando [Report Concerning the Location of Arctic Command].

(home rule) for Greenland in 2009 The Danish military still manages tasks in the maritime region beyond the territorial waters. Through its naval and land-based presence in Greenland, the Danish Defence also assists the civil society whenever needed.[29] The Danish Defence emphasises how they believe that their solution—tasking the military with the whole range of tasks that other Arctic states often divide amongst various civilian authorities—is the most efficient in the case of Greenland.[30]

The Greenlandic Police authority additionally handles all incidents on land and within the territorial waters of Greenland.[31] Albeit highly relevant for Greenlandic emergency response at large, the police are less capable in a large-scale offshore incident. Still, the police operate four vessels for limited offshore use and work with the JRCC and Arctic Command, as needed.[32] Crucially, the presence of *both* the navy (which acts as a coast guard) and the Greenlandic Police has the potential to enable a division of labour depending on the type, scale, and location of the emergency incident. Yet, as the Danish Ministry of Defence's analysis of future missions in the Arctic from June 2016 emphasises, a capacity gap in the waters surrounding Greenland remains.[33] Neither the navy nor the local police has the resources or capacities to sufficiently manage the increasing amount of demands in the north.

On the one hand, requirements to manage fisheries as well as claims to the extended continental shelf might demand more from the Danish Navy; on the other hand, there is a lack of situational awareness in the Arctic. The Arctic Command is understaffed and there is no coherent monitoring of environmental damage at sea.[34] In response, the Danish

---

[29] Kristian Søby Kristensen, Rune Hoffmann, and Jacob Petersen, *Samfundshåndhævelse I Grønland: Forandring, Forsvar Og Frivillighed* [Civil Authorities in Greenland: Change, Defence and Volunteering] (Copenhagen, Denmark: Centre for Military Studies, University of Copenhagen, 2012).

[30] Danish Ministry of Defence, Forsvarsministeriets Fremtidige Opgaveløsning I Arktis [Future Missions of the Danish Ministry of Defence in the Arctic] (Copenhagen, Denmark, 2016), 54.

[31] Unless the ships are registered with the GREENPOS-system.

[32] Skibsfartens og Luftfartens Redningsråd, Mål- Og Resultatkrav for Redningstjenesten I Arktis [Targets and Demands for the Emergency Service in the Arctic] (Copenhagen, Denmark, 2016).

[33] Danish Ministry of Defence, Forsvarsministeriets Fremtidige Opgaveløsning I Arktis [Future Missions of the Danish Ministry of Defence in the Arctic].

[34] Ibid., 66, 116.

Defence is in the process of establishing an Arctic Response Force (*Beredskabsstyrke*). This force will be rapidly deployable from Denmark to improve the capacity of the Arctic Command in responding to any given incident. This force will thus enhance local capacities, although it would still be reliant on initial first-responder capacity due to the deployment time from Denmark.

The *Icelandic Coast Guard* (ICG) is a semi-military institution belonging to the Ministry of Justice. As Iceland does not have a military of its own, the coast guard is central in the Icelandic defence capacities. Up until 2006, the US military had managed the US Iceland Defence Force, operating out of Keflavik Naval Air Station. This exclusive US Defence Force had been present since 1951, established after a joint NATO decision, and predominantly consisted of air and ground defence units. The Icelandic government was openly disappointed with the US decision to leave, and there have been signs that a limited US force might return in the future, albeit with a temporary presence.[35]

The Icelandic Coast Guard thus constitutes the core of the national and local capacity when dealing with maritime incidents. With around five hundred personnel and the whole range of emergency responsibilities, it is—in contrast to the other set-ups in question—a one-stop shop for maritime emergency response as well as security issues in waters around Iceland.[36] Beyond that, however, Iceland does not have a local force operating on behalf of civilian or military authorities dedicated to maritime response. The Icelandic Police is divided into nine districts throughout the country, but their responsibilities exclude the maritime domain.

The core challenge for the Icelandic Coast Guard, however, is a limited budget. When the United States left Keflavik, the helicopter capacity in Iceland was markedly reduced. Not tailored to Icelandic SAR, the American helicopters were still an integral part of capacities present in Iceland. In 2016, around 60% of the coast guard's budget is spent on

---

[35] Josh White, "U.S. to Remove Military Forces and Aircraft from Iceland Base," *The Washington Post*, March 17, 2006, http://www.washingtonpost.com/wp-dyn/content/article/2006/03/16/AR2006031601846.html.

[36] Icelandic Coast Guard, "Icelandic Coast Guard—Always Prepared," *About Us*, 2016, http://www.lhg.is/english/icg/about-us/.

the aviation division, managing its SAR helicopters.[37] It is thus not necessarily the lack of coast guard vessels that constitute a core concern, but the lack of funding for crews to keep the vessels operational, as a considerable portion is spent on airborne capacities. The demand for this capacity—particularly on land—has also grown as the number of tourists has dramatically increased in Iceland from 2006.

Similarly, the coast guard's single surveillance aircraft (Dash-8) could be utilised further to a maximum of 1000 hours annually, but was in 2016 only operating at 300 hours per year due to budget constraints.[38] After the US left is in 2006, the Danes have increasingly become a partner to help fill a capacity gap, and the Danish Defence has considered utilising the aircraft further for domain awareness operations along the east of Greenland. This would serve both the Icelandic Coast Guard's need for continued usage of the aircraft and the Danish Navy's need for improved surveillance around Greenland.[39]

The *Norwegian Coast Guard* (Kystvakten) is part of the Royal Norwegian Navy and thus part of the Norwegian Armed Forces. The coast guard is separated from the regular navy (Kysteskadren) through specific legislation from 1997 which regulated its mandate. The coast guard was established in 1977 based on the recommendations of the Stoltenberg Commission who in 1974 was given the task of exploring possible approaches to exercising national sovereignty in Norwegian waters. The driver for the establishment of the coast guard was increasing petroleum and fishing activity in the 1960s and 1970s, in conjunction with the expansion of the 200-mile economic zone at sea in 1977.[40]

While Kysteskadren is located at Haakonsvern in Bergen, the coast guard's headquarters (SKYS) is at Sortland, North Norway. The Norwegian Coast Guard's main task is to enforce Norwegian

---

[37] Icelandic Coast Guard, "Icelandic SAR and the Coast Guard" (Reykjavik: Interview of Icelandic Coast Guard. By: Andreas Østhagen, 2016).

[38] Ibid.

[39] Ibid.

[40] Willy Knudsen, "Fra Fiskerioppsyn Til Kystvakt - En Studie Av En Beslutningsprosess [From Fisheries Inspections to Coast Guard: A Study of a Decision-Making Process]," *Det Samfunnsvitenskapelige Fakultet* (University of Tromsø, 2008) Thesis; Bjørn Terjesen, Tom Kristiansen, and Roald Gjelsten, *Sjøforsvaret I Krig Og Fred: Langs Kysten Og På Havet Gjennom 200 År* [The Navy in War and Peace: Along the Coast and at Sea through 200 Years] (Bergen: Fagbokforlaget, 2010).

Table 8.3 The various coast guards and their roles, mandates, and organisational affiliation

Region	Name	Tasks	Organisational affiliation
Greenland/Denmark	Royal Danish Navy (*Søværnet*), 1st Squadron	Full spectrum	Danish Defence
Iceland	Icelandic Coast Guard (*Landhelgisgæsla*)	Full spectrum (albeit limited defence capabilities)	Ministry of Justice
Norway	Norwegian Coast Guard (*Kystvakten*)	Full spectrum (albeit separated from the traditional Navy)	Royal Norwegian Navy

sovereignty. In addition, the spectrum of tasks covers all the traditional coast guard tasks from fisheries inspections to environmental protection and search and rescue, as the coast guard is frequently used by other Norwegian public authorities responsible for these areas (Coastal Administration, Customs, JRCC).[41] The coast guard has limited police authority, defined in the Coast Guard Act of 1997, and may thus report and investigate offences related to fisheries.[42]

These tasks and the law separate the coast guard from the regular navy, as the two institutions perform a different set of tasks. The navy has limited presence in Norway's Arctic waters, beyond annual trips north with a frigate and relevant military exercises that take place in northern waters. The coast guard, however, is continuously present in the north, performing a whole range of tasks while also ensuring military presence in northern waters.

Finally, it should be mentioned that Svalbard is a somewhat particular case. Norway was granted sovereignty over the Svalbard archipelago with the Svalbard Treaty, signed in 1920 in Paris, which came into effect in 1925. The Treaty gives all nationals of the signatories the

---

[41] Norwegian Ministry of Defence, *Lov Om Kystvakten (Kystvaktloven)* [Law Concerning the Coast Guard] (Forsvarsdepartementet, 1997), http://lovdata.no/dokument/NL/lov/1997-06-13-42.

[42] Ibid.

right to live and work on the islands, while it places some limitations on Norway's ability to tax and use Svalbard for military purposes. The latter restriction complicates the use of military equipment, although not when the military is performing civilian tasks. The Norwegian Coast Guard, as well as Navy vessels from time to time, makes use of Longyearbyen for bunkering.[43] The coast guard itself constitutes the core public resource in maritime emergency incidents, as it aims to be continuously present in waters around Svalbard. During the summer months, the number of coast guard vessels around Svalbard ranges between two and five, whereas this is slightly reduced in winter months. The various structures are found in the following table (Table 8.3).

Explaining Institutional Outcomes

In the case of these three countries, their institutional structures are a result of the considerable size of the maritime domain they are set to manage, in tandem with relatively modest resources to draw from. In addition to cost-efficiency, the inclusion of the coast guard under the military umbrella adds a security competence, or, as in the case of Denmark, taking a part of the navy and tasking it with coast guard competences.

Resources and Capacities

From the examination of the three coast guard structures, it is apparent that the chosen set-up in each of these Nordic countries is relatively similar. This leads to the question: Why have these three Nordic and North East Atlantic countries converged on a comparable coast guard model? Speaking to the larger theme of this volume, what determines the choice of coast guard model, in conjunction with a country's navy? The following section outlines a few key elements that seem to have determined the choice of institutional structure in these three Nordic countries specifically, which in turn might hint at relevant factors for coast guard structures in general.

First, as is obvious when examining Denmark, Norway, and Iceland, the importance of sheer geographic space cannot be ignored. It is apparent that the larger the maritime domain, the more need there will be for states to manage this domain. As the map of the North East Atlantic

---

[43] Norwegian Ministry of Justice, "St.meld. Nr. 22 (2008–2009): Svalbard," 22–23.

displays, the size of the Danish, Icelandic, and Norwegian EEZs (including the Fisheries Protection Zone around Svalbard) is instructive. This is due to the simple fact that Norway, Denmark (through Greenland and to some extent the Faroe Islands), and Iceland all lie facing relatively open bodies of ocean with few nearby opposing states limiting a full extension of the allowed 200 nautical miles economic zone.

While the concept of occupation is essential in establishing title to land territory, it does not hold relevance in the maritime domain. Contrary to customary international law on sovereignty over land territory, occupation of the continental shelf cannot in itself lead to acquisition of sovereign rights.[44] A marked separation between land and maritime space has arisen, with rights to the latter deriving from the former.[45] Thus, as in the case of Iceland, a relatively small piece of land generates a rather considerable maritime zone which needs to be administered. This is the case across the three countries in focus in this chapter.

What, in turn, do large maritime zones require for coastal states setting up their respective coast guards? Arguably, space itself is less important unless considered in tandem with the size of the relevant country, defined in terms of material capabilities, resources, and population. All three countries in question here are *small* states, in terms of economy and population. Albeit relatively wealthy in terms of GDP per capita and human development,[46] these countries are small in capabilities compared to neighbours such as Canada, the UK, or even Sweden. The combination of large maritime zones in need of administration and relatively limited resources—especially when the coast guards/navies took on their modern form during the first decades after World War II—yields the so-called unitary structure we see in all these North East Atlantic states. As several of the coast guard and navy officials highlight in interviews,

[44] Carole St-Louis, "The Notion of Equity in the Determination of Maritime Boundaries and Its Application to the Canada-United States Boundary in the Beaufort Sea" (University of Ottawa, 2014) Thesis.

[45] Prosper Weil, *The Law of Maritime Delimitation—Reflections* (London: Grotius Publications Limited, 1989), 91–92.

[46] Denmark has a GDP per capita of $48,000 (2016), Iceland $49,200 (2016), and Norway $69,200 (2016). Source: https://www.cia.gov/library/publications/the-world-factbook/rankorder/2004rank.html. Denmark ranks number 5 on the United Nations Human Development Index from 20xx, Iceland number 9, and Norway number 1. Source: http://hdr.undp.org/en/composite/HDI.

this all-purpose set-up is especially suited to small countries with a limited resource base.[47] Crucially, Iceland is closer to a micro-state then a small state, which in turn places even more restrictions on resources and ability to uphold multiple maritime institutions.[48]

It is also worth noting the cultural dimension at play when discussing three Nordic countries. Albeit distinguishable in their own right, it is undisputed that there are cultural similarities between Nordic countries in general.[49] At one point, both Norway and Iceland were also part of a larger Danish Atlantic "empire", which only ended with independence in 1905 (Norway) and 1944 (Iceland), respectively. It is not the purview of this piece to conduct a larger study of the cultural similarities and differences across the coast guard/navy structures in question. Yet, this dimension is still worth pointing out, as another similar feature across these three states.

Defence Tasks and Coast Guards

Moving beyond geography, resources (of the given state), and culture, there are more relevant factors amongst these countries. Given the all-purpose role of these coast guards/navies and their inclusion in each countries' defence structure, security considerations come into play. All states are members of NATO and have been since its founding in 1949. Yet only Norway shares a direct maritime boundary with Russia. The Barents Sea—north of the European continent stretching from Norway and Russia up towards the North Pole—has been central in the relationship between these two countries. In general, the Norwegian Coast Guard—as well as naval officers and military experts in Norway—emphasises the importance of the "grey painted ships" when performing tasks in the Norwegian EEZ and the Fisheries Protection Zone (FPZ) around Svalbard.[50] Being part of the military command chain and being

---

[47] Danish Ministry of Defence, *Forsvarsministeriets Fremtidige Opgaveløsning I Arktis* [Future Missions of the Danish Ministry of Defence in the Arctic]; Icelandic Coast Guard, "Icelandic SAR and the Coast Guard"; Norwegian Coast Guard Official I, "Interview: Norwegian Coast Guard Official I" (Haakonsvern: October 1, 2017).

[48] Icelandic Coast Guard, "Icelandic SAR and the Coast Guard."

[49] See, for example, Mary Hilson, *The Nordic Model: Scandinavia since 1945* (London: Reaktion Books, 2008).

[50] Terjesen, Kristiansen, and Gjelsten, *Sjøforsvaret I Krig Og Fred: Langs Kysten Og På Havet Gjennom 200 År* [The Navy in War and Peace: Along the Coast and at Sea through 200 Years].

armed, albeit lightly, are argued to constitute a factor in the success of the coast guard in managing sovereign rights and keeping tensions at low levels, as the military status infer authority and respect.[51]

For the coast guard, interactions with Russian trawlers have at times been conflictual. Tension concerns reactions from Russia to Norwegian arrests in the FPZ, and the potential escalation from a fisheries incident to a state-state incident. Russian fishing vessels inspected by the Norwegian Coast Guard in the FPZ refuse to sign the inspection documents as a symbolic gesture to highlight how Russia does not recognise Norwegian authority in the Zone—although they allow the Norwegian Coast Guard to perform inspections of the vessels.[52] The Russian Coast Guard has, on occasion, suggested that Norway and Russia conduct joint fisheries inspections in the FPZ around Svalbard.[53] Such cooperation would challenge Norwegian sovereignty and authority in the FPZ, and the Norwegian government has firmly declined all such proposals.[54]

The most severe reactions to Norwegian enforcement in the FPZ came at the end of the 1990s and in the beginning of the 2000s, as scientists reported that fish stocks were in decline and quotas had to be reduced to achieve sustainable fisheries.[55] From around 2000 onwards, there was thus a conscious policy-shift in the Norwegian government, attempting to establish a stronger precedent for the regulatory regime in

---

[51] Svein Kosmo, *Kystvaktsamarbeidet Norge-Russland. En Fortsettelse Av Politikken Med Andre Midler?* [Coast Guard Cooperation Norway-Russia. A Continuation of Politics through Other Means?, *Forsvarets Stabsskole* (Norwegian Joint Staff College, 2010) IS THIS A THESIS; Arild-Inge Skram, *Alltid Til Stede: Kystvakten 1997–2017* [Always Present: Coast Guard 1997–2017] (Bergen: Fagbokforlaget, 2017).

[52] Kosmo, *Kystvaktsamarbeidet Norge-Russland. En Fortsettelse Av Politikken Med Andre Midler?* [Coast Guard Cooperation Norway-Russia. A Continuation of Politics through Other Means?].

[53] Rune T Ege, "Norge Sier Nei Til Russisk Kystvakt-Samarbeid (Norway Rejects Russian Coast Guard Cooperation)," *VG*, July 23, 2012, http://www.vg.no/nyheter/innenriks/forsvaret/norge-sier-nei-til-russisk-kystvakt-samarbeid/a/10059093/.

[54] Østhagen, "Coastguards in Peril: A Study of Arctic Defence Collaboration," 2015, 7–8.

[55] Geir Hønneland and Anne-Kristin Jørgensen, "Kompromisskulturen I Barentshavet [The Culture of Compromise in the Barents Sea]," in *Norge Og Russland: Sikkerhetspolitiske Utfordringer I Nordområdene* [Norway and Russia: Security Challenges in the High North], ed. Tormod Heier and Anders Kjølberg (Oslo: Universitetsforlaget, 2015), 61; Arild-Inge Skram, "Interview: Arild-Inge Skram, Former Chief of the Norwegian Coast Guard" (Drammen: October 24, 2017).

the Barents Sea and the FPZ particularly.[56] The first arrest of a Russian fishing vessel that marked a more stringent enforcement regime came in 1998, with the attempted arrest of the *Novokuybyshevsk*. This was solved at sea in the end.[57] Thereafter, events concerning the arrests and attempted arrests of *Chernigov* in 2001, *Elektron* in 2005, and *Sapphire II* in 2011, caused considerable reactions in Russia amongst local media and politicians, and, at times, at national level in Moscow.[58] In general, these incidents were managed without further escalation, but they highlight the underlying dispute between Norway and Russia in the Svalbard Zone, where the Norwegian Coast Guard is the primary actor operating on behalf of Norway.

Moving further east, Denmark and Iceland have had less severe challenges to their sovereign rights in their maritime zones. Still, during the Cold War, the so-called GIUK-gap (Greenland, Iceland, UK) was deemed a crucial part of NATO's defence strategy to deny Soviet access to the Atlantic.[59] Its importance for the defence alliance led to military presence in the region, as well as investments in both Iceland and Greenland. The mentioned US Keflavik base was established in 1951. Albeit not maritime, Thule Air Base was established in 1952 after an agreement between the Danish government and the United States, to allow early warning and air defence.[60] In general, it has been deemed crucial for both Denmark and Iceland to have naval capabilities in their northern waters.

At the same time, we must recognise that what coast guards primarily spend time and resources on is the protection of sovereign rights through fisheries inspections. There is a gap between security and defence-led tasks, and general resource management. This latter point

---

[56] Hønneland and Jørgensen, *Kompromisskulturen I Barentshavet* [The Culture of Compromise in the Barents Sea].

[57] Skram, *Alltid Til Stede: Kystvakten 1997–2017* [Always Present: Coast Guard 1997–2017], 153–55.

[58] See Geir Hønneland, *Russia and the Arctic: Environment, Identity and Foreign Policy* (London: I.B. Tauris, 2016); Geir Hønneland, *Hvordan Skal Putin Ta Barentshavet Tilbake?* [How Shall Putin Reclaim the Barents Sea?] (Bergen: Fagbokforlaget, 2013); and Skram, *Alltid Til Stede: Kystvakten 1997–2017* [Always Present: Coast Guard 1997–2017].

[59] Julianne Smith, Jerry Hendrix, and Robert D. Kaplan, "Forgotten Waters—Minding the GIUK Gap" Report, (Washington, DC, 2017).

[60] Jørgen Taagholt, "Thule Air Base," *Tidsskriftet Grønland* 2 (2002): 42–112.

is crucial, as what we are discussing with regard to states and maritime space are *sovereign rights* to resources in the water column and on the seabed, not the exclusive right to the whole maritime territory in question. This distinction is at times either ignored in debates concerning territorial conflict, or misunderstood when discussing the conflict potential from maritime disputes.

Still, as highlighted by one interviewee: "By its mere presence and performance of regular resource-related tasks, the coast guard is upholding sovereignty".[61] The coast guards/navy perform multiple roles at once, to the benefit of these small states with large maritime zones and varying degrees of security concerns. We therefore cannot discount such considerations when committees and officials were considering the most purposeful structure of a public branch with a mandate to roam the country's maritime zones. Setting the coast guard up as a part of the navy, as in the case of Denmark and Norway, or as the only naval capability of the state, as in the case of Iceland, seem to correspond with this obvious security need these states faced and still face.

However, we should be aware of purely functionalist explanations (the set-up of a coast guard is a function of the needs of that country). There are alternatives to these structures, as debates ranging in both Denmark and Norway highlight. In Denmark, there have been voices questioning whether it might be more purposeful with a purely civilian coast guard similar to that of Sweden or Germany, as a way of improving effectiveness and saving costs.[62] Tellingly, Greenland only shares a maritime boundary with Canada, a close ally. These voices have not, however, led to policy shifts, but highlight how there is no given structure for any country.

---

[61] Government Official Norway, Interview: Official at Ministry of Defence (Oslo: October 3, 2017).

[62] Erik Holm, "Regeringspartier Positive over for Dansk Kystvagt [Government Parties Positive to Danish Coast Guard]," *Ingeniøren*, 2012, http://ing.dk/artikel/regeringspartier-positive-over-dansk-kystvagt-135103; Erik Holm, "Eksperter Og Fagfolk Vil Samle Maritime Opgaver I Én Kystvagt [Experts and Practitioners Want to Gather Maritime Tasks in One Coast Guard]," *Ingeniøren*, 2012, http://ing.dk/artikel/eksperter-og-fagfolk-vil-samle-maritime-opgaver-i-en-kystvagt-134968.

When the Norwegian Coast Guard was established in 1977, there was also an extensive debate about whether or not it should be organised under the armed forces.[63] In retrospect, some scholars have argued that inclusion in the armed forces—symbolised by grey-painted ships— has given the necessary authority needed in the coast guard's many conflict-filled meetings with foreign fishing vessels in Norwegian waters.[64] Arguments for cost-effectiveness and complementary division of labour with traditional naval forces have also been prominent.[65] Yet, there have been questions asked whether having the coast guard under the military's wings is the best way to manage judicial questions at sea. Is there an added chance of conflict escalation vis-à-vis Russia with a military coast guard?[66] Such debates have not reached far in Norway, but they are not inconsequential. Large-scale incidents like the *Elektron*-case in 2005 could put these questions back on the agenda.

Another central element of the coast guards/navy nexus in these three countries is the relatively positive resource situation they find themselves in compared to other branches of the military. This is most relevant for Norway and Denmark, with larger defence establishments. As budgets have been cut or kept at a standstill over the last decade, the Norwegian Coast Guard and the first squadron of the Danish Navy have received additional funds as well as new equipment. Without

---

[63] Knudsen, *Fra Fiskerioppsyn Til Kystvakt - En Studie Av En Beslutningsprosess* [From Fisheries Inspections to Coast Guard: A Study of a Decision-Making Process]; Gunnar Fermann and Tor Håkon Inderberg, "Norway and the 2005 Elektron Affair: Conflict of Competencies and Competent Realpolitik," in *War: An Introduction to Theories and Research on Collective Violence*, ed. Tor Georg Jakobsen, 2nd ed. (New York: Nova Science Publishers, 2015), 373–402.

[64] Terjesen, Kristiansen, and Gjelsten, *Sjøforsvaret I Krig Og Fred: Langs Kysten Og På Havet Gjennom 200 År* [The Navy in War and Peace: Along the Coast and at Sea through 200 Years].

[65] Norwegian Coast Guard Official I, "Interview: Norwegian Coast Guard Official I"; Terjesen, Kristiansen, and Gjelsten, *Sjøforsvaret I Krig Og Fred: Langs Kysten Og På Havet Gjennom 200 År* [The Navy in War and Peace: Along the Coast and at Sea through 200 Years].

[66] Tor Håkon Inderberg, "Norsk Kystvakt – Politi Eller Forsvar?," [Norwegian Coast Guard—Police or Defence?], *Nordlys*, February 19, 2007, https://www.nordlys.no/kronikk/norsk-kystvakt-politi-eller-forsvar/s/1-79-2594494.

arguing that their resource situation is good, this is a clear sign of the increased attention given to the Arctic by the various governments in Copenhagen, Reykjavik, and Oslo. As maritime traffic has increased in the north, investments in the coast guards/navy have attempted to keep up. Moreover, in Denmark the increased focus on self-governance in Greenland and/or the Faroe Islands is adding to a debate concerning the division of labour and mandates concerning coast guard tasks. Particularly, environmental protection and fisheries inspections are tasks where the local authorities in both nations are developing own competences and capabilities.[67]

We could ask ourselves whether any of these countries had opted for a further institutional separation and specialisation by setting up a completely civilian structure if it had been larger and/or surrounded by only allied nations. Despite debates about the "best" way of organising the coast guard-navy nexus, these three countries seem relatively content with their institutional set-ups, as Arctic maritime activity is set to continue to increase. A larger question, however, is whether or not national investments in coast guards are sufficient to follow the increasing demand in northern waters.

Cooperation Across Boundaries

Another layer relevant to the three coast guards at hand in terms of managing increased activity in the Arctic is *international cooperation*. Beyond efforts such as the agreements signed under the auspices of the Arctic Council or establishing an Arctic Coast Guard Forum, several measures are in development. Efforts to expand already existing cooperation on satellites seem to be a relatively cost-effective way of solving some of the severe communication issues in the Arctic.

For Denmark, Iceland, and Norway, the cooperation related to the European Space Agency already provides a framework in tandem with the EU Satellite Centre (SatCen) in Spain.[68] Moreover, joint efforts

---

[67] Østhagen, "Coast Guard Collaboration in the Arctic: Canada and Greenland (Denmark)."

[68] Danish Ministry of Defence, Forsvarsministeriets Fremtidige Opgaveløsning I Arktis [Future Missions of the Danish Ministry of Defence in the Arctic], 158.

in surveillance, patrolling, and emergency response seem to have great potential. For example, between Nunavut and Greenland, efforts can be expanded. In 2016 alone, Danish vessels around Greenland had to come to the assistance of sinking Canadian fishing vessels twice.[69] The Danish MoD report from 2016 seems to recognise this, as it discusses further formalising the contact between the nearby Arctic countries to improve emergency response and coordination.[70]

There are also obvious advantages in establishing hubs and shared assets in central locations, such as Keflavik Airport, Thule Air Base, and possibly the Norwegian island of Jan Mayen. Denmark and Iceland have already established a system for sharing assets, efforts which hold potential for further development.[71] Finally, the joint procurement of relevant emergency response equipment is being explored. Denmark and Norway are in the process of acquiring new fighter planes (F-35) which will be given a considerable role in their Arctic regions.[72] Similarly, these countries are considering new maritime surveillance aircraft, such as the Boeing P-8 Poseidon (Norway has already decided to acquire it.[73])

In sum, the parallels between these countries and their needs coupled with their memberships in defence organisations tailored for joint procurement (NORDFECO and NATO) entail room for further exploration.[74] There seems to be unexplored potential for further international cooperation, ranging from exercises and the sharing of surveillance data to joint procurement and asset-sharing arrangements.

---

[69] Sima Sahar Zerehi, "Nunavut Officials Press for Arctic Search and Rescue Base," *CBC News: North*, March 7, 2016, http://www.cbc.ca/news/canada/north/arctic-search-and-rescue-needs-1.3477252.

[70] Danish Ministry of Defence, "Forsvarsministeriets Fremtidige Opgaveløsning I Arktis [Future Missions of the Danish Ministry of Defence in the Arctic]."

[71] Østhagen, "Coastguards in Peril: A Study of Arctic Defence Collaboration," 2015.

[72] Jens Ringsmose, "Investing in Fighters and Alliances: Norway, Denmark, and the Bumpy Road to the Joint Strike Fighter," *International Journal* 68, no. 1 (2013): 93–110.

[73] Norwegian Government, "Norway Has Ordered Five Boeing P-8A Poseidon," *Press Release*, 2017, https://www.regjeringen.no/en/aktuelt/norge-har-inngatt-kontrakt-om-kjop-av-fem-nye-p-8a-poseidon-maritime-patruljefly/id2546045/.

[74] A. Østhagen, "Coastguards in Peril: A Study of Arctic Defence Collaboration," *Defence Studies* 15, no. 2 (2015): https://doi.org/10.1080/14702436.2015.1035949.

Conclusion

This chapter has attempted to do many things. First, it showcases and explains a growing Arctic paradox: as the littoral states pursue northern economic adventures and promote the Arctic as a region with untapped potential, they are also forced to invest in, and develop, their coast guard and naval capacities. This has left some Arctic countries in a bit of a squeeze, although those examined here—Denmark (including Greenland and the Faroe Islands), Iceland, and Norway—are better off than some of their North American counterparts.[75]

Another aspect of this chapter was explaining *why* three Nordic countries have chosen dissimilar coast guard models. Yet, by going through each model and set-up in the coast guard/navy balance, it becomes apparent that the models are not that different after all. On paper, they are of different character, but their mandates, tasks, and structures are surprisingly similar (compared to other structures in this volume). What, then, determine how these structures are formed? This chapter has highlighted some core traits that have had an apparent effect in these three countries. They include geography, the resource situation at a national level, and overarching security considerations. Moreover, there is a cultural component to this as well, which lies beyond the scope of this chapter.

Finally, given that the focus here has been on three countries of relatively similar characteristics, located in the same part of the world, there are interesting questions to be asked about the potential for international cooperation across maritime boundaries. This might take on a bilateral or a multilateral form. In turn, cooperation between states cannot only alleviate some of the pressures formed by the described paradox, but might also in turn start shaping the coast guard structures themselves. How coast guards—as an institution—change in response to internal and external pressures are thus an area for further research.

The pressures put on Arctic states and their coast guard structures have led to some questions concerning the most appropriate and cost-efficient way to organise these institutions amongst Arctic countries. For now at least, the one-stop shop model in use by all three countries in question here, seem tailored to an operating environment where actors and incidents are few and far between, but concerns are mounting.

---

[75] Ibid.

CHAPTER 9

Ensuring Security in the Mediterranean Sea: The Italian Navy and Coast Guard

Alessandra Giada Dibenedetto

The Mediterranean Sea is a bridge between some of the world's most ancient territories, cultures and populations. Called *Mare Nostrum* by the Ancient Romans, the Mediterranean was one of the main protagonists of Western history. Today, it maintains its central role, being of great geopolitical and economic importance for a number of European, Middle Eastern and North African (MENA) Countries.

Surrounded by nearly 8000 km of coast, the welfare and security of Italy strongly depends on the Mediterranean Sea. The country's maritime imports and exports via the Mediterranean are worth more than 50 billion euros, the highest value in Europe.[1] Furthermore, commerce by sea represents 80% of the trade between Italy and the MENA area.[2] The latter is of strategic interest for Rome as many of its regions are suppliers of energy resources and raw materials. From Libya, for instance, a natural gas pipeline connects with the coast of Sicily.

---

[1] "Port Indicators," *Maritime Economy*, SRM and Assoporti (March 2017): 27, http://www.economiadelmare.org/wp-content/uploads/2017/03/port_indicators_12017_web.pdf.
[2] Ibid.: 25.

A. G. Dibenedetto (✉)
Centre for International Studies (Ce.S.I.), Rome, Italy

© The Author(s) 2019
I. Bowers and S. L. C. Koh (eds.), *Grey and White Hulls*,
https://doi.org/10.1007/978-981-13-9242-9_9

The Mediterranean is a source of prosperity for the country; nonetheless, there are many threats emanating from its waters. The so-called Arab Spring in 2010 marked the beginning of a wave of instability throughout the MENA region, the consequences of which have reached the Mediterranean waters and the coasts of southern European countries. Nowadays, a number of hybrid threats menaces maritime security and safety in the *Mare Nostrum*: the current migration crisis; increasing radicalization and the spread of jihadist terrorist groups; a surge in organized crime; and the smuggling of weapons and illicit drugs. The untameable migratory flows that have reached European coasts since 2013 pose various humanitarian, political and also operational questions. Furthermore, the related cross-border crimes are challenging the security of the Mediterranean waters. In a period of time in which the terrorist threat remains at its highest, southern European countries such as Italy have to deal with the presence of groups affiliated to the Islamic State in some areas of the MENA coastline along the Mediterranean Sea.

Consequently, guaranteeing maritime security in the *Mare Nostrum* is fundamental for the protection of vital interests of the Italian Republic. This complex task is mostly in the hands of the Italian Navy and Coast Guard.

Maritime Security Agencies in Italy

The Italian Navy and the Coast Guard are the two core maritime agencies in charge of securing the waters of the Mediterranean Sea. Their duties and responsibilities are clearly distinguished and regulated; nonetheless, throughout the years and particularly in the present time, the roles of the two bodies have been increasingly intertwined, blurring the lines between the reciprocal division of labour.

In November 1860, a few months before the proclamation of the Kingdom of Italy, the Italian Navy was born under the name of *Regia Marina*. Following the end of World War II and the proclamation of the Italian Republic, the Navy underwent a process of enlargement and modernization resulting into the currently known *Marina Militare*. The latter is part of the Armed Forces; as such, it hierarchically answers to the President of the Republic, while operationally it is under the command of the Chief of Defence. The Italian Navy is in charge of controlling and conducting naval operations in national and international waters for ensuring the defence of vital interests of the country against threats to its territory, sea lanes used for trade, and citizens abroad. The *Marina Militare* also defends the Euro-Atlantic spaces through its contribution to the North Atlantic Treaty Organization (NATO), handling international crises and safeguarding free institutions.[3] Submarines, surface combatants, amphibious and transport vessels, aircraft and minesweepers provide the core capabilities for the Navy. In order to achieve its mission, the Italian Navy can count on this fleet of multifunctional military naval units that able to perform a multitude of tasks such as: transporting aircrafts and logistic supports, collecting intelligence, reaching difficult and even inhospitable areas, and escorting commercial vessels.[4]

The fleet of the *Marina Militare* is undergoing a process of renewal, which started with the approval of the naval law in 2014 and will be accomplished by the beginning of 2025. The plan is to develop next-generation ships able to perform a wide range of different functions. In particular, the naval programme provides for the building of ten Offshore Multipurpose Patrol Ships (PPA) able to perform, among other tasks, maritime surveillance and control, monitor maritime economic activities at sea, contribute to the protection of the marine environment, and support the Civil Protection in case of natural disaster by providing health support, electricity and drinkable water.[5] These new units will be extremely flexible and will increase the capacity of the Italian Navy to be engaged in "dual-use activities": both military and civilian activities. To this end, three different configurations of the PPA are planned: light, light plus and full. The two light versions, which have a displacement between 4800 and 5800 tons, are equipped with a minimum self-defence capacity and are mostly appropriate for performing patrolling, while the full version, with a displacement between 4900 and 6200, will be fully equipped and thus will be capable of combat missions. One of the peculiarities of these new assets is the presence on board of two modular areas (one at the stern, the other at the centre of the vessel), which will allow for the embarkation of containers designated, according to the mission,

---

[3] "Conosciamoci" [Meet Us], *Marina Militare*, accessed September 1, 2017, http://www.marina.difesa.it/conosciamoci/Pagine/default.aspx.

[4] "Flotta e Mezzi" [Fleet and Assets], *Marina Militare*, accessed September 1, 2017, http://www.marina.difesa.it/uominimezzi/Pagine/default.aspx.

[5] "L'importanza del Mar Mediterraneo" [The Importance of the Mediterranean Sea], *Marina Militare*, accessed September 3, 2017, http://www.marina.difesa.it/uominimezzi/nuoviprogetti/Documents/20160623_ppa.pdf.

for various operative modules (such as logistics and medical). Evidently, once integrated in the Italian Navy fleet, the PPA, thanks to their flexibility and duality, will increase the operational level of the *Marina Militare* as well as its civil role, thus further intertwining its functions with those of the Coast Guard.

The Italian Coast Guard or *Guardia Costiera* is in charge of all aspects concerning the civil use of the sea. Although launched in July 1865 as a law enforcement agency, following the developments of World War I, in 1918 the agency was also tasked with all functions related to military defence and, therefore, militarized for the duration of the war in progress. In 1923, the Coast Guard was reorganized, became part of the *Regia Marina* and thus converted into a military body. The *Guardia Costiera* institutionally and functionally depends on the Ministry of Infrastructures and Transports, nonetheless the Ministry of Environment and Protection of Land and Sea, and the Ministry of Agricultural, Food and Forestry Policies exploit its competencies and skills. As a specialized body of the Navy, the Coast Guard may also perform, under the circumstances provided by the law, military functions. In general, the Italian Coast Guard is involved in a large number of activities, which include: safety of navigation, maritime security, search and rescue (SAR), protection of the marine environment, control over fisheries and commerce, maritime police—namely regulating activities at sea, controlling maritime traffic, guaranteeing safety in ports, carrying out inspections, etc.—supporting the Civil Protection, fighting against illegal immigration and countering terrorism.[6] These tasks are achieved through the use of about 600 vessels that are deployed at over 100 ports across Italy, and an air component composed of reconnaissance aircraft and helicopters. In recent years, the Coast Guard has experienced a process of empowerment; a number of new vessels have been procured to strengthen the Coast Guard's capacity for SAR, maritime police, open sea rescue and the protection of the marine environment.

The Italian Navy and Coast Guard are two maritime security agencies that perform different functions. Nonetheless, reciprocity, interdependence and even overlapping of duties are evident. On the one side,

---

[6] "Capitanerie di Porto" [Port Authorities], *Marina Militare*, accessed September 3, 2017, http://www.marina.difesa.it/conosciamoci/organizzazione/guardiacostiera/Pagine/default.aspx.

as the Coast Guard is under the command of the Navy Chief of Staff, it cooperates with the Navy in a number of activities: maritime and coastal defence, logistics support to its units and assistance in international operations which involve limitations and interdictions of the mercantile traffic. On the other side, the Navy is involved in many civil-related activities. The previously mentioned dual-use capacity is an intrinsic characteristic of the Italian Navy and implies that its technology and assets are deployable both for military and civil ends. As a result, both the Coast Guard and the Navy are involved in activities such as: supporting the Civil Protection, protecting the marine fauna and flora, controlling fishing and pursuing SAR operations (see the chart below). Indeed, the *Marina Militare* is one of the few Western navies that have both normative attributions and the capacities to perform functions typically attributed to the Coast Guard. Nonetheless, considering that the chain of command and control at sea is not entirely clear, this might result into operational overlap a consequent waste of time and financial and human resources.

In this regard, in 2015 the Italian government—at that time led by the central-left party of Matteo Renzi—suggested a public administration reform which would have reshuffled command structures aiming at increasing efficiency and reducing spending. The reform included subordinating the Coast Guard to the Navy: the latter would have taken on the responsibilities of the General Command of the Coast Guard, including the functional relation with the Ministry of Infrastructures and Transports. Such a revision was meant to increase cost-saving and eliminate complicated command and control chains, while continuing to guarantee a strong and efficient maritime presence. The reform soon met resistance: the political opposition talked about an excessive militarization of the country—despite the fact that the members of the Coast Guard already have military status—and the Coast Guard itself firmly opposed the proposal as it was determined to maintain its autonomy. As a consequence, only a few days later, the government modified the initial idea for the reform and simply called for stronger cooperation between the two bodies in the eventuality of possible greater integration in the future.[7] Although the reform proposed by Renzi never turned into law,

---

[7] *New Legislation for Administrative Reorganization of the State*, Italian Law 124/2015, art. 8,1,b.

it indicates that the roles played by both the Navy and the Coast Guard are so similar that the two agencies could merge. Evidently, the current division of labour between them is determined by internal drivers—such as politics and bureaucracy—and external factors—among which the current migration crisis is the most determining—and not the principles of efficiency and efficacy.

Further complicating the picture is the presence of another national agency, namely the naval compartment of the Finance Guard. The Italian Police and Gendarmerie used to have a naval component as well; however, starting from January 2017, the naval services of the Police and the Gendarmerie have been deactivated, and all their relative assets and the full police responsibility of guaranteeing security at sea have been transferred to the Finance Guard.[8] This positive step reduces the number of actors engaged in the Mediterranean and the consequent problems of coordination. Furthermore, it concentrates assets, financial and human resources into one sole police force. The naval service of the Finance Guard relies on 14 operative departments spread throughout various Italian regions and is equipped with naval assets, underwater units, helicopters and fixed-wing aircraft. The functions performed are numerous: economic and financial police tasks, the protection of public order and security at sea, surveillance activities against illicit traffic and in favour of environmental protection, the control and defence of borders, land, ports, national and international waters.[9]

Coordinating the activities of a number of bodies across the sea and along the maritime borders is a hard task, which can only be achieved if the willingness to cooperate is backed by pertinent and effective regulations. The norms administering the work of the naval service of the Finance Guard state that its police role of ensuring security of the sea cannot overlap with the functions attributed to the Coast Guard.[10] Nonetheless, such disposition lacks any details on the specific division of

---

[8] *Provisions for Rationalization of Police Functions and Absorption of the State Forestry Corps*, Legislative Decree, August 19, 2016, n. 177.

[9] "Servizio Navale" [Naval Service], *Guardia di Finanza*, accessed September 9, 2017, http://www.gdf.gov.it/chi-siamo/organizzazione/specializzazioni/comparto-aeronavale/servizio-navale/chi-siamo/cenni-storici/dal-2000-ad-oggi/dal-2000-ad-oggi.

[10] *Provisions for Rationalization of Police Functions and Absorption of the State Forestry Corps*, Legislative Decree, August 19, 2016, n. 177, art. 2,c,1.

labour between the two. The relationship between the Finance Guard and the Navy is even more intricate. While the Finance Guard carries out the operations of the judicial police and controls the borders, the Navy is an armed force engaged in the maritime defence of the national territory. Despite such a clear difference in status and attributions, competition continues to emerge. An example of these dynamics is the debate over the command of the EU FRONTEX Joint Operation Triton—which will be explored in detail in the following sections—which the Italian Navy strongly wanted, although it was already in the hands of the Finance Guard as a police operation.

Evidently, the Italian government needs to further develop a more coherent and efficient division of labour among the agencies involved in the Mediterranean Sea. Even if an impressive step has been taken by empowering the Finance Guard with all police operations at sea, therefore reducing the number of actors, the relationship among the remaining bodies—namely the Navy, the Coast Guard and the Finance Guard—needs to be better regulated. The debate on achieving greater coordination among all institutions active in territorial waters has been ongoing for decades. Currently, however, there are no inter-ministerial decrees governing the mutual relations between the naval units of the various bodies operating at sea. This, added to a very intricate chain of command and control, is leading to discontent, task duplication and waste of resources.

THE MIGRATION CRISIS IN THE MEDITERRANEAN SEA

Dealing with maritime security is an ongoing and evolving challenge for all agencies concerned; this is particularly true in the case of the Mediterranean Sea, which presents a number of both conventional and hybrid threats. In the past five years and particularly problematic for the Italian government has been dealing with the migration flows stemming from North African Countries and reaching Italian coasts through the central Mediterranean. In October 2013, an Italian fishing boat managed to rescue 115 migrants off the coast of Lampedusa, Sicily, while about 368 died.[11] This episode was just the beginning of a series of

---

[11] "Can Europe Stop Migrants Dying in the Mediterranean?" *BBC News*, February 25, 2015, http://www.bbc.co.uk/news/world-europe-31510336.

untameable migratory flows that keep on struggling to reach European coasts. Since January 2017 to September of the same year, in fact, Italy counted almost 100,000 arrivals to the peninsula. The dangers of crossing the Southern Central Mediterranean led to the death of around 2300 migrants in the same time frame.[12] The worse migration crisis that Europe—with Italy on the frontline—is experiencing since 1945 is not only bringing consequences such as acts of terror and a general sense of insecurity, but also posing a number of operational, logistic, political and humanitarian dilemmas. In addition, the roles of the agencies in charge of maritime security have consequentially been reshaped.

The first initiative aimed at dealing with the migratory phenomenon in the Southern Central Mediterranean was the launch by the Italian government of the maritime operation *Mare Nostrum* on 18 October 2013 following the above-mentioned tragic episode off the island of Lampedusa. The scope of the mission was twofold: searching for and rescuing people in distress at sea (also performing sanitary controls and bringing migrants to Sicily) and fighting against human trafficking, with the intent to bring smugglers to justice. The scope of the operation was defined as fulfilling "humanitarian" purposes with "military" means.[13] In fact, the Navy, the Army, the Air Force, Police officers, the Coast Guard, Customs Service and personnel of the Italian Red Cross were involved in the operation. In particular, the units the Italian Navy deployed included: a large amphibious ship with an integrated hospital, two patrol ships, two frigates, an airplane, two helicopters and a coastal radar network. Furthermore, submarines were used to collect evidence of criminal activities. More than 900 personnel were dedicated to *Mare Nostrum*, an operation that cost 9 million euros per month to the Italian government and that covered an area of about 70,000 square kilometres stretching far beyond Italian territorial waters and overlapping with the Maltese and Libyan SAR zones.[14]

---

[12] "Arrivals by Sea and Missing Migrants," *International Organization for Migration*, accessed September 11, 2017, http://www.italy.iom.int/it/arrivi-mare-e-migranti-dispersi.

[13] Sergio Carrera and Leonhard den Hertog, "Whose Mare? Rule of Law Challenges in the Field of European Border Surveillance in the Mediterranean," *CEPS Paper in Liberty and Security in Europe*, no. 79 (2015): 5.

[14] "Operazione Mare Nostrum" [Mare Nostrum Operation], *Marina Militare*, accessed September 15, 2017, http://www.marina.difesa.it/cosa-facciamo/operazioni-concluse/Pagine/mare-nostrum.aspx.

The operation was considered successful for different aspects. First of all in saving lives at sea: around 150,000 men, women and children attempting to cross the Mediterranean Sea were rescued in a total of 421 operations in one year. Moreover, as reported by the Italian Navy, five mother ships were seized and 330 smugglers were brought to justice thanks to the efficient work of the investigative bodies.[15] Nonetheless, *Mare Nostrum* has been heavily criticized. The mission was defined as a "pulling factor": after the launch of the operation, the number of people taking the sea journey increased as well as did its dangers. This was due to the fact that the operation was engaged in proximity to the Libyan coast: smugglers put more and more people on boats with less fuel, food and water, assuming that the Italian Navy would respond to a distress call made after having cruised only few kilometres. Due to this criticism and the international pressure that was emerging from it, in October 2014 Operation *Mare Nostrum* (which was also a large expense for Italy) ended. The Italian government underlined that the mission was closing down because it was meant to be an emergency operation; nonetheless, the country would continue respecting the obligations stemming from the laws of the sea.

Operation *Mare Nostrum* put the complex relationship between the Italian Navy and Coast Guard to the test. Indeed, the two agencies were involved in the same mission together—along with a number of other institutions—and the main reason of controversy laid in the attribution of the SAR task. According to the Hamburg convention of 1979 and article 2 of the Inter-Ministerial Decree of 14 July 2013, the national authority responsible for the coordination of maritime rescue services is the Coast Guard.[16] Despite these dispositions, *Mare Nostrum* put the Navy in charge of managing all SAR events. The request of the Coast Guard to be the main actor entitled to such a task also during *Mare Nostrum* was not embraced by the Navy. As a consequence of such ambiguous provisions on the division of labour, the operative context became extremely blurred and disorganized putting human lives at risk.

---

[15] Ibid.

[16] "Ricerca e Soccorso" [Search and Rescue], *Guardia Costiera*, accessed September 16, 2017, http://www.guardiacostiera.gov.it/attivita/ricerca.

Both the Navy and the Coast Guard, in fact, could intervene in a case in which a migrant boat was considered in peril, leaving the command and control of the rescue and trans-shipping operations in the hands of both agencies. Considering that the chains of command of the Navy and of the Coast Guard follow different paths (as previously illustrated), joint activities at sea were slowed down or even hindered significantly.[17] An emblematic example is the episode of the night between the 31st of October and the 1st of November 2013. A boat full of migrants was found in a highly critical condition given that the sea was extremely rough. Assets of both the Navy and the Coast Guard were on site, but the Navy's patrol boats carried out the trans-shipping operation. Such a decision was strongly criticized by the Coast Guard, which affirmed that the event could have been much better and more safely managed by its smaller patrol boats present during the operation. According to Coast Guard officials, the assets that the Navy deployed for *Mare Nostrum* were too large for performing SAR functions, leading not only to a waste of economic resources and manpower, but also to poor efficacy in the operational context. On the other hand, the Coast Guard possessed all the assets necessary to successfully undertake SAR missions in a timeframe of two hours.[18]

Another example of how the unclear division of labour during Operation *Mare Nostrum* worsened the relationship between the Navy and the Coast Guard can be found in the request of the former to redeploy two units of the latter (which were off the coast of Sicily dealing with the migration crisis) to another area for patrolling activities. The Coast Guard strictly rejected such a request re-affirming that its main function is to perform SAR operations.

The lessons learned from *Mare Nostrum* are numerous. Firstly, an external driver like the migration crisis can fundamentally change the previously established division of labour between two agencies. Secondly, such a division of labour needs to be clear and concrete in order to allow all actors involved to efficiently operate. Finally, the problems that emerged, as the operation progressed, demonstrated that the roles of the Navy and the Coast Guard were not efficaciously assigned.

---

[17] Luca Gambardella, "Mare Nostrum: è scontro tra guardia costiera e militari" [Mare Nostrum: Clash Between Coastguard and the Military], *Linkiesta*, November 6, 2013, http://www.linkiesta.it/it/article/2013/11/06/mare-nostrum-e-scontro-tra-guardia-costiera-e-militari/17540/.

[18] Ibid.

Following the end of Operation *Mare Nostrum*, Italy launched Operation *Mare Sicuro* (Secure Sea) in March 2015. The latter, which is currently still running, is carried out by naval and air assets of the Italian Navy engaged in strengthening maritime security in the central Mediterranean Sea and in proximity of the Libyan coasts. Given the security developments in the Mediterranean waters, six vessels, five aircraft and about 700 soldiers are currently deployed to carry out the mission, which has many goals to achieve. The Navy is in charge of protecting the sea lines of communication (SLOCs) and ensuring a safe environment to maritime trade, as well as monitoring and protecting oil platforms that are of national interest. The assets of the *Marina Militare* are also involved in collecting information on terrorist group movements and illegal maritime traffic.

Concerns migration management, *Mare Sicuro* guards all national vessels—including those of the Coast Guard—engaged in SAR operations by ensuring that they are not effected by any possible action of criminal organizations and can also directly manage SAR activities if the Coast Guard asks for its support. Moreover, they conduct deterrence against human trafficking at sea.[19] The constant surveillance granted by Operation *Mare Sicuro* renders the waters of the Mediterranean Sea safer and more secure. As of June 2016, the Italian Navy contributed to saving 150,000 migrants and refugees' lives, in cooperation with the assets of the Coast Guard. To provide further insight on the scope of the mission, over a period of four months the combined surface units of the Navy are on average engaged in 15,800 sailing hours and its aircraft, almost 400 hours of flight time.[20]

Currently, the mission covers a space of 160,000 square kilometres in the central Mediterranean Sea; an area that extends outside the territorial waters of third states and is bounded to the south by the limit of the Libyan territorial waters. While the auxiliary unit operates mainly remaining moored in port in Tripoli.

---

[19] "Operazione Mare Sicuro (OMS)" [Secure Sea Operation], *Marina Militare*, accessed September 30, 2017, https://www.difesa.it/OperazioniMilitari/NazionaliInCorso/MareSicuro/Pagine/default.aspx.

[20] "Cambio al comando dell'operazione Mare Sicuro" [Change of Command for Secure Sea Operation], *Marina Militare: Press Release nr 41*, June 17, 2016, http://www.marina.difesa.it/conosciamoci/press-room/comunicati/Pagine/2016_041.aspx.

The Italian Coast Guard also conducts an operation called *Mare Sicuro*. Despite having the same name, Operation *Mare Sicuro* carried out by the Coast Guard has totally different mandate from the one of the Navy. In order to avoid misinterpretation, the Coast Guard's Secure Sea occurs only during summer and is aimed at guaranteeing the safety of all beaches and lakes in Italy and of the sea. The operation deploys about 3000 personnel, more than 300 vessels and 15 air assets. During peak tourist months, the Coast Guard safeguards human lives at sea, guarantees safety of navigation and the protection of the environment. By the end of summer 2016, the operation had assisted 3500 people and 700 boats.[21]

It is worth noting, however, that under its duty of carrying SAR operations and being involved in European Union missions, the Italian Coast Guard continues to deal with the migration crisis in the Mediterranean Sea and to be engaged in saving migrants and refugees' lives. Nonetheless, such a commitment is progressively becoming harder to shoulder. Not only has the burden increased in terms of refugee number, also the related dangers have escalated. To cite an example, during summer 2017 a patrol vessel of the Italian Coast Guard was targeted by machine guns while operating 30 miles from the Libyan coasts.[22] The incident turned out to be an accident as the Libyan Coast Guard mistakenly opened fire confusing the Italian vessel with a boat used for human trafficking. While the intention of the local officials was to intimidate the presumed traffickers on board, the risk to personnel of the Italian Coast Guard operating so close to the Libyan territory became increasingly evident. As a consequence of this and a series of other alarming episodes, in June 2017 the General Command of the Italian Coast Guard approved a new measure according to which, its officials will be armed during SAR operations in the context of the migration crisis and, in general, during high-risk assignments (escort activities and counterterrorism, for example). The decision came years after some officials of the Coast Guard had

---

[21] "Mare Sicuro 2017: al via l'operazione estiva della Guardia Costiera" [Mare Sicuro 2017: The Summer Operation of the Coast Guard Starts], *Guardia Costiera*, June 16, 2017, http://www.guardiacostiera.gov.it/stampa/Pages/mare-sicuro-2017-operazione-estiva-guardia-costiera.aspx.

[22] Chiara Giannini, "La svolta: armi alla Guardia costiera" [The Turning Point: Weapons to the Coast Guard], *Il Giornale*, June 2, 2017, http://www.ilgiornale.it/news/politica/svolta-armi-guardia-costiera-1404655.html.

been requiring a minimum number of weapons on board their units in order to defend themselves, if needed, while dealing with the migrants' emergency. The personnel will therefore be equipped with material for protection and defence such as ballistic helmets, bulletproof vests, protective shields, explosives detectors, batons, portable radios, small arms and heavy firearms.[23]

This is an important change in the operational framework of the Italian Coast Guard, which, despite having a military status, has since always operated without weapons and has required the support of the Gendarmerie or Police when in dangerous situations. Once the Coast Guard receives light weapons, it increases the potential for involvement in combat situations and consequently its role and activities may move closer to those of the Navy.

In general, the current migration crisis is not only rendering more complex the division of labour at sea leading to increasingly intertwining roles and competences, but it is also creating tensions among the agencies involved. Hence, it is possible to consider the migratory phenomenon from the MENA area to European coasts as an external driver to the current attribution of duties, especially between the Navy and the Coast Guard. As an overall consequence, it comes naturally to question if the previously mentioned proposal of the Renzi's government in 2015 was correct given the current situation in the Mediterranean theatre. Integrating the Coast Guard with the Navy seems the most feasible solution for efficiently dealing with the migration flows. In fact, maintaining the two agencies as separate bodies becomes unproductive in operational and financial terms, particularly taking into account that they are obliged to communicate and cooperate to efficiently manage the crisis.

THE EUROPEAN UNION FRAMEWORK AND REGIONAL COOPERATION

The stability of the Mediterranean Sea is of crucial importance not only for Italy, but also for most European countries, be they coastal or not. The economy and security of these states are heavily affected by the developments taking place in the Mediterranean area. To cite a few examples, the phenomenon of jihadist terrorism emerging from the

---

[23] Ibid.

MENA region, the energy and oil imports coming from the area, the protection of the SLOC and of maritime trade, and the migrant flux reaching European coasts. These are the most immediate challenges that European countries, with the European Union at the forefront, have to deal with in order to guarantee security to their citizens.

Navies and the coast guards of EU member states are the main actors responsible for ensuring security in the Mediterranean waters and providing for situational awareness and high operability at sea. This goal is pursued both by the actions of individual states—as in the Italian case previously examined—and bilateral or multilateral cooperation under the normative and operational framework of the EU.

The following section will introduce the European Union engagement in the Mediterranean Sea giving an overview of its main maritime operations, namely the Frontex Joint Operation Triton (and the institutional arrangements such as the establishment of an EU Coast Guard) and its successor Frontex Operation Themis, and EUNAVFOR Operation Sophia. It is worth noting that this type of engagement is predominantly aimed at tackling the migration crisis as it remains among the top priorities on the EU agenda. The migratory phenomenon, in fact, is not only increasing the general sense of insecurity inside the Union, but it is also becoming the main source of political instability in the EU. This section will also give a close focus on how Italian maritime security agencies fit in this communitarian framework and how they interact with their European counterparts. Overall, is argues that under the umbrella of EU operations, the division of labour between the Italian Navy, Coast Guard and the other maritime agencies involved is well delineated and effective. Hence, contrary to national missions, the Italian maritime institutions are able to achieve a high level of coordination when operating under the EU structure.

Prior to the ending Operation *Mare Nostrum*, Italy urged the EU to establish a new SAR operation in order to guarantee a constant presence in the Mediterranean Sea and reducing the number of deaths at sea. At the end of August 2014, after having had a meeting with Mr. Alfano, the Italian former Minister of Interior, the then European Commissioner for Home Affairs, Ms Malström, announced the creation of Joint Operation (JO) Triton, led by the EU agency tasked with border control of the Schengen Area,[24] Frontex. JO Triton was born from

---

[24] The Schengen Area comprises 26 European States that, by signing the Schengen Agreement in 1985, abolished all types of border controls at their mutual frontiers therefore granting the freedom of movement to their citizens inside the area.

the merging of Operations Hermes and Aeneas, previous Frontex operations, which respectively covered the south of Sicily and the coasts of two Italian regions, Calabria and Puglia. The mission was aimed at coordinating the operational activities at the Union's sea borders in the Central Mediterranean "in order to control irregular migration flows towards the territory of the European Union and to tackle cross border crime".[25] Under its mandate, JO Triton supported Italy with border control, surveillance and SAR in the central territory of the Mediterranean Sea. It operated under the command of the Italian Ministry of Interior in an area stretching up to 138 nautical miles from the southern Sicilian coastline.[26]

Nonetheless, on many occasions the Italian Coast Guard redirected the assets of JO Triton in areas far away from their operational perimeter for assisting migrants and refugees in distress thus fulfilling the obligations provided by the UN Convention on the Law of the Sea and avoiding the umpteenth disgrace at sea. Although the Italian Coast Guard and Finance Guard were part of the operation, while the Navy did not deploy any assets. In general, JO Triton could count on the presence of 350 officials, 11 vessels and five aircraft. In 2016, the operation contributed to rescuing more than 48,000 migrants in the Central Mediterranean Sea.[27]

In October 2016, Frontex was upgraded, becoming the European Border and Coast Guard Agency. As an evident response to the migration crisis, this new structure is aimed at giving Frontex a stronger role in monitoring and supporting national border guards. The agency, in fact, focuses on early detection and prevention of weaknesses in managing EU borders utilizing the tools of risk analysis, vulnerability assessment and training. From an operative perspective, Frontex can now quickly deploy border and coast guard officers from the rapid reaction pool made up of

---

[25] Frontex Operations Division Joint Operations Unit, *Concept of Reinforced Joint Operation Tackling the Migratory Flows Towards Italy: JO EPN-Triton* (Warsaw: European Agency for the Management of Operational Cooperation at the External Borders of the Member States of the European Union, 2014), 10, https://deathbyrescue.org/assets/annexes/2.Frontex_Concept_JO_EPN-Triton_28.08.2014.pdf.

[26] "EU Operations in the Mediterranean Sea," *European Commission*, October 4, 2016, 2017, https://ec.europa.eu/home-affairs/sites/homeaffairs/files/what-we-do/policies/securing-eu-borders/fact-sheets/docs/20161006/eu_operations_in_the_mediterranean_sea_en.pdf.

[27] "Joint Operation Triton (Italy)," Frontex, accessed January 9, 2019, https://frontex.europa.eu/media-centre/focus/joint-operation-triton-italy--ekKaes.

at least 1500 officers.[28] At land and at sea, Frontex's capacity for intervention has increased. Maritime operations, in particular, account for the largest share of the budget available to the agency with over 100 million Euro spent per annum.[29]

The efforts at sea of the European Border and Coast Guard Agency are extensive; besides border control, they include activities of SAR, customs, law enforcement, maritime security and safety, environmental protection and fisheries control. An initiative worthy of notice carried out by Frontex is the establishment of the European Coast Guard Cooperation Network, which brings around the table a number of European and international authorities operating in the maritime realm. The aim of the initiative is to improve the dialogue between these actors about law enforcement at sea in the fields of border management, SAR, migration, countering terrorism and cross-border crime.

In November 2016, the Network held its first meeting in Warsaw with the intent of highlighting the expanded role the new Frontex has in the maritime arena. Representatives of the navy, coast guard, border police, customs and other maritime agencies coming from more than 40 different national authorities of EU member states joined the gathering, together with delegates of various EU bodies, as well as Interpol, NATO, the United Nations Refugee Agency, and non-EU countries such as the USA, Libya and Morocco. During the meeting, the Commander of the Italian Coast Guard, rear Admiral Vincenzo Melone, as the national authority responsible for the coordination of SAR operations at sea, gave a speech on the topic. In the context of the migration crisis, he explained the modalities of rescuing human lives at sea and the criticalities related to this activity and its coordination.[30] The Italian Finance Guard joined the European Coast Guard Cooperation Network with the goal of enhancing close cooperation and inter-agency coordination with coastal

---

[28] "European Border and Coast Guard Agency (Frontex)," accessed January 9, 2019, https://europa.eu/european-union/about-eu/agencies/frontex_en.

[29] "Leggeri: Revamped Frontex Will Be 'Game Changer'," Euroactive, accessed January 9, 2019, https://www.euractiv.com/section/justice-home-affairs/news/leggeri-revamped-frontex-will-be-game-changer/.

[30] "A Varsavia il primo meeting dell'European Coast Guard Cooperation Network" [In Warsaw the First Meeting of the European Coast Guard Cooperation Network], *Guardia Costiera*, December 7, 2016, http://www.guardiacostiera.gov.it/stampa/Pages/Varsavia-meeting-European-Coast-Guard-Cooperation-Network.aspx.

Countries of the European Union and other non-EU states willing to develop a common security framework at sea. The air and naval component of the Finance Guard has always been on the frontline in countering illegal migration to Europe since the very start of the problem. After this Frontex initiative, the Finance Guard now provides for surveillance of territorial and international waters near the Libyan coasts and it supports the numerous flag vessels present in the area.

Frontex's JO Triton could, therefore, count on the support of numerous agencies coming from different states, and trying to achieve the same goal: guaranteeing security to the waters of the Mediterranean Sea. Italy was the country in charge of coordinating and directing the activities of all the maritime institutions involved. The command of JO Triton, in fact, was in the hands of the Italian Ministry of Interior in cooperation with the Italian Finance Guard and Coast Guard. In this context, the involvement of the Italian Navy was only marginal. As explained in the previous section, during the first year of existence of the operation, the Italian Navy deployed one vessel in support and requested the control of the entire mission. After an intense debate, Triton being a police operation focused on border control and SAR, the Finance Guard remained the main actor in charge. Hence, the principal Italian agencies involved in the activities of JO Triton were both the Finance and the Coast Guard. They were also responsible for deciding about the deployment and allocation of assets. Furthermore, Italian officials were constantly onboard of all vessels and helicopters participating in the operation. Evidently, being part of Frontex and at the command of JO Triton gave Italy and its institutions involved a significant responsibility. Coordinating the activities of not only national maritime agencies, but also those of other EU states, in fact, is a hard task that further complicates the division of labour at sea.

The same regulatory and institutional framework and division of work within Italian agencies applies to the new Frontex mission, Operation Themis which was launched on the 1st of February 2018 and replaces JO Triton. At the centre of Themis' mandate there is a triple commitment: assist Italy in the activities of control of maritime borders, continue performing SAR at sea, and ensure that the international norms are respected in the Mediterranean waters.

Themis has two operational zones: one in the eastern part of the Mediterranean Sea for controlling the fluxes coming from Egypt, Turkey and Albania and a more western one for tackling the traffics in route from Algeria, Tunisia and Libya. Compared to Triton, the new Frontex operation better reflects the changed patterns of migration. Furthermore, the operation has a strong security component aimed at guaranteeing internal security to all Member States thanks to a constant work of monitoring migratory fluxes, eventual infiltrations of foreign fighters through the Tunisian route (the most credible for possible jihadist to reach Europe)[31] and drugs smuggling.

What makes operation Themis stand out is the renewed effort in applying the law of the sea as established by the Hamburg convention: migrants rescued will have to be accompanied and disembarked in the European port closer to the spot in which the rescue has taken place.[32] In contrast during JO Triton's, people saved at sea were indiscriminately conducted to Italy, ignoring geographical vicinity of other States.

A completely different operation in scope and mandate was already launched in 2015, when the leaders of the European Union, following a drastic increase in the number of lives lost in the Mediterranean Sea, realized that a SAR operation (like Triton at that time) was not sufficient to deal with a phenomenon like the migration crisis, which has profound origins and is related to the crime of human trafficking. Hence, in April 2015 the European Council committed to mobilizing all efforts at its disposal to prevent additional drowning in the Mediterranean Sea and to tackle the root causes of the human emergency by fighting human smugglers. Three months later the EU launched a new Common Security and Defense Policy (CSDP) mission: EUNAVFOR MED, later renamed Operation Sophia—after the birth of a baby aboard one of the ships involved in the mission. This new maritime operation differs from the ones previously analysed in the EU's decision to deal with the migration crisis by adding a military component. Such an approach should be understood as innovative: the EU shifted from merely providing humanitarian assistance to fighting against migrant smugglers. In fact, the mission consists of disrupting the business model of human smuggling networks in the Southern Central Mediterranean in accordance

---

[31] The route that connects Tunisia to the costs of eastern Sicily is the safest to travel: it has a much shorter duration than the journeys that depart from Libya and wooden boats and motorboats are used for the crossing, proving for a real "shuttle service".

[32] "Frontex Launching New Operation in Central Med," *Frontex*, February 1, 2018, https://frontex.europa.eu/media-centre/news-release/frontex-launching-new-operation-in-central-med-yKqSc7.

with United Nations Convention on the Law of the Sea and the relative Security Council Resolutions.[33] The mandate of Operation Sophia provides for sequential phased missions that will engage in: monitoring and gaining information on migrant networks and patrolling on the high seas (phase 1); conducting boarding, search, seizure and diversion of vessels suspected of being used for human smuggling or trafficking on the high seas (phase 2A) and in Libyan territorial and internal waters (phase 2B); operating in the territory of Libya by taking all necessary measures against a vessel and related assets, which are suspected of being used for human smuggling or trafficking (phase 3).[34] Besides its core mandate, Operation Sophia also performs SAR at sea following international obligations: during its first year of mandate it contributed to saving 15,000 people.[35]

The mission is composed of a number of ships that rotate according to the will of the EU States participating and the needs of the Operation Commander. At the time of writing the operation can count on three surface vessels and five air assets. More than twenty-five countries contribute to the mission, among those Italy, France, Germany, Luxemburg and the UK, have taken most of the burden. Throughout the years, the mandate of Operation Sophia has been modified and extended according to the necessities of the time. In October 2015, the operation transitioned to phase 2A, during which apprehended smugglers were brought to Italy for juridical processes and eventual prosecution. At the end of June 2016, the mandate of Operation Sophia was extended by one year, and two new tasks were added to reinforce its core mission: training the Libyan Coastguard and Navy and, on the basis of the UNSC Resolution 2292, supporting the implementation of the UN arms embargo on the high seas off the Libyan coast by sharing information and countering illegal arms trafficking.

In July 2017, the European Council extended the mandate of Operation Sophia until the end of December 2018 and amended it by adding (1) a monitoring mechanism of the trainees of the Libyan

---

[33] "Council Decision (CFSP) 2015/778 on a European Union Military Operation in the Southern Central Mediterranean (EUNAVFOR MED)," *Council of the European Union*, May 18, 2015, 2.

[34] Ibid.: 3.

[35] "Statement by the HR/VP Federica Mogherini on the Adoption of Resolution 2292 by the UN Security Council," European Union External Action, June 14, 2016, https://eeas.europa.eu/headquarters/headquarters-homepage/4993/statement-hrvp-federica-mogherini-adoption-resolution-2292-un-security-council_en.

Coastguard for ensuring long-term efficiency in the training programme; (2) the conduct of new surveillance activities for gathering information on illegal trafficking of oil exports from Libya; (3) the possibility of sharing information on human trafficking with the agencies Frontex and Europol.[36] While in December 2018 the mandate of the operation was extended once again until the end of March 2019.[37]

Italy is once again on the forefront of all EU initiatives dealing with security in the Mediterranean Sea: it commands Operation Sophia, it hosts its headquarters in Rome, and Rear Admiral Enrico Credendino of the Italian Navy is currently appointed as Operation Commander. Moreover, at the time of writing, the Italian frigate *Luigi Rizzo* is the flagship of the mission. The operational and logistic support that Operation Sophia gives to *Mare Sicuro* and vice versa, as well as the constant official visits between respective officials, emphasizes the existing ties between the EU mission and the broader Italian effort in the Mediterranean Sea. The two operations, despite having a different mandate, are intrinsically tied; as such, they coordinate their activities at sea and share information.

From the brief analysis provided on the activities performed at sea under the umbrella of the European Union, it is evident that there are a multitude of actors involved in contributing to securing the waters of the Mediterranean Sea. Not only there are different states, but also each of them charges various maritime agencies to support the efforts of the EU. As a consequence, Italy—being one of the main countries responsible for most maritime actives in the Mediterranean—has to manage, coordinate and maintain dialogues with numerous institutions. In order to facilitate such an exchange, the EU provides for diverse networks and fora in which the protagonists present in the Mediterranean Sea can share best practices and information. The above-described European Coast Guard Cooperation Network is a clear example.

---

[36] "EUNAVFOR MED Operation Sophia: Mandate Extended Until 31 December 2018," *European Council*, July 25, 2017, http://www.consilium.europa.eu/en/press/press-releases/2017/07/25-eunavformed-sophia-mandate-extended/.

[37] "EUNAVFOR MED Operation Sophia: Mandate Extended Until 31 March 2019," *European Council*, December 21, 2018, https://www.consilium.europa.eu/en/press/press-releases/2018/12/21/eunavfor-med-operation-sophia-mandate-extended-until-31-march-2019/.

For what concerns the internal coordination between the various Italian maritime agencies participating in EU operations, the division of labour is well defined, despite the broke out of some disputes like the one regarding the command of JO Triton. While the Italian Navy is responsible for the activities of EUNAVFOR Operation Sophia, the Finance and Coast Guard were involved in Frontex JO Triton, and now they are in operation Themis. Moreover, all three agencies are engaged in the training of the Libyan Navy and Coast Guard. Overall, it is possible to argue that the Italian maritime institutions are able to achieve a high level of coordination, both internal and external, when operating under the EU structure, regardless of the large number and the variety of actors involved.

CONCLUSION

Guaranteeing stability to the Mediterranean Sea is of crucial importance to both Italy and other European Countries for security and economic reasons. Nonetheless, safeguarding its waters is becoming increasingly challenging as the number and level of threats including untamable migration flows, the spread of jihadist terrorism, and the smuggling of weapons and illicit drugs continue to increase. In Italy, the Navy and the Coast Guard, together with the support of the Finance Guard are the main agencies in charge of securing the Mediterranean Sea. Throughout the years, and given the challenges posed by the worsening of the maritime security situation, the roles of these bodies have been progressively intertwining, blurring the lines in the reciprocal functions and roles, and leading to, in some cases, the duplication of tasks and institutional competitiveness.

As this chapter has outlined, internal and external drivers have determined the current division of labour at sea. Domestic politics and intra-agency dynamics have shaped the functioning and tasks assigned to each maritime body. However, the Italian structures administering the work of the various agencies operating in the Mediterranean Sea are very broad and lack specific details on reciprocal duties. The Italian government needs to elaborate upon inter-ministerial decrees managing the mutual relations between the units of the various bodies in charge of securing the waters surrounding the Country.

The main external factor that is decisive in attributing tasks and duties at sea is the migration crisis. The migratory flows stemming from the MENA area and reaching European coasts have forced political and military leaders to revise and reshape the work of the Navy, Coast Guard and Finance Guard, also in order to make them fit within the broader EU framework dealing with the crisis. Indeed, internal and external drivers are merging dynamics that generally result into the latter dictating the developments of the former.

Overall, it is possible to argue that among Italian maritime agencies reciprocity and overlapping of duties prevail over efficacy and efficiency when tailor-made dispositions are not provided. The Italian government's decision of charging the Finance Guard with all police operations at sea is valuable and represents a remarkable progress in simplifying maritime activities. Nonetheless, the relationship between the Navy, the Coast Guard and the Finance Guard trio necessitates further regulations and arrangements in order to increase coordination and avoid wasting assets, monetary and human resources. Furthermore, Italy could exploit its successful leadership role in operating in the Mediterranean Sea under the EU framework for strengthening internal leadership and inter-agency coordination. As the Chief of the Italian Navy, Admiral Valter Girardelli, stated in occasion of the 11th symposium of Venice in which all the Navies of the broader Mediterranean area gathered: "in order to face the increasing panoply of operations and tasks related to maritime security, it is necessary to maximize the esteem of the naval component within the complex inter-forces, inter-institutional and inter-agency structure".[38]

---

[38] Admiral Valter Girardelli, "L'11° simposio di venezia. Prefazione" [The 11th Symposium of Venice. Preface], *X-tra gli speciali di RiD*, n. 015 (October 2017).

CHAPTER 10

Russia's Navy-Coastguard Nexus

Ingvill Moe Elgsaas and Liv Karin Parnemo

Russia commands vast maritime areas, and two-thirds of Russia's 60,932 km-long national border is maritime.[1] Moscow also considers maritime activities and offshore resources as a bulwark that will ensure the country's socio-economic development as well as its aspirations for international standing. The importance of the maritime domain translates into an ambitious maritime policy with the overall objectives to implement and protect Russia's national interests at sea,[2] and to

---

[1] 38,807 km of borders at sea, 7,141 km borders along rivers, and 475 km borders across lakes, according to Dmitry Boltenkov, "The Russian Coast Guard," *Moscow Defense Brief* 35, no. 3 (2013), http://mdb.cast.ru/mdb/3-2013/item3/article1/.

[2] The term used is the 'World Ocean', *Mirovoy Okean*, which refers collectively to all the world's oceans. This term appears throughout the Russian sources cited in this chapter and is translated as 'the world's oceans', 'the oceans' or, as here, 'at sea'.

I. M. Elgsaas (✉)
Norwegian Institute for Defence Studies (IFS), Norwegian Defence University College (NDUC), Oslo, Norway
e-mail: Ingvill.Elgsaas@ifs.mil.no

L. K. Parnemo
Department of Long-Term Planning and Defence Policy, Norwegian Ministry of Defense, Oslo, Norway

© The Author(s) 2019
I. Bowers and S. L. C. Koh (eds.), *Grey and White Hulls*,
https://doi.org/10.1007/978-981-13-9242-9_10

strengthen Russia's position in the maritime domain so that Russia can become a leading maritime power.[3]

Russia's aspirations in the maritime domain create broad responsibilities and tasks for the Navy and the Coastguard. Together, these organisations make up the "sharp end" of Russia's comprehensive effort to utilise the Arctic as a strategic reserve and secure Russia's ambitious national interests. Naval and coastguard capabilities in the Arctic and the organisations' diverse portfolios make them central contributors to Arctic safety as well as to Russia's defence and security. This places them at the centre of Arctic affairs, whether the sign of the times is international cooperation or rivalry. Today, the geopolitical context is marked by Russia being at odds with the West, including its Arctic neighbours.

The Arctic is one of two focus areas in Russia's maritime policy and serves as a focal point for this discussion of Russia's Navy-Coastguard nexus. In addition to the military-strategic importance of the region, Russia is economically dependent upon its natural resources. Russia also places great emphasis on ensuring transport to and from the region, as well as turning the Northern Sea Route into a viable competitor for international shipping.

Russia's rather broad threat perception increases the need for security and control over both its national borders and natural resources. Among the outcomes of Russia's focus on, and wide understanding of, national security, is the reopening and modernising of military bases along the Arctic coast—a development many see as a decisive step towards a militarisation of the Arctic.[4] To meet the demands produced by increased activities in the region, Russia is pursuing comprehensive safety and security in the Arctic with a focus on interagency cooperation where the Northern Fleet and the Coastguard are central participants.

The Russian Navy and Coastguard play central roles in the formulation and implementation of Russia's maritime policy. Both organisations'

---

[3] *Maritime Doctrine of the Russian Federation* [Morskaya doktrina Rossiyskoy Federatsii] approved by presidential decree July 26, 2015, Section II Article 6, http://docs.cntd.ru/document/555631869. Henceforth, *the Maritime Doctrine* (2015).

[4] E.g. Robbie Gramer, 2017, "Here's What Russia's Military Build-Up in the Arctic Looks Like," *Foreign Policy*, January 25. https://foreignpolicy.com/2017/01/25/heres-what-russias-military-build-up-in-the-arctic-looks-like-trump-oil-military-high-north-infographic-map/; Sergey Sukhankin, "Russia's Push for Militarization of the Arctic Continues," *Eurasia Daily Monitor*, 15, no. 93 (2018), https://jamestown.org/program/russias-push-for-militarization-of-the-arctic-continues/.

composition and hardware are influenced by their Soviet predecessors, and this chapter takes brief retrospective looks at the Soviet experience to frame the current discussion. The Soviet legacy of militarism gave way to the unintentional "demilitarisation" of the Navy through decay and neglect in the 1990s. The Coastguard, on the other hand, was deliberately demilitarised in the 2000s. Russia's replenished coffers coupled with its maritime and Arctic ambitions have resulted in the partial restoration of both navy facilities and activities in recent years. As maritime activities have increased following geopolitical changes and an upswing in the Russian economy in the early 2000s, expensive hardware and vast operational areas require cooperation between the Navy and the Coastguard.

The post-Soviet reforms in Russia's security and defence sector have created uncertainties about different actors' responsibilities and tasks, and even their organisations. Today, the Russian Coastguard is a department in the Border Service of the Federal Security Service (FSB). The portfolio of the FSB is both immense and varied, yet the FSB's Coastguard Department is mainly responsible for civilian tasks, such as inspections of fishing vessels and rendering assistance to ships in distress. Unlike its predecessor, the maritime units of the Soviet KGB Border Troops that were seen as a "Navy reserve",[5] the Russian Coastguard is a law-enforcer, resource manager and rescuer.[6] Yet, as we shall see in the section on Russia's maritime policy, according to Russia's most recent strategic document on maritime activities, the Navy and the FSB are jointly responsible for Russia's *military*-maritime activities. The latter, we argue, indicates that Russian authorities are opening up for a diversification of the Coastguard to also cover tasks in the military domain. We also see that maritime exercises aim to improve interagency operability between the Navy and the Coastguard. Such a pooling of resources makes sense considering Russia's ambitions in the global maritime domain, and particularly in the Arctic, coupled with the challenges relating to expensive hardware and extensive operational areas to cover.

[5] Dmitry Boltenkov, "The Russian Coast Guard."

[6] Kristian Åtland, Law Enforcer, Resource Manager and Rescuer—The Making of the RUSSIAN Coastguard [Myndighetsutøver, ressursforvalter og livredder—den russiske kystvakten i støpeskjeen], *Nordisk Østforum* 30, no. 1 (2016), https://tidsskriftet-nof.no/index.php/noros/article/view/390/662.

The Kremlin's threat perception might serve as justification to use all available means to meet the perceived threat.

The chapter is organised into four sections. The first section discusses the evolution of the Russian Navy from the late Soviet period to the present, focusing on decay followed by rearmament and the creation of an Arctic military district. The second section discusses the evolution of the Russian Coastguard from the late Soviet period to the present, focusing on its reform from a military formation to a law enforcement agency and on the recently created coastguard administrations in the Arctic. Section three discusses Russia's maritime policy with particular attention to the Arctic as a priority direction and to military-maritime activities. In the fourth and concluding section, we speculate that developments in the Navy and the Coastguard coupled with the latest development in Russia's maritime policy open for a possible diversification of the Coastguard to once again become a "Navy reserve", in addition to its primary role as a law-enforcer.

THE NAVY: DECAY FOLLOWED BY MILITARISATION OR NORMALISATION?

The Russian Navy is the principal heir to the Soviet Navy and was formally founded in January 1992. It is organised into four service branches: surface forces, submarine forces, naval aviation, and coastal forces, and two additional troop branches: the coastal rocket-artillery forces and naval infantry.[7] It is divided into what is in effect four and a half fleets—the Northern Fleet, the Pacific Fleet, the Black Sea Fleet, the Baltic Fleet and the Caspian Flotilla. According to Russia's Ministry of Defence, the Navy is "responsible for the armed protection of Russia's interests and conduct of operations in the maritime theatre of war" and should be "capable of attacking enemy land-based facilities with nuclear weapons, destroying enemy naval forces at sea and on bases, disrupting its maritime lines of communication and protecting friendly maritime shipping operations".[8] It can also support the ground forces during

---

[7] Ministry of Defence of the Russian Federation, *Navy Main Command* [Glavnoye komandovaniye Voyenno-Morskogo Flota], n/d, https://structure.mil.ru/structure/forces/navy/structure.htm.

[8] Ministry of Defence of the Russian Federation, *Navy*, n/d, http://eng.mil.ru/en/structure/forces/navy.htm.

operations in a continental theatre of war, insert maritime forces into operational areas and repel enemy assaults.[9]

However, while the Navy's tasks are first and foremost military in nature, there is also overlap with the tasks of civilian organisations. For example, the Navy is responsible for protecting Russia's underwater and air border and supports the FSB in its duties to protect the maritime border, the territorial sea and the exclusive economic zone. The Navy responds to emergencies and supports the civilian organisation in charge of emergency response, the Ministry for Emergencies.[10] Navy search and rescue forms part of Russia's national emergency system, which is overseen by the Ministry for Emergencies, and the Northern Fleet is an important participant in exercises and rescue operations in the Arctic. All the while, responsibility for search and rescue at sea is under the jurisdiction of the Russian Ministry of Transport.

Russia's Armed Forces are organised into military districts. Since the end of the Soviet period, there was a gradual reduction in the number of military districts from nine[11] in 1991 to four in 2010: The Western, Southern, Central and Eastern. In December 2014, a fifth military district was created that is variously referred to as military district "North", Russia's "Arctic military district" or—as it is presented on the Russian Ministry of Defence's home page—the "Northern Fleet military district".[12] The Northern Fleet, which was previously part of the Western military district, now commands the Western Russian Arctic as well as Arctic archipelagos further east (Severnaya Zemlya and Novosibirsk Islands) that previously belonged to the Central and Eastern military districts. Severnaya Zemlya and Novosibirsk Islands both house Soviet bases that are currently being refurbished.

The Northern Fleet is essential to Russia's military power. It is the largest of Russia's fleets and alongside the Pacific Fleet in the Eastern military district, one of two with strategic nuclear capabilities. The Northern Fleet's bases are concentrated in the Western Russian Arctic, but include bases in the Eastern Russian Arctic, such as the "Northern Clover" on Kotelny Island (Novosibirsk Islands). The "Northern

---

[9] Ibid.

[10] Ibid.

[11] Eight regular military districts, plus a special district for the Kaliningrad enclave.

[12] Ministry of Defence of the Russian Federation, *Military Districts* [Voyennyye okruga], n/d, http://mil.ru/.

Clover" is part of a drive to reopen and modernise military bases along Russia's Arctic coast. In 2015, it was announced that Russia's Special Construction Troops (*Spetsstroy*) would deploy 1500 workers to build six military facilities in the Arctic.[13] Speaking on the third anniversary of the creation of the Arctic military district, Commander of the Northern Fleet Admiral Nikolay Yevmenov congratulated its military and civilian staff and declared that the military district created to protect Russia's national interests in the Arctic had significantly increased its combat potential over these three years.[14] There is no doubt that Russia's Armed Forces, and especially the Navy represented by the Northern Fleet, have expanded their presence and activities in the Arctic over recent years. There is disagreement, however, on whether this constitutes a militarisation or is merely a normalisation in Russian defence posture.

Russia's efforts to modernise and strengthen the Russian military in the 2000s, operationalised in the military reform set upon in 2008 by then Defence Minister Anatoly Serdyukov, are often interpreted as Russia pursuing a policy of militarisation. The *State Armament Programme towards 2020 (GPV-2020)* designated approximately 26% of the funds to the Navy.[15] According to this programme, the frequency of campaigns and exercises was to increase, and so too was Russia's naval presence in prioritised ocean areas. Accordingly, there has been a general

[13] Spetsstroy of Russia: About 1.5 Thousand Workers Are Building Military Facilities in Six Locations in the Arctic [Spetsstroy Rossii: okolo 1,5 tysyach rabochikh stroyat voyennyye ob"yekty v shesti tochkakh Arktiki], *TASS*, September 29, 2015, http://tass.ru/armiya-i-opk/2300055. The locations of these objects were listed as: Aleksandra Land (Franz Josef Land), Rogachevo (Novaya Zemlya), Sredny Island (Sedov Archipelago within the Novosibirsk Islands), the above-mentioned Kotelny Island (Novosibirsk Islands), Wrangel Island and Cape Schmidt.

[14] Ministry of Defence of the Russian Federation, *The Northern Fleet's Joint Strategic Command Marks Its Third* Anniversary [Ob"yedinennoye strategicheskoye komandovaniye Severnogo flota otmechayet tret'yu godovshchinu so dnya obrazovaniya], 2017. https://function.mil.ru/news_page/country/more.htm?id=12155012@egNews&_print=true.

[15] Julian Cooper, "Russia's State Armament Programme to 2020: A Quantitative Assessment of Implementation 2011–2015," *FOI Report 4239-SE* (March 2016), 20, https://www.researchgate.net/profile/Julian_Cooper2/publication/299338379_Russia%27s_state_armament_programme_to_2020_a_quantitative_assessment_of_implementation_2011-2015_FOI_Report/links/56f11db508aecad0f31f235d/Russias-state-armament-programme-to-2020-a-quantitative-assessment-of-implementation-2011-2015-FOI-Report.pdf.

increase in naval activity.[16] This development evolved alongside an increased Russian geopolitical assertiveness on the global stage, as well as a growing distrust towards NATO and the West. This geopolitical framework strongly contributed to an impression of a more aggressive Russia, supporting its ambitions by striving to rebuild its former military might.

On the other hand, the military reform and the naval modernisation in the 2000s can be interpreted as a normalisation that compensates for the decline in capabilities the Russian military suffered in the 1990s. In the Navy's case, there is a stark contrast from the golden age under Commander-in-Chief Admiral Gorshkov in the 1950s-1980s to the detrimental 1990s. In the 1990s, the main military objectives were to maintain Russian sovereignty, preserve Russia's status as a nuclear superpower and deal with conflicts in the post-Soviet space and in the North Caucasus in particular.[17] Since the most pertinent tasks fell outside the Navy's realm, it lost out in the competition over scarce funding and personnel. Compared to the Soviet Navy, the Russian Navy lost naval bases, industry, infrastructure and its recruitment pool shrank.[18]

Therefore, the decay of naval capacities in the 1990s should not be considered a demilitarisation in terms of political intent. It was rather a result of a politically turbulent period, where a combination of low priorities, a lack of financial resources and lag from the Soviet period led to the inevitable downscaling of Russian military capacity. A surge of oil-money in the 2000s then allowed Russia to once again put serious funding towards a military in dire need of modernisation, and as a result, the Navy has begun to slowly recover from the dramatic decay of capacities in the 1990s.[19]

---

[16] Dmitry Gorenburg, 2015, "Is It Possible to Fulfil Kremlin's Grand Expectations," *PONARS Eurasia, Policy Memo No. 395* (October 2015), http://www.ponarseurasia.org/memo/russian-naval-shipbuilding-it-possible-fulfill-kremlins-grand-expectations.

[17] Mikhail Tsypkin, "The Challenge of Understanding the Russian Navy," in *The Russian Military Today and Tomorrow: Essays in Memory of Mary Fitzgerald*, ed. S. Blank and R. Weitz (Carlisle: Strategic Studies Institute, U.S. Army War College, 2010), 331–357, 332.

[18] Katarzyna Zysk, "Russia's Naval Ambitions: Driving Forces and Constraints," in *Twenty-First Century Seapower: Cooperation and Conflict at Sea*, ed. P. Dutton, R. Ross and O. Tunsjo (Routledge: London, 2012), 112–135.

[19] Liv Karin Parnemo, "Russia's Naval Development—Grand Ambitions and Tactical Pragmatism," *The Journal of Slavic Military Studies* 32, no. 1 (2019): 41–69, https://doi.org/10.1080/13518046.2019.1552678.

This is not to say that the effort to modernise the Navy has been successful in remedying the decay of the transition period. Russia's stagnating economy, sanctions, ineffective and corrupt naval industry, and a considerable lag in production produce delays in the development of new vessels and the number of write-offs exceeds the acquisitions. Instead of prioritising larger ocean-going vessels, such as aircraft carriers, the vessels being built today are mainly smaller, highly manoeuvrable vessels for coastal waters. This force structure does not just reflect a lack of funding; it is also a result of Russia's current strategic focus on waters closer to home, such as the Baltic, Black, Azov and Mediterranean seas in the Atlantic policy area. This trend is further supported by developments in long-range missile and submarine technologies as well as layered defence strategies.[20]

THE COASTGUARD: FROM DEMILITARISATION TO DIVERSIFICATION

The Russian Coastguard is a department in the Border Guard Service of the FSB. The FSB is the chief heir to the Soviet KGB. It is the largest and most powerful among Russia's security services, with a broad and diverse mandate. Its main areas of activity are counter-intelligence, counterterrorism, crime prevention, intelligence, information security; and, since 2003, border security including in the maritime domain.[21]

The Navy's continuing material and financial challenges, the diversity of its tasks and its expanding activities in the Arctic are all factors that open up for the Coastguard potentially acting as a support element to the Navy. The same could be said of the geographical challenges facing the Navy. The vast distances separating the Russian naval bases and maritime theatres make power transfers cumbersome. The limited possibility for transferring capacities from one fleet to another potentially increases the need for readily available support in conflict situations, as well as to increase presence.

Supporting the Navy is no new task to the Russian Coastguard. In the Soviet period, the border troops, including their maritime units,

[20] Ibid.
[21] *Federal Law No. 40, On the Federal Security Service* [O Federal'noy sluzhbe bezopasnosti], April 3, 1995. Article 8.

were part of the colossal committee for state security, the KGB. In 1993, the border troops became a separate service, the Federal Border Service (FPS). A few years later, the maritime units in the FPS were organised into a Maritime Guard (*Morskaya okhrana*) and a corresponding department was set up within the service. Then, in July 2003, the FPS was dissolved, and its functions transferred to the FSB, thus creating the FSB's Border Guard Service.[22] What had been the Maritime Guard Department in the FPS was reorganised into a Coastguard administration (*Beregovaya okhrana*) in the FSB's Border Guard Service in 2004. In 2007, the Coastguard was elevated to a department within the FSB.

The maritime units in the Soviet border troops were highly militarised, and their tasks were narrowly defined. Their primary task was to prevent border violations at sea, unauthorised ingress to Soviet territory and unauthorised egress by Soviet citizens.[23] Aleksey Nikolsky has argued that the Soviet siege mentality coupled with the state's monopoly on foreign trade made the Soviet government keep its borders "locked and barred", which translated into unprecedented militarisation of the Soviet border troops.[24] According to Dmitry Boltenkov, the Soviet military command considered the border troops' maritime units as the Soviet Navy's reserve for wartime.[25]

Since it was the Navy that was in charge of Soviet ship design institutes and procurement programmes, the border troops' maritime units were equipped with slightly modified versions of the Navy's own vessels, many of them with excessive weaponry for border guard tasks.[26] Starting in the late 1970s, the border troops' tasks were extended to include protection of maritime economic resources to prevent foreign fishing boats from "plundering" Soviet resources.[27] Despite its broadening portfolio,

---

[22] *Presidential Decree No. 308*, On Measures to Improve the State's Administration of Security in the Russian Federation [O merakh po sovershenstvovaniyu gosudarstvennogo upravleniya v oblasti bezopasnosti Rossiyskoy Federatsii], March 11, 2003, http://ivo.garant.ru/#/document/185629/paragraph/8888:11 and http://base.garant.ru/185629/c3b40f620a0805943a2028ba274f1c13/#block_1.

[23] Dmitry Boltenkov, "The Russian Coast Guard."

[24] Aleksey Nikolsky, "The Invisible Reform of the Border Guard Service." *Moscow Defense Brief* 34, no. 2 (2013), http://mdb.cast.ru/mdb/2-2013/item4/article1/.

[25] Dmitry Boltenkov, "The Russian Coast Guard."

[26] Ibid.

[27] Ibid.

the connection between the border troops and the military remained strong. This continued into the post-Soviet period. Even as a separate service in the 1990s, the Federal Border Service "essentially remained an armed force".[28]

In the late 1990s and early 2000s, the FPS' Maritime Guard's civilian activities continued to grow. Management of economic resources increased in importance. Unlike the Navy, in the case of the Coastguard, demilitarisation was a central component in a conscious plan for reform. According to Nikolsky, the FPS' subordination to the FSB marked the beginning of a radical reform aiming to demilitarise the border service and transform it into a law enforcement agency.[29] In 2005, references to border "troops" in Russian legislation were removed.[30] This shows deliberate efforts to sever the link between the Border Service and the Armed Forces, including between the Coastguard and the Navy. This change coincided with the service beginning to phase out conscripts among its ranks.

In 2006, the head of the FSB's Coastguard, Vice Admiral Vyacheslav Serzhanin, described the Coastguard as a complex, multifunctional system designed to defend and guard Russia's state border at sea, the country's economic and other legitimate interests in the maritime border area, in the Exclusive Economic Zone and on the continental shelf, as well as anadromous fish species outside the EEZ.[31] When asked about the Coastguard's ability to perform its tasks, Serzhanin admitted that the past 20 years had witnessed a steady decline in both quality and quantity of ships and that the pace of write-offs far exceeded the pace of

---

[28] Aleksey Nikolsky, "The Invisible Reform of the Border Guard Service (2013)."

[29] Ibid.

[30] *Federal Law No. 15*, On the Introduction of Amendments to Some Legislative Acts of the Russian Federation and the Exclusion of Certain Provisions in Legislative Acts of the Russian Federation in Connection with the Implementation of Measures to Improve State Administration in the Sphere of Protection and Guarding of the State Border of the Russian Federation [O vnesenii izmeneniy v nekotoryye zakonodatel'nyye akty Rossiyskoy Federatsii i priznanii utrativshimi silu otdel'nykh polozheniy zakonodatel'nogo akta Rossiyskoy Federatsii v svyazi s osushchestvleniyem mer po sovershenstvovaniyu gosudarstvennogo upravleniya v sfere zashchity i okhrany Gosudarstvennoy granitsy Rossiyskoy Federatsii], March 7, 2005.

[31] Nikita Ussurysky, 'Frontier' Prevented Damages of 64 Million Rubles ['Rubezh' predotvratil ushcherb v 64 milliona rubley], *Voenno-Promyshlennyy Kuryer*, August 9, 2006, https://vpk-news.ru/articles/5125.

construction. Consequently, Serzhanin said, the existing composition of ships does not fully allow for effective performance of the Coastguard's tasks.[32]

In 2015, two new bodies, the border administration for the Western Arctic and for the Eastern Arctic, were set up within the FSB's Border Guard Service. The Arctic border administrations stand apart from the other border administrations that follow the territorial-administrative organisation of the Russian Federation, each covering the territory of one or two regions (federal subjects).[33] The Arctic border administrations' orientation to the maritime domain is underscored by responsibility for the Western Arctic land border (between the Murmansk region and Norway) being transferred to the Kareliya border administration when the Western Arctic border administration was created.[34]

According to Head of the FSB Border Guard Service's Administration for the Western Arctic, Mayor General Igor Konstantinov, the new organisation reflects the Arctic region's geostrategic and economic significance, an increasing interest in the region's "currency-intensive" bio-resources, hydrocarbons and the Northern Sea Route.[35] When asked if this interest was accompanied by a growing appetite for the Russian Arctic, Konstantinov contended that leading powers such as the USA, Canada and Norway seek to increase their influence in the Arctic while trying to force Russia out of its zone of strategic interests.[36] Adversarial rhetoric aside, Russia participates in international coastguard cooperation through the Arctic Coast Guard Forum.

Both modified navy ships and specialist coastguard ships form the Coastguard's fleet.[37] According to Kristian Åtland, there has been less

---

[32] Ibid.

[33] Border Service of FSB Russia, Map of Locations of FSB Russia's Border Administrations [Karta raspolozheniya pogranichnykh upravleniy FSB Rossii], n/d, http://ps.fsb.ru/regions.htm.

[34] Elizaveta Desnitskaya, The Arctic Under the Borderguard's Protection [Arktika—pod shchitom. Pogranichnym], *Murmanskiy Vestnik*, August 14, 2015, http://www.mvestnik.ru/army/pid2015081451/.

[35] Interview by Leonid Slavin, The Arctic's Border Shield [Pogranichnyy shchit Arktiki], *Naryana Vynder*], July 23, 2015, http://nvinder.ru/article/vypusk-no-76-20278-ot-23-iyulya-2015-g/8660-pogranichnyy-shchit-arktiki.

[36] Ibid.

[37] "Russian Federation Coast Guard 2018," *RussianShips.info*, December 24, 2018, http://russianships.info/eng/coastguard/.

political will to spend money on modernising the Coastguard compared to the Navy.[38] However, the Coastguard's capacity in the Arctic has recently been increased by the commission of new vessels. In 2016, the Coastguard commissioned the *Polar Star* (*Polyarnaya Zvezda*), its first *Okean* class (Project 22100) patrol vessel with icebreaker capability and helicopter. There is talk of as many as six to be constructed in total, but so far only another two have been laid down. The *Polar Star* set its course for Murmansk in the Western Arctic in December 2016 where it is now based. In 2017, the Coastguard in the Western Arctic received another fresh acquisition, a *Rubin* class (Project 22460) patrol vessel, *Predanny*. Upon its arrival in Murmansk, *Predanny* was described as a versatile ship designed to perform a wide range of tasks assigned to the Coastguard. These include patrolling the territorial waters of near and far sea areas, protecting the state border and the continental shelf, carrying out emergency rescue operations and disaster relief and combatting terrorism and piracy.[39] Several more vessels are planned for the Arctic; however, the state of the shipbuilding industry and the Russian economy cause delays in production.

Since 2013, the FSB Border Service has been led by Army General and first deputy FSB director Vladimir Kulishov. In an interview with Interfax in May 2017, Kulishov emphasised the growing importance of the Coastguard's tasks in the Arctic including controlling movement along the Northern Sea Route and participating in the development of resources on the shelf.[40] Kulishov's background from the FSB's counterterrorist units illustrates the Coastguard's diversification and puts emphasis on the complexity and cross-sectoral nature of threats and challenges facing the Coastguard, and the Border Service, at present.

Over the course of the post-Soviet period, the Coastguard has evolved from the KGB border troops' specialised maritime units to an FSB

---

[38] Kristian Åtland, "Law Enforcer, Resource Manager and Rescuer—The Making of the Russian Coastguard," 52.

[39] A New Coastguard Ship 'Predanny' Arrived in Murmansk [V Murmansk pribyl novyy pogranichnyy storozhevoy korabl' 'Predannyy'], *TV21*, October 16, 2017, http://www.tv21.ru/news/2017/10/16/v-murmansk-pribyl-novyy-pogranichnyy-storozhevoy-korabl-predannyy.

[40] Head of FSB Border Service: Our Strategic Goal is a Gradual Transition to Remote Control Over Border Areas [Glava Pogransluzhby FSB: nasha strategicheskaya tsel'—posledovatel'nyy perekhod k distantsionnomu kontrolyu za okhranyayemoy granitsey], *Interfax*, March 26, 2017, http://www.interfax.ru/interview/563807.

Coastguard with a broad portfolio. The former was highly militarised and even considered a reserve for the Soviet Navy before its activities were expanded to include civilian tasks, such as sustainable management of fish stocks. In the post-Soviet period, the civilian tasks grew in importance and became the Coastguard's main activities. As will be shown in the next section, a sign of the current times is emphasis on cooperation between the Coastguard and the Navy.

Russia's Maritime Policy: The Arctic and Military-Maritime Activities

This section discusses Russia's maritime policy with a focus on the Arctic as a priority and on the roles and tasks attributed to the Navy and to the FSB. A central tenet in Russia's policy in the maritime domain, and also in its Arctic policy, is to address complex challenges in a comprehensive manner and through cooperation between the Navy and the Coastguard. While the Navy remains the principal actor in Russia's military-maritime activities, the most recent official documents assign a significant role to the FSB in this field. Close cooperation between the Navy and the FSB in military-maritime activities translates into practical joint exercises on the tactical level. A central component in the organisations' joint exercises, whether they aim to protect oil transport, harbour facilities, or indeed, the Northern Fleet's own facilities and assets, is to practice interagency operability.

In 2001, Russia adopted a *Maritime Doctrine for the period until 2020*.[41] While this document is still in effect, an updated and more detailed version, the *Maritime Doctrine of the Russian Federation* was adopted in 2015.[42] The new edition of the *Maritime Doctrine* was presented by President Vladimir Putin on 26 July 2015, at a meeting on-board the frigate *Admiral Gorshkov*.[43] President Vladimir Putin described the new doctrine as a big event for the Navy and for the shipbuilding industry. In this doctrine, the Navy—described by Putin as "the main customer"—formulates its needs, and it is up to the shipbuilding

---

[41] *Maritime Doctrine of the Russian Federation until 2020* [Morskaya doktrina Rossiyskoy Federatsii na period do 2020 goda] approved by presidential decree July 27, 2001, http://docs.cntd.ru/document/902010411. Henceforth, the *Maritime Doctrine* (2001).

[42] *The Maritime Doctrine* (2015), op.cit.

[43] President of the Russian Federation, *Russian Federation Marine Doctrine*, July 26, 2015, http://en.kremlin.ru/events/president/news/50060, February 16, 2018.

industry to meet these needs. Putin also emphasised that, as a first, the new doctrine includes social provisions. Then Deputy Prime Minister and chairman of the Maritime College, Dmitry Rogozin, who also chaired Russia's Arctic Commission at the time, stated that among the participants in the drafting process the Navy played the leading role. However, the Russian fleet (*Rossiyskiy flot*) described in the *Maritime Doctrine* comprises several other organisations including the FSB.[44]

Russia's national maritime policy is operationalised into four functional and six regional policy areas. The functional policy areas are: shipping, development and conservation of resources in the oceans, maritime scientific research and military-maritime activities.[45] The Arctic and the Atlantic are singled out as priorities among the regional policy areas.[46] Focus on the Atlantic centres on a perceived need to counter NATO and on the strategic situation in Crimea. The *Maritime Doctrine* (2015) states that Russia's interests in the Arctic region centre on the vast natural resources (such as fish, minerals and hydrocarbons) of the exclusive economic zone and the continental shelf, the increasing importance of the Northern Sea Route, and the decisive role of the Northern Fleet.[47] The importance of the Arctic is further enhanced by the fact that all four of the doctrine's functional areas have particular impact on the development of the region, in terms of the Northern Sea Route, resource potential, scientific research and, not least, military-maritime activity, which we shall turn to below.

The most recent strategic document laying down Russia's maritime policy is the *Foundations of the Russian Federation's State Policy for Military-Maritime Activities until 2030* adopted in 2017.[48] With the

---

[44] *Maritime Doctrine* (2015). General Provisions. *Maritime Doctrine* (2001). General Provisions.

[45] *The Maritime Doctrine*, 2015. Article 18. The regional policy areas are: the Atlantic region, the Arctic region, the Pacific region, the Caspian region, the Indian region and the Antarctic region. Ibid. Article 50.

[46] Maritime Collegium of the Government of the Russian Federation, Russia's Maritime Doctrine—The Arctic and Crimea in Focus [Morskaya doktrina Rossii—v prioritete Arktika i Krym], *Russia's Maritime Policy: People, Events and Facts*, no 13 (2015), http://marine.gov.ru/publication/russian-maritime-policy/23/.

[47] Articles 59–61.

[48] *Foundations of the Russian Federation's State Policy for Military-Maritime Activities until 2030*, 2017, http://pravo.gov.ru/proxy/ips/?docbody=&firstDoc=1&lastDoc=1&nd=102438738, Henceforth, the *Foundations*.

adoption of this new document, the previous *Foundations of the Russian Federation's State Policy for Military-Maritime Activities until 2020* from 2012 was voided. The *Foundations* aims to concretise other strategic documents, including the *Maritime Doctrine*.[49] The *Foundations* describes the period leading up to its adoption as a time when competition over the oceans' natural resources has intensified and prompted several states to assert control over strategically important maritime transport routes.[50] Looking towards 2030, the prediction is military-political instability with further rivalry between states in a climate marked by political and economic instability, deteriorating international relations and international terrorism.[51]

Dangers and threats to Russia's national security are listed[52] and include several provisions that reveal Russia's arguably inflated view on conflict potential in the Arctic and Atlantic regions. Russia feels threatened by foreign states' domination at sea, and their efforts to achieve superior naval forces, with particular mention of the USA and its allies. Potential sources of contention are territorial claims of foreign states with respect to Russian coastal territories and adjacent waters. Also troubling Russia is other states' efforts to limit its access to the oceans' resources and to vital maritime transport routes. Another concern is the pressure exerted on Russia to lower the effectiveness of its maritime activities in the oceans and weaken its control over the Northern Sea Route. Faced with such a treacherous environment, Russia must provide military-maritime presence, permanent or periodic, in strategically important regions across the world's oceans.

Against this potentially adversarial backdrop, the *Foundations* upholds that Russia's Navy is a fundamental foreign policy instrument.[53] The Navy should ensure the national interests of Russia and its allies at sea by military means, maintain military and political stability globally and regionally and repel aggression against Russia in the maritime domain.[54] The Navy should also uphold appropriate conditions for Russia's maritime activities, ensure military-maritime presence, fly the flag and

[49] *Foundations*, 2017. Articles 4 and 5.
[50] Ibid. Article 20.
[51] Ibid. Article 23.
[52] Ibid. Article 24.
[53] Ibid. Article 28.
[54] Ibid. Article 12.

demonstrate Russia's military strength at sea, participate in the fight against piracy, participate in international peacekeeping and humanitarian actions, protect Russia's state borders (underwater), including anti-subversive and anti-sabotage defence.[55]

The FSB is responsible for implementing Russia's border policy, defending and protecting the border and Russia's economic and other interests in the border area, in the EEZ, and on the continental shelf, as well as implementing state control on protection of marine biological resources.[56] The FSB implements international treaties on national security in the border area and coordinates activities of executive bodies pertaining to protection of internal waters, the territorial sea, the EEZ, the continental shelf and their natural resources.[57]

Russia's fundamental tasks to achieve its state policy for maritime activities are divided into eight categories: defence and national security; state and societal security; economy; foreign policy; science, technology and education; ecological security and natural resources; strategic stability; and social security and recruitment to the Navy and to the FSB.[58] True to established form, the FSB and the Navy are invoked throughout the listed tasks. For example, under state and societal security, we find ensuring border security, including improving interagency cooperation and interstate border cooperation, and the Navy's participation in emergency preparedness. Under economy, we find the use of the Navy and the FSB to ensure the security of Russia's economic activities in the world's oceans and the development of dual-use infrastructure in the Arctic to ensure bases for civilian vessels as well as those of the Navy and the FSB. The first order of business under science, technology and education is to develop the military-industrial complex to support the Navy's and the FSB's combat potential. This contrasts with the Coastguard's prior demilitarising reforms and opens for closer ties between the Coastguard and the Navy.

As we note above, the Navy is the shipbuilding industry's main customer and it played a leading role in drafting the new *Maritime Doctrine*. The *Foundations* also pays additional attention to the Navy

[55] Ibid. Article 13.
[56] Ibid. Article 14.
[57] Ibid. Article 15.
[58] Ibid. Article 29.

with two sections devoted entirely to the Navy: Section IV considers the Navy as an effective instrument for strategic deterrence, and section V considers strategic demands on the Navy. The document does, however, represent a notable departure from the *Maritime Doctrine*'s Navy domination. The initial pages of the *Foundations* treat the two actors as equals. Throughout the document, both the Navy and the FSB are treated in much more detail. Cooperation between the Navy and the Coastguard is emphasised in both the *Maritime Doctrine* and in the *Foundations*,[59] with the former making specific reference to providing ships and other assets as needed.

The Navy and the Coastguard carry out tasks and exercises in the Arctic both separately and in collaboration. An example of a joint exercise took place in early August 2018 when a detachment of Northern Fleet vessels set out from Severomorsk, along the Northern Sea Route, with course for the Novosibirsk Islands.[60] The detachment was led by a helicopter-carrying destroyer, the *Vice Admiral Kulakov*, and included a couple of large landing crafts, the *Alexander Obrakovsky* and the *Kondopoga*; a sea trawler, the *Vladimir Gumanenko*; an icebreaker, the *Ilya Muromets*; a tanker, the *Sergey Osipov*; a rescue tug, the *Pamir*; and a crane ship, the KIL-143. Along the way, the detachment carried out various tasks and exercises, including ice monitoring in the Kara Sea and rescue drills along the Northern Sea Route. During the first leg of the journey, in the Barents Sea, the detachment practised "safeguarding economic activities and resolving crisis situations" in a joint exercise with the FSB's coastguard administration for the Western Arctic.[61]

The Coastguard heavily emphasises the protection of marine resources and the prevention of illegal fishing. In July 2018, the FSB detained six offending vessels; two of them were fishing illegally in the Barents Sea.[62] Fisheries inspections, tracking and apprehending poachers is part of

---

[59] *Maritime Doctrine*, 2015. Article 48. *Foundations*, 2017. Article 17.

[60] Detachment of Northern Fleet Ships and Vessels Entered the Kara Sea [Otryad korabley i sudov obespecheniya Severnogo flota zashel v Karskoye more], *TV21*, August 13, 2018, http://www.tv21.ru/news/2018/08/13/otryad-korabley-i-sudov-obespecheniya-severnogo-flota-zashel-v-karskoe-more.

[61] Ibid.

[62] Border Guards Detained Six Poacher-Vessels [Pogranichniki zaderzhali shest' brakon'yerskikh sudov], *FSB*, July 31, 2018, https://www.osfsb.ru/materialy/news/pogranichniki-zaderzhali-shest-brakonerskikh-sudov/.

everyday operations for the Coastguard in the Russian Arctic. Another aspect of the Coastguard's activities in the region is to prepare against more exotic threats, such as terrorism. The FSB plays a central role in Russia's system for countering terrorism, and the Coastguard is central to maritime counterterrorism. Arctic energy facilities and infrastructure are seen as potential targets that must be protected from terrorists and other threats, according to the Russian authorities. As a result, recent years have seen regular counterterrorism exercises in the Russian Arctic. One such exercise took place in June 2017 and exercised the following scenario: terrorists have infiltrated the crew of an oil tanker en route from Arkhangelsk to Murmansk. As the tanker enters Kola Bay, the terrorists take control of the vessel and make "unreasonable political demands". In a joint effort involving Coastguard vessels and vessels of the Northern Fleet as well as FSB aviation, the situation is diffused. The tanker is intercepted and blocked in, then boarded by special forces repelling from a helicopter while combat divers approach from the water.[63]

Counterterrorism may seem a surprising choice for the Arctic; however, the threat posed by domestic and international terrorism is very much present in the minds of Russian authorities—even in the remote Russian Arctic.[64] Terrorism is a diverse threat and countering it allows for joint exercises practising different scenarios that involve the whole security-safety spectrum in Russia's comprehensive approach to the Arctic. Indeed, many counterterrorist scenarios include other emergency fields. A similar joint counterterrorism exercise to the one described above took place in June 2015 with participation from the Northern Fleet and FSB as well as the Ministry of the Interior and the Ministry for Emergencies and included search and rescue, oil spill response, firefighting, detonating explosive devices under water, and releasing hostages in its scenario.[65]

---

[63] Border Guards Neutralized 'Terrorists' Who Seized the Tanker in the Barents Sea [V Barentsevom more pogranichniki obezvredili uslovnykh terroristov, zakhvativshikh tanker], *TV21*, June 07, 2017, http://www.tv21.ru/news/2017/06/07/v-barencevom-more-pogranichniki-obezvredili-uslovnyh-terroristov-zahvativshih-tanker.

[64] See Ingvill Moe Elgsaas, "Counterterrorism in the Russian Arctic: Legal Framework and Central Actors," *Arctic and North*, no 29 (2017), 110–132.

[65] Counter-Terrorism Exercise [Ucheniye po antiterroru], *Federal Fisheries Agency*, July 27, 2015, http://fish.gov.ru/otraslevaya-deyatelnost/bezopasnost-moreplavaniya/avarijno-spasatelnye-otryady/novosti-avarijno-spasatelnykh-otryadov/5821-uchenie-po-antiterroru.

Comprehensive safety-security is central to Russia's Arctic policy. The Navy, represented by the Northern Fleet, and the FSB, with its Arctic Coastguard administrations, are responsible for the security end of the spectrum. Both organisations are also central contributors to ensure safety in the region as well.[66] The regular counterterrorism exercises in the Russian Arctic allow the Navy and the Coastguard to hone their cooperation practising a variety of scenarios in a challenging climate. All the while, the Navy rebuilds and demonstrates Russia's military power in the region and the Coastguard protects the resource base and economic activities that will support Russia on its intended course to become a leading maritime power.

CONCLUSION

In this chapter, we have discussed the development of the Russian Navy and Coastguard and the relationship between them across the post-Soviet period. Our starting point was the Soviet experience. Militarism was a central feature in the Soviet polity and antagonism between the Soviet Union and the West during the Cold War also underscored the central role and prestige of the Soviet Navy. The Soviet border troops and its maritime units were specialised and highly militarised. Their tasks were to prevent border violations at sea and, if needed, to support the Navy. The Russian Navy was hard hit by the turmoil and economic hardship that followed the demise of the Soviet Union. While it is the principal heir to the Soviet Navy, compared to its predecessor, the Russian Navy lost bases, industry and personnel. Empty coffers and a new geopolitical climate resulted in the Navy being "demilitarised" through decay—procurement stalled while assets decayed. In the 2000s, much-needed funding has been put towards remedying some of the Navy's decay. Military reform and rearmament programmes are most accurately described as a normalisation rather than militarisation. The current state of the Russian Navy's surface fleet still suggests that the use of coastguard assets may be a viable option in a case of emergency.

The Coastguard also suffered due to financial restraints in the 1990s yet was subsequently subjected to deliberate demilitarisation. Since 2003, the Coastguard has been part of the FSB. The FSB Border Guard

[66] See Ingvill Moe Elgsaas, "The Arctic in Russia's Emergency Preparedness System," *Arctic Review on Law and Politics* 9 (2019), 287–311.

Service's Coastguard is a very different organisation than its Soviet predecessor. Unlike the specialised and militarised maritime units in the Soviet border troops, the current Coastguard has a broad portfolio and many of its core activities are in resource management and law enforcement. The Coastguard also participates in activities of other agencies, notably search and rescue, as well as activities of other FSB departments, such as counterterrorism.

The broadening portfolio of the Coastguard reflects the growth and diversification of activities in the Arctic. Among the most recent reorganisations in the security and defence sector are the creation of an Arctic military district centring on the Navy's Northern Fleet and two FSB Border Guard Service administrations for the Western and Eastern Arctic. These unifying organisations cut across several administrative-territorial borders and underscore Russia's comprehensive approach to safety and security in the Arctic. Safety and security cooperation is laid down in Russia's strategic documents for the maritime domain and with particular focus on the Navy and the Coastguard.

The latest *Foundations* document lists the Navy and the FSB as jointly responsible for Russia's military-maritime activities. While the Navy retains a clear principal role, the explicit inclusion of the FSB in military activities in the maritime domain underscores the hard security component in the Coastguard's broad and diverse portfolio. This opens for a return to the Soviet precedent with the Coastguard functioning as a "Navy reserve". This is also in line with the broad threat perception of the current Russian regime. Meeting the many and varied security challenges, as perceived by the Kremlin, in the maritime domain and in the Arctic in particular requires a comprehensive toolbox. That being said, law enforcement and other civilian tasks remain the Coastguard's main functions and its new status as an important military-maritime actor is secondary. It is also unlikely that the latter will supplant the Coastguard's civilian portfolio in the near future.

PART IV

North and South America

CHAPTER 11

The United States

Jonathan G. Odom

This chapter seeks to inform the reader about the nature of the relationship between the US Navy (USN) and the US Coast Guard (USCG), and the ways in which they work together to protect the maritime security interests of the United States. First, this chapter will describe the different mindsets of the USN and USCG. Second, this chapter will examine how these two maritime security agencies work together in a cooperative manner, leveraging the unique legal-policy authorities and resource-capacities that each possesses. Third, this chapter will explain the command structures and mechanisms that the USN and USCG utilize in order to coordinate decision-making and promote unity of effort. Fourth, this chapter will highlight several interagency challenges that the USN and the USCG overcame for such cooperation and coordination. Ultimately, this chapter concludes that the USN and USCG have developed a number of lawful and practical ways to not only overcome their different mindsets, authorities, and capacities, but also leverage those unique characteristics by working together effectively and efficiently to achieve US national security objectives in the maritime context.

J. G. Odom (✉)
George C. Marshall European Center for Security Studies,
Garmisch-Partenkirchen, Germany
e-mail: jonathan.odom@usa.mil

The Different Mindsets of the USN and USCG

Before examining the actions and decision-making of these two US maritime security agencies, it is important to recognize and understand the different mindsets of these two organizations. Their respective mindsets and the established parameters of behavior are predominant drivers on the ways in which US maritime forces conduct operations, activities, and actions to protect the maritime security interests of the United States. These mindsets are formalized through contemporary US laws, administrative regulations, policy directives, and organizational doctrines. On a more fundamental level, however, they are a reflection of the history of the nation and legacies of these two organizations within that national history. Much like the proverbial chicken and egg, it is difficult to know precisely where the national history and organizational legacies shaped those regulatory authorities and where those authorities have driven that history and legacy. Nonetheless, understanding these different mindsets helps to provide a context for the restraints applied to their actions and decision-making and better appreciate the innovative ways of how the two agencies cooperate with one another when appropriate.

The history of the United States as a nation has included a series of negative experiences of occupation by military units and personnel. When the States were English colonies in the mid- to late-eighteenth century, the American colonists experienced mistreatment by British soldiers who were deployed to maintain order in Great Britain's overseas colonies.[1] These experiences led directly to one of the bases for the American colonies' Declaration of Independence,[2] as well a provision in the Bill of Rights of its new Constitution.[3] Even after the United States gained its independence as a nation and established its own Army and Navy, American citizens continued to have negative experiences from

---

[1] For a general discussion of the British army's mistreatment of American colonists, see John M. Blum et al., *The National Experience: A History of the United States to 1877* (San Diego: Harcourt Brace Jovanovich, 1989), 93–94.

[2] Declaration of Independence (1776), https://www.archives.gov/founding-docs/declaration-transcript (citing, inter alia, abuses of the colonies to include the King "kept among us, in times of peace, Standing Armies without the Consent of our legislatures"; "affected to render the Military independent of and superior to the Civil Power"; "quartering large bodies of armed troops among us").

[3] US Const. amend. III, https://www.archives.gov/founding-docs/bill-of-rights-transcript#toc-the-u-s-bill-of-rights.

the forceful presence of military forces, including in the maritime context. During the years leading up to the War of 1812, the British Royal Navy stopped merchant ships in the waters along the coast of the United States, inspected the crews, and "pressed" crewmembers of unproven origins to serve involuntarily aboard British warships.[4] Thereafter, these negative experiences of military occupation and enforcement continued into a third formative era of US history involving the US Civil War and the subsequent Reconstruction period. After the controversial election of the Republican Rutherford B. Hayes in 1876 to become the nation's president, there were allegations[5] of improper use of federal troops at the polling stations. In June 1878, the US Congress enacted and President Hayes signed into law the Posse Comitatus Act prohibiting the Army from "executing" US laws,[6] a statute that remains in effect.[7] In the modern era of US history, these restrictions on US military personnel enforcing laws have been affirmed and strengthened by additional laws. In 1981, the US Congress prohibited all Department of Defense (DoD) military forces, including the Navy, from "direct participation" in law enforcement activities.[8] The net result of these US federal statutes and implementing policies[9] is that they memorialize the historical mindset of and codify restrictions upon DoD personnel and units, including the Navy, when operating within the United States.

Contrast this restrictive mindset of the USN with the mindset of the USCG. The USCG has what could be described as a blended or hybrid mindset on its identity and its responsibilities as a government agency.

[4] John P. Deeben, "The War of 1812: Stoking the Fires," *Prologue* 22, no. 2 (Summer 2012), https://www.archives.gov/publications/prologue/2012/summer/1812-impressment.html.

[5] See, e.g., Mark L. Bradley, *The Army and Reconstruction 1865–1877* (Washington, DC: US Army Center of Military History, 2015), 71, https://history.army.mil/html/books/075/75-18/cmhPub_75-18.pdf.

[6] An act making appropriations for the support of the Army for the fiscal year ending June thirtieth, eighteen hundred and seventy-nine, and for other purposes, Pub. L. No. 45-263, 20 Stat. 145 (June 18, 1878), § 15, https://www.loc.gov/law/help/statutes-at-large/45th-congress/session-2/c45s2ch263.pd.

[7] 18 U.S.C. § 1385.

[8] 10 U.S.C. § 375.

[9] See US Department of Defense Instruction 3025.21, *Defense Support of Civilian Law Enforcement Agencies* (February 27, 2013), https://www.esd.whs.mil/Portals/54/Documents/DD/issuances/dodi/302521p.pdf.

The opening provision of Title 14 of the US Code declares that the USCG "shall be a military service *and* a branch of the armed forces of the United States *at all times*."[10] Then, the next provision of Title 14 directs that the USCG "shall enforce or assist in the *enforcement of all applicable Federal laws* on, under, and over the high seas and waters subject to the jurisdiction of the United States."[11] While some observers might assume this would lead to the equivalent of a split personality disorder for a government agency, the functional duality of the USCG has been an organizational way of life for over a century. While the default mindset of the other four armed services of the United States allows for limited exceptions in specific circumstances to enforce US laws, the fifth armed service of the USCG is a literal and perpetual exception.[12] Additionally, the USCG has long been empowered to seek assistance from and provide assistance to other government agencies, including agencies within the federal government, state and local governments, and foreign governments.[13]

The Nexus via Cooperative Actions Between the USN and the USCG

Many of the maritime threats facing the United States are not compartmented neatly into categories requiring purely a military response or a law enforcement response. Nevertheless, they are serious threats that the US government must effectively counter. Given the different mindsets and codified authorities for the USN and the USCG, how do these two maritime security agencies operate together to protect the maritime security interests of the United States? As the heads of the USN and USCG have acknowledged, "Merging our individual capabilities and capacity produces a combined naval effect that is greater than the

---

[10] 14 U.S.C. § 1 (emphasis added); see also 10 U.S.C. § 101(a)(4). ("The term 'armed forces' means the Army, Navy, Air Force, Marine Corps, and Coast Guard.")

[11] 14 U.S.C. § 2 (emphasis added).

[12] See U.S. Department of Defense Joint Publication 1, *Doctrine for the Armed Forces of the United States* (March 25, 2013), II-7, http://www.jcs.mil/Portals/36/Documents/Doctrine/pubs/jp1_ch1.pdf?ver=2017-12-23-160207-587. ("[The U.S. Coast Guard] is the only military Service not constrained by the Posse Comitatus Act or its extension by [Department of Defense] directive.")

[13] 14 U.S.C. §§ 141–154.

sum of its parts."[14] This meets the classic definition of synergy.[15] What exactly does that mean? Perhaps the best way to explore USN-USCG cooperation in practice is to examine two real-world examples.

As the first example, consider the efforts to counter the maritime trafficking of illegal drugs into the southern coast of the United States. In terms of geography, the United States has one of the longest coastlines of any nation in the world, a significant portion of which is located along its southern shores.[16] Having such a large coastline presents a vulnerability to the security of the United States from a number of threats, including but not limited to the importation of foreign-produced illegal drugs for distribution and use within the sovereign territory of the United States. Looking southward from the continental United States, a significant percentage of the world's illegal drug supply is grown or produced in the nations located in the subregion of Latin America.[17] A significant amount of those illegal drugs is trafficked by sea via the Gulf of Mexico and the Caribbean Sea.[18] Not surprisingly, the southern coastline and territorial seas of the United States are a common entry point. Given the nature of these smuggling methods and the maritime entry points, it is understandable that US maritime security forces would play a vital role in countering this particular security threat. Consequently, three decades ago, the US government escalated the effort to counter the trafficking of illegal drugs as a national policy priority, to include increasing the role of the US military in such efforts.[19]

[14] Commandant of the US Marine Corps, Chief of Naval Operations, Commandant of the US Coast Guard, *A Cooperative Strategy for 21st Century Seapower* (March 2015), 2, http://www.navy.mil/local/maritime/150227-CS21R-Final.pdf.

[15] See *Cambridge Dictionary*, s.v. "synergy," accessed February 1, 2018, https://dictionary.cambridge.org/us/dictionary/english/synergy (defining synergy as "the combined power of a group of things when they are working together that is greater than the total power achieved by each working separately").

[16] The World Factbook, US Central Intelligence Agency, https://www.cia.gov/library/publications/the-world-factbook/fields/2060.html.

[17] Clare Ribando Seelke et al., "Latin America and the Caribbean: Illicit Drug Trafficking and U.S. Counterdrug Programs," *Congressional Research Service* (May 12, 2011), 1, https://fas.org/sgp/crs/row/R41215.pdf.

[18] US Department of Justice, National Drug Intelligence Center, *National Drug Threat Assessment* (February 2010), 21, https://www.justice.gov/archive/ndic/pubs38/38661/38661p.pdf.

[19] President Ronald W. Reagan, National Security Decision Directive 221, *Narcotics and National Security* (April 8, 1986), 1, https://fas.org/irp/offdocs/nsdd/nsdd-221.pdf.

The authority of the USCG to detect and interdict the trafficking of illegal drugs, including maritime smuggling, is derived from a combination of national laws and international law. For the USCG's authority to detect and interdict at sea, US law is long-standing in existence, explicit and clear in wording, and broad in scope. As discussed previously, Title 14 of the US Code authorizes the USCG to "enforce or assist in the enforcement of all applicable Federal laws on, under, and over the high seas and waters subject to the jurisdiction of the United States."[20] Additionally, the USCG is authorized to "engage in maritime air surveillance or interdiction to enforce or assist in the enforcement of the laws of the United States."[21] Logically, "all applicable Federal laws" and "the laws of the United States" would include US counter-drug statutes.[22] As a matter of international law, the USCG has entered a number of agreements on behalf of the United States with other nations, which are focused on cooperative efforts to counter maritime trafficking of illegal drugs.[23]

Relative to the USCG's authorities under national law and international law to counter maritime drug trafficking, the authority of DoD forces is newer and more limited. In the mid-1980s, Congress amended Title 10 of the US Code, to include several significant authorities for DoD military forces and USCG cooperation with those DoD forces. Specifically, the DoD was designated as the lead federal agency for "the detection and monitoring of aerial and maritime transit of illegal drugs into the United States."[24] Additionally, DoD military forces were authorized to provide logistical and operational support to counter-drug operations, including the use of military equipment and facilities.[25] Also, of note, the USCG was mandated to provide personnel for law enforcement purposes "on board every appropriate surface naval vessel at sea in a drug-interdiction area."[26] These USCG personnel were required to be

[20] 14 U.S.C. § 2(1).
[21] 14 U.S.C. § 2(2).
[22] See, e.g., 21 U.S.C. § 841(a).
[23] See US Department of State, Bureau of International Narcotics and Law Enforcement Affairs, *International Narcotics Control Strategy Report* (2016), https://www.state.gov/j/inl/rls/nrcrpt/2016/vol1/253221.htm.
[24] 10 U.S.C. § 124.
[25] 10 U.S.C. § 272 and § 274.
[26] 10 U.S.C. § 279(a).

"trained in law enforcement" and have law enforcement powers including "the power to make arrests and to carry out searches and seizures."[27] These USCG personnel assigned aboard USN ships were mandated to perform "law enforcement functions (including drug-interdiction functions)."

Given these complementary authorities, what is the operational feasibility for these two maritime security agencies to detect and interdict maritime drug smuggling? Not only is the southern coastline of the United States lengthy, but the two adjacent bodies of water are geographically large and therefore difficult to monitor and police. The USCG has the legal authority and capability to conduct maritime interdiction operations in these bodies of water, but it does not have the full capacity to do so. The USN has the capability and additional capacity to conduct such operations, but it is limited in its legal authority to do so. In light of these respective limitations and enablers, these two US maritime security agencies recognized a necessity to bridge their differing authorities and capacities in order to counter this maritime security threat lawfully, effectively, and efficiently.

Following US policy guidance and leveraging US legal authorities, these two US maritime security agencies have developed a joint operating concept to detect and interdict the trafficking of illegal drugs, including maritime smuggling via the Gulf of Mexico and the Caribbean Sea. These standard operating procedures[28] can be summarized as follows: USCG Law Enforcement Detachments (LEDETs) are embarked aboard USN warships patrolling the open waters along the southern coastline of the continental United States. From the outset of their voyages, these warships are executing the authorized DoD mission of detection and monitoring. If a boat suspected of trafficking illegal drugs is detected, one of these warships "switches from detection and monitoring to supporting law enforcement" and closes with the suspicious boat. As appropriate, the accompanying USCG LEDET will conduct law enforcement actions against the boat, including a potential at-sea boarding, and thereafter "determines the disposition of suspected traffickers

---

[27] 10 U.S.C. § 279(b).

[28] Evan Munsing and Christopher J. Lamb, *Joint Interagency Task Force-South: The Best Known, Least Understood Interagency Success* (Washington, DC: National Defense University, 2011), 40, http://ndupress.ndu.edu/Portals/68/Documents/stratperspective/inss/Strategic-Perspectives-5.pdf.

and seized evidence." After the LEDET has secured the suspected traffickers and any seized evidence onboard the USN warship, the ship "resumes" its detecting and monitoring mission. This standard practice fuses the legal authorities and resource-capacities of both maritime security agencies to achieve a US maritime security policy objective.

As a second example of synergized action, consider the US efforts to counter illegal, unreported, and unregulated (IUU) fishing in the South Pacific. In addition to the United States having a long coastline to protect, it also has a large exclusive economic zone (EEZ) to police. A significant portion of the US EEZ is derived from those portions of the EEZ surrounding the US islands located in the Pacific.[29] Of note, several of these portions of the US EEZ located in the South Pacific share a maritime boundary with the EEZs of Pacific island nations. Within the South Pacific Ocean and among the South Pacific island nations, one of the greatest security challenges arises from IUU fishing. The consequences of IUU fishing to individual nations, including the South Pacific island nations, and the greater international community can be quite significant.[30] These include environmental, economic, security, and governance consequences. The challenge to counter the problem of IUU fishing faces both the flag States of the fishing vessels and the coastal States who have jurisdiction over the waters in which the fishing occurs. But the unfortunate reality of "flags of non-compliance" means that the burden for countering IUU fishing tends to fall disproportionately upon coastal States. Therefore, coastal States must work together to gain efficiencies, build capabilities, and augment capacity. This is particularly true for small island nations, including many of the Pacific island nations, who are both blessed with large EEZs but overwhelmed to police them effectively.

The USCG has the legal authority to address the challenge of IUU fishing and other maritime security threats in the South Pacific cooperatively under both US law[31] and international law. As a matter of US

---

[29] "Exclusive Economic Zone," *Sea Around Us*, last accessed February 1, 2018, http://www.seaaroundus.org/data/#/eez.

[30] See, e.g., Agreement on Port State Measures to Prevent and Eliminate Illegal, Unreported, and Unregulated Fishing, preamble; see also ASEAN Guidelines for Preventing Fish and Fishery Products from IUU Fishing Activities Into the Supply Chain (2015), para. 5.

[31] 14 U.S.C. § 149(b).

law, one of the primary legal authorities for fisheries enforcement is the Magnuson–Stevens Fisheries Conservation and Management Act, which authorizes the USCG to enforce its provisions.[32] As a matter of international law, the USCG has entered a series of bilateral shiprider agreements on behalf of the United States with neighboring Pacific island nations.[33] Traditionally, maritime security operations executed under these shiprider agreements have been conducted by the vessels, aircraft, and maritime law enforcement personnel of the USCG. But, as a practical matter, these operations typically occur when USCG ships are "already patrolling nearby U.S. waters and high seas."[34] The reason for this selective level of maritime security cooperation in the South Pacific is clear, especially when one considers the simple mathematical facts: The USCG command responsible for operating in this part of the world is District 14, which has an area of responsibility spanning more than 12.2 million square miles of land and sea, but is equipped with only three 225-foot buoy tenders, four 110-foot patrol boats, and two 87-foot patrol boats.[35]

Compared to the USCG, the USN is resource-rich in the Pacific. The Pacific Fleet of the USN has a large number of surface ships that do have the appropriate specifications to support at-sea boarding operations.[36]

[32] An Act to provide for the conservation and management of the fisheries, and for other purposes, Pub. L. No. 94-265, 90 Stat. 331 (April 13, 1976), https://www.gpo.gov/fdsys/pkg/STATUTE-90/pdf/STATUTE-90-Pg331.pdf.

[33] As a matter of international law, the US government has negotiated and concluded a number of bilateral "shiprider agreements" to conduct cooperative maritime law enforcement. "U.S. Coast Guard Fisheries Enforcement Shiprider Operations," US Agency for International Development, last accessed February 1, 2018, https://rmportal.net/biodiversityconservation-gateway/legality-sustainability/fisheries-development/project-search/add-a-project-activity/u.s.-coast-guard-fisheries-enforcement-shiprider-operations.

[34] James Hurdell, "The Value of Ship Rider Agreements in the Pacific," *cogitASIA* (December 10, 2014), last accessed February 1, 2018, https://www.cogitasia.com/the-value-of-ship-rider-agreements-in-the-pacific/.

[35] "Welcome to the Fourteenth Coast Guard District Honolulu, Hawaii," US Coast Guard District Fourteen, last accessed February 1, 2018, http://www.pacificarea.uscg.mil/Our-Organization/District-14/.

[36] "U.S. Pacific Fleet, Ship Count," Commander, Naval Surface Force, last accessed February 1, 2018, http://www.public.navy.mil/surfor/Pages/USNavyPacificFleetShipsbyClass.aspx#.WnX5A_mnGUk.

These Navy assets and personnel are operational resources that could help to protect US maritime interests in countering IUU fishing in the Pacific. Relative to the USCG's national and international legal authorities to counter IUU fishing in the Pacific, the authority of DoD operational forces to participate in such fisheries enforcement is extremely limited.

In the early 2010s, US Pacific Command, US Pacific Fleet, and USCG Pacific Area collaborated to develop a concept of operations to assist Pacific island nations in their efforts to counter IUU fishing within their respective EEZs. The name for the proposed effort was to be the "Oceania Maritime Security Initiative" (OMSI). Since 2012, these two US maritime security agencies have conducted OMSI operations on a regular basis. The concept of operations for OMSI can be summarized as follows: Foreign maritime law enforcement personnel and USCG personnel embark together on USN ships operating in EEZs of the Pacific island nations. The combined operations detect and monitor maritime activities within the EEZs for potential IUU fishing. If a particular fishing boat is suspected of engaging in IUU fishing, the USN closes with the boat. Then, the USCG and foreign law enforcement team board and inspect the boat, and take any appropriate actions under the laws and regulations of the partner nation. Similar to the countering of maritime trafficking of illegal drugs, this standard practice countering IUU fishing fuses the legal authorities and resource-capacities of both maritime security agencies to achieve a US maritime security policy objective.

The Nexus via C2 and Coordinated Decision-Making between USN and USCG

In addition to understanding the different mindsets of the USN and the USCG and examining how these two maritime security agencies execute cooperative actions to protect US maritime security interests, it is also worth exploring how the executive decisions and directions among these two agencies are commanded, controlled, and coordinated. This includes command and control (C2) in times of war and routine maritime security operations, as well as situations when both agencies are taking separate actions but for a common US policy objective.

Usually, these two US maritime security agencies do not operate under the same parent organization within the US government. Under normal, peacetime conditions, the USN is organized within the DoD[37] and the USCG is organized within the Department of Homeland Security (DHS).[38] Yet US law specifies that the USCG "shall operate as a service in the Navy" if either Congress declares war and "so directs" a transfer in the war declaration, or "when the President directs" a transfer.[39] During World Wars I[40] and II,[41] the entire USCG was transferred to the USN, and USCG forces played an active role in each of them. Following World War II, however, the practice shifted to transferring only select USCG units to the DoD, instead of the entire USCG. For example, when the United States led a coalition of nations for combat operations in the 1991 Persian Gulf War, neither Congress nor the President transferred the entire USCG to the USN.[42] Instead, at the request of the DoD, the USCG transferred 10 four-person LEDETs to serve with USN forces to conduct maritime interception operations (MIOs) to enforce U.N. Security Council sanctions against Iraq, primarily through at-sea boardings of suspect vessels.[43] A decade later, following the September 11 attacks, the USCG moved from the Department

---

[37] 10 U.S.C. § 111(b).

[38] 14 U.S.C. § 3(a).

[39] 14 U.S.C. § 3(b).

[40] "The U.S. Coast Guard & U.S. Lighthouse Service in World War I," US Coast Guard Historian's Office, last accessed February 1, 2018, http://www.history.uscg.mil/Commemorations/World-War-I/.

[41] President Franklin D. Roosevelt, Executive Order 8929, 6 Fed. Reg. 5581 (November 1, 1941), http://www.presidency.ucsb.edu/ws/index.php?pid=60917.

[42] Connie Terrell, "The Long Blue Line: Coast Guard Operations During the Persian Gulf War," Coast Guard Compass: Official Blog of the U.S. Coast Guard (July 14, 2016), last accessed February 1, 2018, http://coastguard.dodlive.mil/2016/07/the-long-blue-line-coast-guard-operations-during-the-persian-gulf-war/.

[43] US Department of Defense, *Conduct of the Persian Gulf War, Final Report to Congress* (April 1992), 61–81, https://ia801407.us.archive.org/3/items/ConductofthePersianGulfWarFinalReporttoCongress/Conduct%20of%20the%20Persian%20Gulf%20War%20Final%20Report%20to%20Congress.pdf (describing the maritime interception operations to enforce the U.N. Security Council resolution sanctions against Iraq).

of Transportation to the newly formed DHS.[44] Additionally, the Executive Branch of the US government bifurcated the protection of US maritime space into two missions: maritime homeland defense[45] and maritime homeland security,[46] with the DoD being the lead federal agency for the former and the DHS for the latter. To execute these two missions, these departments entered two memoranda of agreement (MOA) for the rapid flow of commands and forces. One of these MOAs facilitated the rapid flow of DoD forces, including USN commands and forces, to the USCG in support of maritime homeland security operations.[47] The other MOA facilitated the rapid flow of USCG forces to the DoD, particularly the USN, for maritime homeland defense operations.[48]

For more routine maritime security operations, consider the C2 structure for the US counter-drug operations off the southern coast of the continental United States. Three decades ago, the White House established several regional Joint Interagency Task Forces (JIATFs) and tasked JIATF-South with the counter-drug mission in the Caribbean.[49]

[44] See Homeland Security Act, Pub. L. No. 107-296, 116 Stat. 2135 (November 25, 2002) §§ 888 and 1704, https://www.gpo.gov/fdsys/pkg/STATUTE-116/pdf/STATUTE-116-Pg2135.pdf.

[45] US Department of Defense Joint Publication 3-27, *Homeland Defense* (July 29, 2013), http://www.jcs.mil/Portals/36/Documents/Doctrine/pubs/jp3_27.pdf. ("The protection of United States sovereignty, territory, domestic population, and critical infrastructure against external threats and aggression or other threats as directed by the President.")

[46] US Department of Defense Joint Publication 3-27, *Homeland Defense* (July 29, 2013), http://www.jcs.mil/Portals/36/Documents/Doctrine/pubs/jp3_27.pdf. ("A concerted national effort to prevent terrorist attacks within the United States; reduce America's vulnerability to terrorism, major disasters, and other emergencies; and minimize the damage and recover from attacks, major disasters, and other emergencies that occur.")

[47] Memorandum of Agreement Between the Department of Defense and Department of Homeland Security for Department of Defense Support to the US Coast Guard for Maritime Homeland Security, *cited in* US Department of Defense Joint Publication 3-27, *Homeland Defense* (July 29, 2013), D-11, http://www.jcs.mil/Portals/36/Documents/Doctrine/pubs/jp3_27.pdf.

[48] Memorandum of Agreement Between Department of Defense and Department of Homeland Security for the Inclusion of the US Coast Guard in support of Maritime Homeland Defense, *cited in* US Department of Defense Joint Publication 3-27, *Homeland Defense* (July 29, 2013), D-11, http://www.jcs.mil/Portals/36/Documents/Doctrine/pubs/jp3_27.pdf.

[49] Even Munsing and Christopher J. Lamb, *Joint Interagency Task Force-South: The Best Known, Least Understood Interagency Success*, 18–19.

Under this arrangement, the partnering US agencies retain operational control (OPCON)[50] of their units, but JIATF-South was given tactical control (TACON)[51] over those units.[52] This OPCON-TACON arrangement enables JIATF-South with a "potent package of legal authorities."[53] A study of JIATF-South arrangement described the intertwined relationship between C2 and legal authorities as follows:

> What one component does not have authority to do, another has. For example, DOD cannot make arrests or conduct criminal investigations, but other partners can. Along with its tactical control of other agencies' assets during operations, these diverse authorities mean that JIATF-South does not 'have to ask 'mother may I' when chasing smugglers.' When law enforcement officials are about to interdict or arrest traffickers, tactical control is shifted to the appropriate U.S. Coast Guard law enforcement authority [Coast Guard District Seven in Miami, Florida]. If the Coast Guard law enforcement officers are on board the U.S. or partner nation naval vessel, the vessel will actually take down its own flag and fly the U.S. Coast Guard flag, at which point the senior law enforcement officer exercises the Coast Guard's law enforcement authority until the case is concluded.[54]

Additionally, the JIATF-South staff is manned with liaison officers from the various partner agencies, including the USN and the USCG, who are "empowered by their parent organizations to make decisions that commit their agencies to action."[55] Time can be of the essence, especially when the perpetrators of this threat are driving vessels known as "go-fast boats."

---

[50] US Department of Defense, *Dictionary of Military and Associated Terms* (August 2017), 226, http://www.jcs.mil/Portals/36/Documents/Doctrine/pubs/dictionary.pdf. ("The authority over forces that is limited to the detailed direction and control of movements or maneuvers within the operational area necessary to accomplish missions or tasks assigned.")

[51] US Department of Defense, *Dictionary of Military and Associated Terms* (August 2017), 173, http://www.jcs.mil/Portals/36/Documents/Doctrine/pubs/dictionary.pdf. ("The authority to perform those functions of command over subordinate forces involving organizing and employing commands and forces, assigning tasks, designating objectives, and giving authoritative direction necessary to accomplish the mission.")

[52] Evan Munsing and Christopher J. Lamb, *Joint Interagency Task Force-South: The Best Known, Least Understood Interagency Success*, 37.

[53] Ibid., 39.

[54] Ibid.

[55] Ibid.

Thus, a cooperative C2 structure with authorities delegated to the local level help these two US maritime security agencies counter this type of maritime threat effectively on a routine basis.

In addition, the Executive Branch of the US government has also developed mechanisms and protocols for coordinating decision-making by the USN and the USCG in maritime security missions. To "enhance the security of and protect U.S. interests in the Maritime Domain," then-President George W. Bush issued National Security Presidential Directive (NSPD) 41 in December 2004.[56] One of the policy objectives identified by NSPD 41 was "[e]nsuring seamless, coordinated implementation of authorities and responsibilities relating to the security of the Maritime Domain by and among Federal departments and agencies." To coordinate such actions effectively, the Executive Branch also developed the Maritime Operational Threat Response (MOTR) Plan, which was finalized in 2006.[57] The MOTR Plan has been described as follows:

> The Maritime Operational Threat Response (MOTR) is the presidentially approved Plan to achieve a coordinated U.S. Government response to threats against the United States and its interests in the maritime domain. The MOTR Plan contains operational coordination requirements to ensure quick and decisive action to counter maritime threats.[58]

What is important to understand is that the MOTR protocols and procedures are a coordination mechanism to promote unity of effort,[59] not unity of command.[60] In other words, US maritime security agencies

---

[56] President George W. Bush, National Security Presidential Directive 41, *Maritime Security Policy* (December 21, 2004), https://fas.org/irp/offdocs/nspd/nspd41.pdf.

[57] "Global MOTR Coordination Center," US Department of Homeland Security, last accessed February 1, 2018, https://www.dhs.gov/global-motr-coordination-center-gmcc.

[58] Ibid.

[59] US Department of Defense, *Dictionary of Military and Associated Terms* (August 2017), 242, http://www.jcs.mil/Portals/36/Documents/Doctrine/pubs/dictionary.pdf. ("Coordination and cooperation toward common objectives, even if the participants are not necessarily part of the same command or organization, which is the product of successful unified action.")

[60] US Department of Defense, *Dictionary of Military and Associated Terms* (August 2017), 242, http://www.jcs.mil/Portals/36/Documents/Doctrine/pubs/dictionary.pdf. ("The operation of all forces under a single responsible commander who has the requisite authority to direct and employ those forces in pursuit of a common purpose.")

such as the USN and the USCG are not given greater authorities via the MOTR process, nor are they given any "veto" authority over the decisions or actions of one another.[61] Instead, each US government agency operates under its existing legal and policy authorities, and merely informs one another of their internal decisions and actions, so that the Executive Branch of the US government can collectively respond to maritime threats that might arise.

As a practical example of this MOTR coordination, consider how the Executive Branch enforces US immigration laws in the maritime domain. Every year, thousands of people attempt to migrate illegally into the United States by sea. The first line of security in the US government's efforts to prevent illegal immigration by sea is the USCG, which is authorized to enforce "all applicable Federal laws on, under, and over the high seas and waters subject to the jurisdiction of the United States."[62] The sheer numbers of interdicted migrants can sometimes overwhelm the capacity of the USCG to transfer individuals to the appropriate immigration offices ashore for processing.[63] Consequently, the Secretary of Homeland Security is authorized by executive order to "maintain custody, at any location he deems appropriate, of any undocumented aliens he has reason to believe are seeking to enter the United States and who are interdicted or intercepted in the Caribbean region."[64] To effectuate this custody, the Executive Branch is further authorized to "operate a facility, or facilities, to house and provide for the needs of any such aliens" and specified one of these facilities to be located aboard Guantanamo Bay Naval Base.[65] Under these circumstances,

---

[61] Brian Wilson, "The Complex Nature of Today's Maritime Security Issues: Why Whole-of-Government Frameworks Matter," in *Handbook on Naval Strategy and Security*, ed. Joachim Krause and Sebastian Burns (Oxon: Routledge, 2016), 157. ("As a horizontal coordinating mechanism, those involved in MOTR have no authority to direct or compel another agency to take (or not take) action, regardless of who is designated lead. The Department of Justice could not direct the Navy to use a specific ship to rescue a pirated vessel, and conversely, the Navy couldn't direct the Department of Justice to prosecute.") Of note, Mr. Wilson is the Deputy Director of the Global MOTR Coordination Center.

[62] 14 U.S.C. § 2.

[63] See, e.g., White House, *National Strategy for Maritime Security* (September 01, 2015), 6, https://www.state.gov/t/pm/rls/othr/misc/255321.htm.

[64] President George W. Bush, Executive Order 13,276, 67 Fed. Reg. 69985 (November 15, 2002), § 1.

[65] Ibid.

one US maritime security agency (i.e., USCG) has the authority and responsibility to interdict migrants at sea, while another maritime security agency (i.e., USN) has the authority and responsibility for housing a migrant operations center aboard one of its secure installations. Thus, when migrants are interdicted, the transfer of those personnel from sea to shore in a safe, humane, and expeditious manner necessitates coordination between the US government agencies involved. To ensure such coordination occurs, a MOTR telephone conference call is convened among the interested US government agencies. Each of the agencies represented in the conference call retains its legal and policy authorities. If there is no policy difference between the participating agencies over the "desired national outcome"[66] and the appropriate course of action for this particular situation, then the agencies' representatives discuss practical arrangements for the date, time, location, and method of transferring the migrants from the interdicting agency to the holding agency.[67] These MOTR calls and the MOTR process more generally help to ensure that all of the interested government agencies contribute to the unity of effort within the Executive Branch of the US government. For these situations involving the USN and the USCG, the coordination mechanism of MOTR process helps to synchronize the decision-making among each of the agencies to respond effectively to a maritime threat or situation.

OVERCOMING INTERAGENCY CHALLENGES

In their current form, these concepts of cooperative action between the USN and the USCG are effective and efficient in protecting US maritime security interests. But it would be erroneous for an observer to assume that these structures and approaches were successful either immediately or in their initial form. In reality, each of these concepts of cooperative action had to overcome its own set of interagency challenges and be refined. Some of those challenges and refinements are worth highlighting.

---

[66] Brian Wilson, "The Complex Nature of Today's Maritime Security Issues: Why Whole-of-Government Frameworks Matter," 157.

[67] If the government agencies have a policy difference over the desired national outcome or appropriate course of action for a particular maritime threat or situation, then the MOTR discussions would terminate and the issue would be elevated to policy decision-makers within the appropriate interagency policy process established by the White House. Ibid., 157.

Consider some of the interagency challenges to counter the maritime trafficking of illegal drugs in the Caribbean. Following Presidential policy direction and Congressional legislative amendments in the mid-1980s to fight the US "war on drugs" more effectively, the US military established several regional joint task forces (JTFs) focused on that specific mission. The DoD established these JTFs, but the JTF responsible for the Caribbean was first commanded by a retired USCG admiral recalled to active duty, interestingly because "no Service was willing to give up a flag officer to take charge of an untested idea."[68] Additionally, that same JTF "had no dedicated assets for the counterdrug mission; nor could it secure assets in advance."[69] In terms of C2, the JTF commander had command authority only over assigned military personnel.[70] While these JTFs led to some successes in the "war on drugs," these challenges experienced and lessons learned resulted in a new C2 structure in the early 1990s. On April 7, 1994, President Bill Clinton issued the first National Interdiction Command and Control Plan (NICCP), which included transitioning these JTFs into JIATFs and tasking JIATF-South with the counter-drug mission in the Caribbean.[71] Regarding C2, these JIATFs were to "remain inside the military chain of command," but they were "national task forces," which empowered them to "control assets from any department or agency."[72] At the operational level of command, USN fleet commanders and the USCG area commanders for the Atlantic and Pacific areas entered MOAs to govern USCG LEDET procedures for these maritime counter-drug operations, thereby enabling C2 to shift rapidly between the USN and the USCG chains of command and leverage their associated legal authority.[73]

[68] Evan Munsing and Christopher J. Lamb, *Joint Interagency Task Force-South: The Best Known, Least Understood Interagency Success*, 12.

[69] Ibid., 13.

[70] Ibid., 15.

[71] Ibid., 18–19.

[72] Ibid., 19.

[73] US Department of Defense, Joint Publication 3-07.4, Joint Counterdrug Operations (June 13, 2007), Appendix G, https://fas.org/irp/doddir/dod/jp3-07-4.pdf. On August 14, 2013, this version of the joint publication has been superseded by a publication with the same title, but that version is not publicly available. See U.S. Department of Defense, Joint Electronic Library, http://www.jcs.mil/Doctrine/Joint-Doctrine-Pubs/3-0-Operations-Series/.

Consider also some of the interagency challenges for the cooperative effort between the USN and the USCG to counter IUU fishing in Oceania. When OMSI was proposed initially, the DoD faced a challenge of how to fund these operations, given that Congress generally does not appropriate funds in the US budget for the USN to conduct law enforcement missions. Yet several rarely used provisions of US law do authorize the USN to support the USCG in fisheries enforcement, including enforcement operations in the South Pacific. Of note, one section of the Magnuson–Stevens Fisheries Conservation and Management Act authorizes agencies of the US government, including the DoD, to support the USCG's efforts.[74] Similar provisions of US law have also been enacted to authorize the DoD and other federal agencies to support the USCG's enforcement of obligations under fisheries treaties, including the Western and Central Pacific Fisheries Convention[75] and the South Pacific Tuna Treaty.[76] These laws empower the USN to use its appropriated funds to support fisheries enforcement, but only if a formal arrangement ("by agreement") is entered between the DoD and the DHS. In April of 2012, the DoD and the DHS entered a memorandum of understanding (MOU) for that specific purpose.[77] By invoking these obscure provisions of the US fisheries laws authorizing elements of the DoD to support the USCG, the OMSI concept of operations became more viable. Developing and negotiating that interagency MOU took time, which delayed the USN and the USCG from initiating OMSI operations. Ultimately, the finalized MOU enabled the two agencies to lawfully cooperate in this mission and fully leverage their respective authorities.

For the USN and the USCG to overcome these interagency challenges, they had to refine their concepts of cooperative action. These refinements were in the form of amendments to national laws, new presidential policy directives, new implementing interagency agreements, and new command

---

[74] 16 U.S.C. § 1861(a).

[75] See Western and Central Pacific Fisheries Convention Implementation Act, 16 U.S.C. § 6905(a)(2)(A).

[76] See South Pacific Tuna Act, 16 U.S.C. § 973 h(a).

[77] Memorandum of Understanding Among the United States Coast Guard, the National Oceanic and Atmospheric Administration, and the Department of Defense Concerning the Use of Department of Defense Resources in Support of Fisheries Law Enforcement Efforts in the United States Pacific Command and Coast Guard District Fourteen Areas of Operational Responsibility (April 30, 2012).

structures. Once these refinements were completed, the operational forces from these two US maritime security agencies were able to cooperate and coordinate their efforts more effectively and efficiently.

Conclusion

Those who perpetrate security threats at sea and from the sea do not ignore the gaps and seams in authorities, capabilities, and political will that might exist within and among the governments of coastal nations. If anything, these perpetrators are keenly aware of such gaps and seams, and intentionally exploit them to their advantage. Bureaucratic concepts such as "stove piping"[78] and "rice bowls"[79] are vulnerabilities within governments that present opportunities for bad actors to achieve their political and pecuniary goals. In the maritime context, the question is how the governments of individual nations can reduce gaps and seams, bridge stove piping, and share rice bowls. Success requires concerted direction from the political levels of a nation's government, both through legislation and policy directives. But success also requires the individual maritime security agencies within each government to innovate ways that counter maritime security threats in a cooperative and collective manner, through a fusion of those agencies' authorities, capabilities, and capacities.

The United States has nearly two and a half centuries of historical experience in addressing maritime threats, including ones posed by state actors as well as others by non-state actors. By no means is the US maritime security architecture perfect, nor are the individual maritime

---

[78] See, e.g., National Commission on Terrorist Attacks Upon the United States, *9-11 Commission Report* (July 22, 2004), 403, https://www.9-11commission.gov/report/911Report.pdf (discussing the "stovepipe" phenomenon among intelligence and operational agencies with the executive branch of the US government that created a vulnerability for the September 11th attacks).

[79] See, e.g., Linda E. Brooks Rix, "Low and Slow: The Process of Reforming Government," *Huffington Post*, November 23, 2011, https://www.huffingtonpost.com/linda-e-brooks-rix/low-and-slow-the-process-_b_974571.html (describing a "rice bowl" issue as one in which a government agency's parochial interests take greater priority than the overall good of the agency or the government).

agencies within that architecture perfect. What matters is whether a nation's maritime agencies can work together to respond to maritime threats effectively. The experiences of the USN and the USCG have demonstrated innovative, legal, and practical ways for the maritime security forces of a nation to answer that emergency call.

CHAPTER 12

Ready to Secure: A Sea Control Perspective on Canadian Fisheries Enforcement

Timothy Choi

Canadian naval history has often been told as one of struggle for control of the Atlantic sea lanes. From its formative years in the First World War through the end of the Cold War, the Royal Canadian Navy (RCN) has dedicated itself to the challenging task of anti-submarine warfare.[1] Accordingly, discussions of sea control in the Canadian context have tended to emphasize the wartime RCN. Yet, sea control, this chapter argues, has a much longer and broader peacetime history in Canada than purely naval histories would suggest. This can be seen in the shared and shifting responsibilities for Canada's fisheries enforcement between the country's various maritime agencies.

To understand the shifting responsibilities of the RCN and Canadian Coast Guard (CCG) and their predecessors, this chapter examines their histories through the lens of a broadened definition of sea control. From

---

[1] W. A. B. Douglas, "The Prospects for Naval History," *The Northern Mariner* 1, no. 4 (October 1991): 23.

T. Choi (✉)
Centre for Military, Security and Strategic Studies,
University of Calgary, Calgary, AB, Canada
e-mail: thtchoi@ucalgary.ca

© The Author(s) 2019
I. Bowers and S. L. C. Koh (eds.), *Grey and White Hulls*,
https://doi.org/10.1007/978-981-13-9242-9_12

its origins in Mahan's seminal work as "command of the seas", the general concept of sea control has been used almost exclusively to describe and analyse naval actions in times of war.[2] This chapter begins by asserting that sea control should be conceptualized as a spectrum with differing levels of intensity during both its contestation and exercise phases, with clear applicability in peacetime.

In the rest of the chapter, this broadened concept of sea control will be used to analyse the shifting responsibilities of Canada's various maritime services. Cases are selected from three periods in Canadian naval history: the years before and during RCN's formation in 1910, the time period surrounding the end of the Cold War, and the near future. Reflecting dramatically different levels of institutionalization and capabilities, this selection allows the reader to see how differences in sea control responsibilities and manifestations vary as a state's maritime services mature.

Adapting Sea Control for Peacetime Sea Power

Sea control traditionally has been broadly defined as the ability to use the seas and deny an opponent the same.[3] Not all sea powers (actors who possess some sea power—the ability to influence behaviour at and/or from the sea) are able to or interested in making use of the sea per se, and some are content with possessing sea power only in permissive and uncontested contexts: sea control is not synonymous with sea power. For those that do pursue sea control, Ian Speller argues that in its positive form, it is the ability for both to use the sea and to deny others its use, while the pure pursuit of sea denial is primarily a negative form.[4]

In further conceptualizing the phenomenon of sea control, two distinct dimensions should be attributed to the positive form at the operational level—contesting and exercising sea control.[5] Meanwhile, the negative form, sea denial, consists only of the contestation element.

---

[2] Geoffrey Till, *Seapower: A Guide for the 21st Century* (Frank Cass: London, 2003), 149–150.

[3] Ibid., 149.

[4] Ian Speller, "Introduction," in *The Royal Navy and Maritime Power in the Twentieth Century*, ed. Ian Speller (London: Frank Cass, 2005), 5–6.

[5] Colin S. Gray and Roger W. Barnett, *Seapower and Strategy* (Annapolis: Naval Institute Press, 1989), x.

This is not to say that sea denial lacks a purpose beyond the operational level, only that any such higher purpose does not involve actively using the seas that have been contested.

Extant discussions of sea control's attributes imply applicability only for wartime scenarios. Yet, the fundamental activity of denying another user's ability to operate on the seas and, if necessary, take advantage of that ability for further objectives, has substantial peacetime relevancy, especially for maritime constabulary operations. To understand how this is the case, I begin by establishing sea control as a spectrum, with "command of the seas", plural, to describe the ultimate, but idealized, form of sea control at the far positive end: the complete ability to exercise sea control in any sea on the globe by ensuring no enemy can contest that control and thereby interfere with its exercise.

But because sea control consists of both its contestation and exercise, my sea control spectrum takes on two dimensions: an axis for contestation and another for exercise. Both of these terms are variable and can be had in greater or lesser amounts, as measured through the level of resources required. Theoretically, a situation of no contestation and no exercise can exist, which I term "null command". Although maximizing one's ability to contest sea control can maximize that party's ability to exercise it, the two are not always concurrent, as will be shown in the empirical section (Fig. 12.1).

An event's inclusion under the sea control concept requires both the following: (1) contestation, or the ability to challenge (not necessarily with violence) another actor's use of the seas by any means; and (2) exercise, the ability to make use of the seas, which include any of the following: the sea as a source of resources, the sea as a medium of transport, the sea as a basis for projecting influence landwards, and the sea as a source of information.[6] Any attempt to apply the spectrum to more than one of these uses of the seas should be done with great care to avoid qualitatively incomparable resource requirements.[7] Having established a concept of sea control and its criteria, I now turn to explore how sea control has manifested in Canada's maritime services.

[6]These four uses of the seas are adapted from Till, *Seapower*, 6–17.

[7]For example, attempting to use this spectrum for sea control whose exercise takes both the form of using the sea as resource and as a base for projecting landward power may result in trying to compare ten oil rigs with ten amphibious assault ships—likely inappropriate.

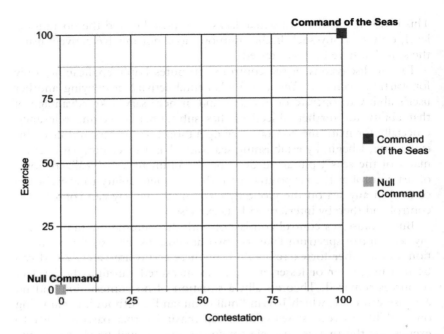

Fig. 12.1 A two-dimensional spectrum for sea control, with the ideal forms "Command of the Seas" and "Null Command" on opposite corners. Any sea control phenomenon can have varying degrees of contestation and exercise, falling somewhere within this spectrum. The numbers are ordinal reference points for resource requirements. The spectrum should only be used with one of the four ways of making use of the seas for a given series of phenomena to avoid qualitatively different resources requirements

Sea Control Responsibilities in Canada

In the decades preceding the CCG's creation, responsibility for the whole range of maritime security issues—such as mariner safety, environmental protection, aids to navigation, and fishery protection—belonged to a number of different agencies. For example, while the running of some harbours had long belonged to local commissions, it was not until 1936 that they eventually fell under the responsibility of the Minister of Transport. When the Department of Transport was established, hydrography duties, which had been carried out by the Department of Naval

Service between 1910 and 1922, were shifted to the Department of Mines and Resources.[8] But of the many agencies, perhaps the one that best reflects the core principles of how, when, and over what Canadian sea control activities would be undertaken was the Department of Marine and Fisheries (DMF), established in 1867 shortly after Canada's confederation.

Beaver and the Eagle: The Early Years

As the RCN's official history notes, "Any discussion of the role that naval power has played in Canadian history" has to acknowledge Canada's alliance with the "two dominant sea powers of the nineteenth and twentieth centuries"—the UK and the United States—and the protection this alliance provided for Canadian maritime interests.[9] With this security guarantee against major foreign predations, Canada had little initial need for its own ability to control what happens on the high seas during wartime. Yet, control was nonetheless required, albeit closer to home and against challengers less threatening than the German or, later, Soviet battle fleets.

Demonstrating the influence of the Royal Navy's global presence on Canadian maritime security arrangements, the DMF initially only took on responsibilities relating to safety issues on and around Canadian waters, from lighthouses to sailors' welfare.[10] Meanwhile, the Department of Militia and Defence (DMD) shied away from anything to do with naval defence, refusing to spend limited Canadian resources on sustaining permanent naval forces or militias despite their demonstrated worth during the Fenian raids just prior confederation. Even as London reduced funding for Canadian defence post-confederation, the Canadian government continued to see little value in maintaining a maritime force under the auspices of the DMD.[11]

---

[8] Thomas E. Appleton, *Usque ad Mare: A History of the Canadian Coast Guard and Marine Services* (Ottawa: Department of Transport, 1968), 95, 273.

[9] William Johnston et al., *The Seabound Coast: The Official History of the Royal Canadian Navy, 1867–1939*, volume 1 (Toronto: Dundurn Press, 2010), xiii.

[10] Appleton, *Usque ad Mare*, 31.

[11] Johnston et al., *The Seabound Coast*, 4–6.

This dependency on the assumption that the Royal Navy (RN) would come to Canada's aid in any future conflict could be justified if Canadian maritime concerns were limited to only high-intensity interstate wars where threats to Canadian maritime communications also affected the empire and Britain. At the day-to-day level of peacetime maritime security issues, however, such an assumption proved to be a miscalculation. More interested in keeping "harmonious relations" with the United States than the economic welfare of Canadian fisherfolk, the 1860s London did little to support the latter when Americans began fishing from Canada's inshore fisheries.

In response, Peter Mitchell, Minister of Marine and Fisheries, established the "Marine Police", commissioning six armed schooners to patrol the fishery zones. After arresting twelve American vessels in 1870, the Marine Police demonstrated its ability to contest sea control in peacetime so that Canadian fishermen could exercise that control for the ultimate goal of food security. It is noteworthy that this contestation did not necessarily require the use of force, but only the threat thereof, and the contest put up by American fishermen was limited to refusal to adhere to Canadian legal fishing rights.

A year later, the United States was brought to the negotiating table and the resultant 1871 Treaty of Washington not only ensured peaceful relations between Great Britain and the United States, but also enshrined mutual fishing rights between Canadians and Americans in the Gulf of St. Lawrence and the maritime provinces.[12] This accomplished, the Marine Police was subsequently disbanded. Greater concerns such as financial pressures and European geopolitical developments were likely the prime drivers behind why the US and Great Britain agreed to the Treaty. However, the role of the Marine Police in forcing both sides to include a fisheries agreement in the Treaty cannot be ignored.[13] To borrow James Cable's gunboat diplomacy framework, this appeared to be purposive force, where Canada's use of armed force at sea was able to convince the United States to alter its behaviour for political objectives.[14]

---

[12] Johnston et al., *The Seabound Coast*, 6; United States and Great Britain, Articles 18–21, *The Treaty of Washington* (May 8, 1871): 23–24, https://archive.org/details/cihm_27720.

[13] Joseph Gough, *Managing Canada's Fisheries: From Early Days to the Year 2000* (Sillery, Quebec: Septentrion, 2006), 88–90.

[14] James Cable, *Gunboat Diplomacy: Political Applications of Limited Naval Force* (New York: Praeger, 1971), 21.

However, just 1 fifteen years later, the United States abrogated the fisheries agreement in that 1871 Treaty, causing Canada to re-establish a fishery protection force as a "formal Fisheries Protection Service" (FPS) comprised of eight newly built armed vessels.[15] These soon proved their worth, with over 1300 boardings in 1887; 1894 saw the newly commissioned Canadian Government Ship (CGS) *Petrel*, a "screw ram-bowed gunboat", arrests some fifty American sports fishermen who had been fishing without licences on Lake Erie.[16] Demonstrating the multifaceted tasks faced by the FPS and foreshadowing future maritime security roles, *Petrel* also employed arms to ensure environmental security when it fired a shot across the bow of an American garbage tug on its way to dumping Detroit garbage in Canadian waters. But *Petrel*'s ability to successfully contest sea control against such targets offering minimal resistance and thereby enable Canada's exercise of its maritime rights would not last forever: by 1905, civilian vessels had become nimble enough to outrun the heavier and older patrol ship, and the American poacher *Silver Spray* managed to escape *Petrel* despite rifle shots.[17]

In these formative years of confederation, the Canadian approach to sea control in peacetime can therefore be categorized generally as extremely limited contestation against unarmed threats (fishermen and garbage scows) with the limited exercise of that control for domestic civilian use. The only element of contestation would be in non-violent forms, such as outrunning patrol ships when possible. The main areas of operations were the Great Lakes, the Gulf of St. Lawrence, and the territorial seas around the maritime provinces.

Lacking a formal naval service, the Canadian government did not expect to *independently* pursue sea control in wartime.[18] But the lack of independent Canadian naval forces in this period was a conscious

---

[15] Johnston et al., *The Seabound Coast*, 10, 19; Gough, *Managing Canada's Fisheries*, 98.

[16] Johnston et al., *The Seabound Coast*, 21; Gough, *Managing Canada's Fisheries*, 98.

[17] Gough, *Managing Canada's Fisheries*, 101.

[18] This is a situation that comes close to the "null command" form of sea control, at least as far was Ottawa-directed control was concerned. This is not to say that Canada, as a country overall, had no roles in wartime sea control: concerned about enemy cruisers in the Pacific, the British Admiralty had 4.7-inch guns stockpiled in Hong Kong and Vancouver for use on the Canadian Pacific Railway's *Empress* ocean liners, which were duly converted into armed merchant cruisers under Royal Navy command in August 1914. Johnston et al., *The Seabound Coast*, 26–27; Robert D. Turner, *The Pacific Empresses: An Illustrated History of Canadian Pacific Railway's Empress Liners on the Pacific Ocean* (Winlaw, BC: Sono Nis Press, 2004), 85–87.

decision of Prime Minister Macdonald, who recognized the existing relationship with Britain meant any warship capable of contributing to imperial war efforts abroad could be called away by the Admiralty, leaving Canadian coasts defenceless. Instead, by keeping its patrol forces under the DMF, the ships fell squarely under Canadian domestic control.[19] Additionally, the Rush–Bagot Agreement that forestalled a peacetime naval arms race on the Great Lakes after the War of 1812 prohibited the development of heavily armed warships. This further reduces the attractiveness of developing means for contesting sea control beyond fishery patrol vessels operated under civilian command[20]—even if the strict technical limits of the Agreement kept being pushed by both sides resulting in *faits accomplis* and then renegotiated terms.[21]

Within such legally and strategically constrained conditions, how did the RCN come to be in 1910? In the decade following the United States' defeat of the Spanish fleet at Manila Bay, the Royal Navy grew increasingly aware of its inability, in the words of Admiral Lord Walter Kerr, "to be a superior force everywhere".[22] Meanwhile, Canada's militia performed admirably in the South African (Boer) War, demonstrating to both Canadians and the British that dominions can field effective fighting forces.[23] This provided the strategic room for Canada to develop its maritime force from one that could contest and exercise sea control against and for peacetime civilian objectives to one that could operate against armed vessels beyond coastal waters.

To start, growing recognition by successive Ministers of Marine and Fisheries, as well as Militia and Defence, of the Royal Navy's declining willingness to intercede on behalf of Canadian local interests saw the gradual accumulation of additional shipboard weaponry meant for Fishery Protection Service vessels. To ensure the aforementioned Rush–Bagot Agreement was not violated, these weapons were stored in warehouses on shore, such as Quebec City by 1899. Fisheries protection sailors were then sent for artillery training with the militia during the winter off-seasons.

---

[19] Johnston et al., *The Seabound Coast*, 34.

[20] Christopher Mark Radojewski, "The Rush-Bagot Agreement: Canada-US Relations in Transition," *American Review of Canadian Studies* 43, no. 3 (2017): 281.

[21] Johnston et al., *The Seabound Coast*, 53.

[22] Johnston et al., *The Seabound Coast*, 65.

[23] Johnston et al., *The Seabound Coast*, 69.

These initial attempts at increasing Canada's ability to contest sea control were hardly formal—federal opposition leader Henri Bourassa's efforts to learn more about rumours regarding the government's "organization of a naval school, training vessels, and of a naval reserve" resulted in no documentary response.[24] Through the first decade of the new century, the FPS fleet further modernized to keep pace with the increased capabilities of their main "adversary": American fishing tugs on the Great Lakes that were now able to steam faster than some of the 1890s-era FPS patrol ships like the *Petrel*. Addressing this, two new high-speed "warlike" ships were procured: the *Canada* from the famous Vickers yard in England and the *Vigilant* from Polson Iron Works in Toronto, the "first 'modern' warship" built in Canada. At 200 and 175 feet long, respectively, these relatively large fast "cruisers" were suitable for not just contesting control of coastal fisheries, but also for deploying on training expeditions to the Caribbean in the winter months.[25]

While such efforts to increase Canada's potential ability to contest sea control along the American border were taking place, efforts to *exercise* sea control without having to yet contest it also took place in the Arctic. Prime Minister Laurier was particularly concerned that ongoing territorial disputes regarding the British Columbia–Alaska boundary would set a precedent of "possession by right of settlement" and that this would not be to Canada's favour in the sparsely administered Arctic. To pre-empt attempts by the Americans to assert ownership of Arctic islands by virtue of greater use by their fishermen, Laurier sent the DMF on an Arctic expedition. Unlike previous expeditions focusing on scientific or exploratory objectives, this one was commanded by the North-West Mounted Police (NWMP). In the winter of 1903–1904, NWMP constables on the *Neptune* established a series of permanent stations along the eastern Arctic so as to exercise Canadian sovereignty over customs, justice, and law enforcement.[26] In so doing, Canada exercised sea control to pre-empt the potential need to contest it vis-à-vis the Americans in a prospective territorial jurisdiction dispute.

---

[24] Johnston et al., *The Seabound Coast*, 78–79.
[25] Johnston et al., *The Seabound Coast*, 84, 94; Appleton, *Usque ad Mare*, 80.
[26] Johnston et al., *The Seabound Coast*; Gough, *Managing Canada's Fisheries*, 104.

But while Canada performed admirably in its creative use of the DMF to contest and exercise sea control in local waters, there remained the issue of why a formal navy would be established. Appropriately, this, too, would be the result of a sea control question, albeit on a much larger and expensive scale. Admiral Jacky Fisher, in his quest to rationalize and reform the Royal Navy towards his vision of sea control, recognized it could no longer support so many far-flung naval stations, especially around the relatively peaceful North American shores. Canadian concerns over American fishermen or boundary disputes notwithstanding, the RN sought to divest responsibility for its naval bases at Esquimalt and Halifax and instead put those sailors to work on new warships that were straining the RN's manpower. By May 1906, therefore, both bases were transferred to Ottawa's control with Canadian troops raised to man them.[27]

Thus was formed the "nucleus" of the future RCN: the naval bases on the Pacific and the Atlantic combined with the expanded fleet of fishery protection cruisers and their crews created the physical elements of sea power suitable for not only fisheries protection but also naval diplomacy and tactical naval training.[28] In 1909, Laurier's government finally managed to approve the establishment of a naval militia under the DMF, an effort that had been attempted by multiple personalities for over a decade prior.[29] The year after, the *Naval Service Act* passed, establishing the RCN as a distinct service.[30]

But the role played by the DMF in safeguarding Canada's maritime interests and contesting sea control in peacetime would not end with the RCN's creation. Unlike the expectations of those who argued for the naval militia, the creation of the RCN did not mean the straightforward conversion of the DMF's Fisheries Protection Service into that military force.[31] Instead, the RCN began with two new, but used, ships: the protected cruiser HMCS *Rainbow* for the West Coast, and the armoured

---

[27] Johnston et al., *The Seabound Coast*, 95.

[28] The term "nucleus" was used by Minister of Marine and Fisheries Préfontaine, cited in Johnston et al., *The Seabound Coast*, 101.

[29] Gough, *Managing Canada's Fisheries*, 103; Johnston et al., *The Seabound Coast*, 83.

[30] The term "Royal Canadian Navy" would not actually be employed until royal authorization on August 29, 1911. See Marc Milner, *Canada's Navy: The First Century* (Toronto: University of Toronto Press, 1999), 23.

[31] Johnston et al., *The Seabound Coast*, 85.

cruiser HMCS *Niobe* on the east. Nevertheless, the RCN would occasionally carry out domestic law enforcement duties that would usually be done by the DMF. The most infamous example took place only a few short years after the RCN's formation, when in May 1914, the West Coast cruiser HMCS *Rainbow* escorted the steamship *Komagata Maru* from Vancouver after her 400 Indian passengers were rejected for immigration.[32]

During the First World War, the limitations of a nascent small navy on even the peripheries of a high-intensity conflict were demonstrated. As Germany commenced unrestricted submarine warfare in January 1917, the RCN began to do more to protect Canadian shores from German submarines. Despite a significant construction programme involving 148 steel trawlers and wooden drifters between 84 and 130 feet in length, the urgency required that much of the RCN's sea control activities in the war be carried out by a combination of purchased private yachts and existing vessels from other departments, such as the DMF. CGS *Canada*, for example, was utilized as an "auxiliary patrol ship" and, along with seven other transferred vessels so designated, "formed the backbone of the Canadian patrols until the end of the war".[33] The auxiliary patrol ships operated along the St. Lawrence as convoys made their way from Quebec to the Atlantic, providing a continued presence deterring German submarines.[34] In times of war, then, fundamental requirements for contesting sea control required creative allocation of resources between organizations dedicated to fighting foreign military forces as well as organizations assigned for domestic law enforcement duties. In this context, it was perhaps for Canada's benefit that the RCN and the DMF fell under the authority of the same cabinet-level minister at this time.[35]

The war's end resulted in a surplus of coastal patrols ships. Illustrating again the close relationship between the RCN and the DMF, some of the excess RCN anti-submarine trawlers became used for fishery patrol. On the Pacific coast, HMCS *Thiepval* patrolled extensively along the western shore

---

[32] Milner, *Canada's Navy*, 35.

[33] Roger Sarty, "Hard Luck Flotilla: The RCN's Atlantic Coast Patrol, 1914–18," in *The RCN in Transition: 1910–1985*, ed. WAB Douglas (Vancouver: The University of British Columbia Press, 1988), 106–107.

[34] Johnston et al., *The Seabound Coast*, 707–708.

[35] Johnston et al., *The Seabound Coast*, 162.

and northern end of Vancouver Island, where she authorized US fishing vessels to take shelter as needed or to remove them when they lacked appropriate papers.[36] HMCS *Patrician*, one of two destroyers acquired post-war, was also employed on the West Coast for fisheries protection duties, ensuring bilateral arrangements such as the Pelagic Sealing Treaty were being adhered to via tactics similar to those used by DMF vessels.[37]

Peacetime Sea Control: Cold War and Beyond

In those early years of the RCN, the delineation of duties between it and the DMF was quite ambiguous. Organizationally, this dichotomous approach does not quite reflect the nuances involved in the plethora of agencies involved in affairs maritime. Even at the creation of the CCG in 1962, there were thirteen different governmental departments which had waterborne capabilities.[38] It would not be until the mid-1990s that Canada's maritime capabilities could be clearly delineated between the military vessels of the RCN and civilian assets in the CCG. As a result, even though this volume is focused on the "coast guard-navy nexus", this section will rarely reference the CCG per se as it was the Department of Fisheries (and its successors) that was responsible for fisheries protection until 1995.[39]

It is perhaps surprising that fisheries protection is being cited here to exemplify sea control during and after the Cold War. Certainly, the RCN's core duty as guardian of North Atlantic sea lanes of communication versus the Soviet submarine threat was a clear example of the highly contested end of the sea control concept. But as the Cold War never turned "hot", RCN efforts to secure the North Atlantic and enable its use for US and Canadian reinforcements to Europe remained more potential than actual. Such was not the case, however, for that lowly duty of fisheries protection.

---

[36] Johnston et al., *The Seabound Coast*, 778–779.

[37] Johnston et al., *The Seabound Coast*, 843–844.

[38] Charles D. Maginley, *The Canadian Coast Guard, 1962–2002* (St. Catherine's, ON: Vanwell Publishing, 2003), 221.

[39] The fishery protection vessels would also subsequently fall under the Department of Fisheries and Forestry (1969), the Department of Environment (1970), the Department of Fisheries and Environment (1976) and the Department of Fisheries and Oceans (1979). Maginley, *The Canadian Coast Guard*, 219–222.

While the preceding section's focus on the DMF (with occasional RCN assistance) patrols took place primarily within the three-nautical-mile territorial seas that Canada was permitted to have in the early 1900s, the third United Nations Conference on the Law of the Sea and its resulting 1982 Convention (UNCLOS) dramatically increased the area of responsibility out to 200 nautical miles.[40] This had extensive effects on not just the operations and tactics required of Canada's fisheries protection fleet, but also strategies and policies.

On January 1, 1977, Canada declared its 200-nautical-mile exclusive fisheries zone (EFZ).[41] Anticipating the 200-nautical-mile exclusive economic zone (EEZ) then being discussed at the UNCLOS negotiations, Canada helped push for EEZ acceptance despite resistance from other powers. The Soviet Union, for example, had the world's largest distant-fishing fleet and was initially disinclined to support any measure that would so drastically regulate available fisheries. Through bilateral negotiations, however, Canada managed to convince the Soviet Union to accept reduced total allowable catches (TACs) limits off Canadian shores in return for surplus stocks. This acceptance of Canadian jurisdiction out to 200 NM was reciprocated by the other major states which fished in Canadian soon-to-be-waters: Poland, Spain, Portugal, and Norway.[42] Although minor issues at the start of this new regime required sea control actions, such as the arrest of an unlicensed Norwegian longliner by the Coast Guard ship *John Cabot*, on the day the 200 NM zone came into effect, the overall reception and behaviour by foreign fishing fleets was acquiescence.[43] Canadian fishermen, ecstatic about the dramatic expansion of fisheries they no longer had to compete for, were encouraged by optimistic stock yields and biomass projections from the scientists of the Department of Fisheries and Oceans (DFO). For the first decade after the EFZ was put into place, all seemed well.[44]

---

[40] Parzival Copes, "Canadian Fisheries Management Policy: International Dimensions," in *Canadian Oceans Policy: National Strategies and the New Law of the Sea*, ed. Donald McRae and Gordon Munro (Vancouver: University of British Columbia Press, 1989), 6.

[41] Gough, *Managing Canada's Fisheries*, 298.

[42] Ibid., 297–298.

[43] Gough, *Managing Canada's Fisheries*, 298. In anticipation for violators at the initial stages of implementation of the new regime, vessels from the fishery protection fleet were augmented with CCG and RCN assets.

[44] Douglas Day, "Fishing Beyond the Limits: The Canada-European Union Dispute," *IBRU Boundary and Security Bulletin* 3, no. 1 (1995): 52.

However, these fish stock sustainability estimations were in error, and it eventually became apparent that the fishing had to be dramatically curtailed. While this was easily enough done for stocks wholly within Canada's 200 NM EFZ, challenges became apparent when a fishery straddled the outer limits of that zone. Specifically, the problem resided in turbot, a type of halibut dwelling on/close to the seabed. The turbot stock in question lived across the 200 NM line on the parts of Canada's Grand Banks continental shelf that went beyond the 200 NM boundary, called the "Nose and Tail". This meant the health of the fishing stock outside the limit was key to the sustainability of the stock overall.

Recognizing the potential for such an issue, a new international fisheries organization was also established soon after the EFZ to help manage fishing stocks straddling and just beyond Canada's EFZ boundary: the Northwest Atlantic Fisheries Organization (NAFO). A primarily scientific organization, its main role was to identify and set total allowable catches and quotas for relevant fisheries.[45] Member states could, however, object to these quotas and not be bound by them.[46] This fundamental weakness to NAFO would cause what became known as the "Turbot War".

As the fish stock situation deteriorated, Canada passed amendments to its Coastal Fisheries Protection Act in 1994, which granted the power to arrest foreign vessels working in the nose and tail. The primary users of the turbot stock in the nose and tail were trawlers from Spain and Portugal, which were represented on the NAFO committees by the European Union. Objecting to Canadian attempts to impose restrictions on their activities, Spanish trawlers, in particular, continued to well exceed the quotas set by the NAFO.

In Canada, fishermen and industry increasingly pressured the Canadian government to take further actions to ensure the future viability of the turbot stock. As Canadian Fish, Food, and Allied Workers Union President Earle McCurdy eloquently stated: "We in Atlantic

---

[45] Gough, *Managing Canada's Fisheries*, 299.
[46] Day, "Fishing Beyond the Limits," 53–54.

Canada expect to be protected from foreign invasion on the fishing grounds in the same way that people on the Prairies would expect to be protected from foreign invasion of their farmlands".[47]

Thus, on March 9, 1995, the Spanish trawler *Estai* was arrested. Selected due to previous infractions and her continued presence on the Grand Banks well after the quota was estimated to have been exceeded, the *Estai*'s crew's reaction to Canadian officials demonstrated the wisdom of the DFO adopting an "armed boarding" programme for its patrol fleet in 1987.[48] Instead of allowing DFO officers from the fishery patrol vessel *Cape Roger* to board safely, the *Estai*'s crew threw the boarding ladder into the sea, and the officers with them. A second attempt with Royal Canadian Mounted Police officers also met with a similar fate. Meanwhile, nearby Spanish trawlers attempted to dissuade the Canadians from further attempts, setting collision courses with the other patrol ship, the *Leonard J. Crowley*, and the CCG ship *Wilfred Grenfell*. A third attempt to board also met with failure. In the face of such inability to maintain sea control without the use of violent force, the only option remaining was to escalate. The use of warning shots, however, had to be approved by the Deputy Minister of Fisheries and Oceans, Bill Rowat. Approval was relayed to the captain of the *Cape Roger* after discussion with the Minister of Fisheries and Oceans, Brian Tobin, and other high-level members of the government. At 17:55, after three hours of chasing, *Cape Roger* opened fire with her .50 calibre machine guns, expending a total of twenty-three rounds of ammunition into the waters ahead of the *Estai*. This was finally enough to convince the *Estai* to surrender the chase, and she was brought into St. John's Harbour.[49]

---

[47] Donald Barry, Bob Applebaum, and Earl Wiseman, *Fishing for a Solution: Canada's Fisheries Relations with the European Union, 1977–2013* (Calgary: University of Calgary Press, 2014), 58–59.

[48] Gough, *Managing Canada's Fisheries*, 385. This programme armed fishery patrol ships with .50 calibre machine guns and trained their crews to conduct opposed boardings.

[49] Adam Gough, "The Turbot War: The Arrest of the Spanish Vessel Estai and Its Implications for Canada-EU Relations" (Master's thesis, University of Ottawa, 2009), 59–62.

Minister Tobin stayed out of the limelight as the *Estai* came in undertow, wanting the event to be no more than merely halting the act of illegal fishing in and of itself.[50] In the days after *Estai*'s arrest, Canadian government ships were equipped with warp cutters to enable them to continue Tobin's definitive force mission without tripping the rules of engagement of Spanish Navy patrol vessels *Vigia* and sister ship *Serviola*, which had arrived to stop further Canadian boardings.[51]

Amidst claims by Spain that the Canadian government were conducting piracy on the high seas, negotiations dragged on over the next months, and the RCN deployed the destroyers *Gatineau* and *Nipigon* to counter the Spanish patrol vessels should they uncover their weapons; Tobin also publicly revealed that a Canadian submarine was carrying out surveillance duties in the area.[52] This role played by the RCN gave Canada escalation dominance. By escalating the risk of outright naval battle between NATO members, Canada encouraged negotiators to accept the proposals that had been stalled, resolving the issue through such measures as permanent full-time observers on ships and new quotas.[53]

We see here how a sea control operation has dramatic political consequences for ensuring a state's environmental and economic security. The complex multi-layered efforts of the Royal Canadian Mounted Police, the DFO, the CCG, and the RCN enabled Canada to maintain control over its fisheries at both the tactical and operational levels via direct interdiction and deterrence, respectively. Through this integrated law enforcement effort, sea control established the conditions required, as well as providing the physical evidence necessary, to conclude a permanent political solution. The sea control resources required for this

---

[50] Gough, "The Turbot War," 65.

[51] Gough, "The Turbot War," 70; Rhiannon Stromberg, "Unilateralism in Canadian Foreign Policy: An Examination of Three Cases," (Master's thesis, University of Saskatchewan, 2006), 44; "Patrol Boat SERVIOLA (P-71)," *Armada Espanola*, 2017, http://www.armada.mde.es/ArmadaPortal/page/Portal/ArmadaEspannola/buquessuperficie/prefLang-en/08patrulleros--03patrulleros-clase-serviola.

[52] Nicholas Tracy, "Canada's Naval Strategy: The Record and the Prospects," in *Canadian Gunboat Diplomacy: The Canadian Navy and Foreign Policy*, ed. Ann Griffiths, Peter T. Haydon, and Richard Gimblett (Halifax: Dalhousie University, 1998), 236.

[53] Tracy, "Canada's Naval Strategy," 236–237.

effort reflected the greater resistance provided by the opponent, placing it further right on the sea control spectrum than most day-to-day activities.

Return to the North: Maritime Security in the Canadian Arctic

On September 15, 2018, the first of Canada's Arctic and Offshore Patrol Vessels (AOPVs), *Harry DeWolf*, was launched in Halifax, Nova Scotia.[54] The helicopter-carrying 6600-ton ship and its five sisters will provide the RCN with its first armed capability in ice-covered waters since the transfer of HMCS *Labrador* to the CCG in the mid-1950s. Belying their namesake's storied career as a Second World War destroyer captain, the *DeWolf* class are not designed for conventional naval warfare, being armed with only a 25-mm gun and a pair of .50 calibre machine guns.[55] Within the sea control framework described in this chapter, the ships are meant for the low-intensity side of the contestation element against non-state actors, but with a substantial capability to exercise sea control in support of whole-of-government missions as required.[56] Their ability to operate throughout the Arctic shipping season will greatly increase the RCN's role in addressing Canada's Arctic maritime security responsibilities, heretofore led by the CCG. Given the generally cooperative atmosphere between Arctic states within the Arctic realm, this is a reasonable match of means and ends. However, in combination with the CCG's own icebreaker recapitalization problems, the introduction of the six *DeWolfs* may well mean a de facto shift in Arctic maritime responsibilities to the RCN.

---

[54] Royal Canadian Navy, "Future HMCS Harry DeWolf Launches," *Royal Canadian Navy*, September 24, 2018, http://www.navy-marine.forces.gc.ca/en/news-operations/news-view.page?doc=future-hmcs-harry-dewolf-launches/jmc3wpez.

[55] Department of Defence, *AOPS—SRD—DRAFT* (Department of National Defence, September 15, 2010), 187.

[56] The *DeWolf* class has substantial sealift capabilities for a patrol ship, with bays for landing craft, rescue boats, and modular containers to assist in a variety of government missions—from humanitarian assistance to scientific research. Department of Defence, *AOPS—SRD—DRAFT*.

Despite some media coverage of the Arctic as a region of future interstate competition and conflict, many Arctic security and politics scholars tend to hold a more optimistic view regarding the ability of the five Arctic Ocean states to keep "Arctic" issues isolated from other political concerns arising elsewhere.[57] As for issues within the Arctic itself, it is unlikely that a "race" for hydrocarbons and minerals in disputed areas will occur due to the financial and practical difficulties of resource extraction in ice-covered waters. Although climate change is reducing the amount and thickness of sea ice overall, significant ice will remain for much of the year in the as-yet undelimited extended continental shelf beyond the 200 NM EEZ. It would make little economic sense to expend resources on such unlucrative endeavours when the majority of resources lie within already-accepted boundaries.[58] From a sea control perspective, contestation over seabed resources in the Central Arctic Ocean is unlikely to be necessary, given the minimal ways in which control, even if successfully contested, could be exercised.

However, there may be some requirement for minimal sea control capabilities where the resources in the water column are concerned. On October 3, 2018, the five Arctic Ocean states as well as Iceland, Japan, South Korea, China, and the European Union signed a legally binding agreement instituting a moratorium on commercial fishing in the Central Arctic Ocean for the next 16 years while further scientific studies are conducted. The signatories promise to monitor the area and ensure that "nobody undercuts the agreement", in the words of the Canadian negotiator, Nadia Bouffard.[59] However, private actors and countries outside the agreement may still attempt to exploit the

---

[57] Jørgen Staun, "Russia's Strategy in the Arctic: Cooperation, Not Confrontation," *Polar Record* 53, no. 270, 314–315; Andreas Østhagen, "High North, Low Politics—Maritime Cooperation with Russia in the Arctic," *Arctic Review on Law and Politics* 7, no. 1, 83–100; and Elizabeth Riddell-Dixon, "Canada and Arctic Politics: The Continental Shelf Extension," *Ocean Development & International Law* 39, no. 4, 343.

[58] Riddell-Dixon, "Canada and Arctic Politics: The Continental Shelf Extension," 344–345.

[59] Levon Sevunts, "Canada, EU and 8 Other Countries Sign 'Historic' Arctic Fisheries Moratorium Agreement," *Radio Canadian International*, October 3, 2018.

waters if fish stocks migrate north into the warmer waters,[60] and a sea-based ice-capable platform like the *DeWolf* class can help enforce the moratorium.

But although the RCN's *DeWolf* vessels provide Canada with a significant degree of offshore presence to help maintain maritime domain awareness, as well as minor weapons to help coerce potential opponents, they will have to operate in conjunction with other Canadian agencies for any law enforcement duty. Because the RCN does not have arrest authority, their ships will have to embark Fisheries and Oceans Canada inspectors if functioning in the offshore fisheries enforcement role—similar to current arrangements off the Atlantic and Pacific coasts, where such inspectors carry out "Monitoring, Control and Surveillance Activities" from CCG vessels. Where and when such activities occur outside Canada's 200 NM EEZ, the officers operate under the authority of the relevant regional fisheries management organization, such as the NAFO or the North Pacific Anadromous Fish Commission (NPAFC).[61]

The latter is similar to the 2018 Ilulissat Declaration and therefore a likely model—NPAFC hosts *Operation Driftnet*, which sees member and partner states patrol four million square kilometres of the North Pacific for illegal high seas driftnet fishing in accordance with a 1993 United Nations-imposed moratorium.[62] For this role, Canada employs the air force's CP-140 *Aurora* maritime patrol aircraft, illustrating the close relationship between Canadian military and civilian assets when it comes to fishery operations.[63] Although the aircraft do not contest and exercise sea control

---

[60] Susanne Kortsch, Raul Primicerio, Maria Fossheim, Andrey V. Dolgov, and Michaela Aschan, "Climate Change Alters the Structure of Arctic Marine Food Webs Due to Poleward Shifts of Boreal Generalists," *Proceedings of the Royal Society B: Biological Sciences* 282 (2015): 1546; Jørgen S. Christiansen, Catherine W. Mecklenburg, and Oleg V. Karamushko, "Arctic Marine Fishes and Their Fisheries in Light of Global Climate Change," *Global Change Biology* 20 (2014): 352–359.

[61] Fisheries and Oceans Canada, "Canada's High Seas Monitoring, Control and Surveillance Activities," *Fisheries and Oceans Canada*, November 10, 2015, http://www.dfo-mpo.gc.ca/international/mcs-activities-eng.htm.

[62] Fisheries and Oceans Canada, "Operation Driftnet," *Fisheries and Oceans Canada*, April 8, 2015, http://www.dfo-mpo.gc.ca/international/mcs-npafc-eng.htm.

[63] Fisheries and Oceans Canada, "Operation Driftnet's 20th Anniversary," *Fisheries and Oceans Canada*, November 14, 2013, http://www.dfo-mpo.gc.ca/international/media/Driftnet-eng.htm.

directly in such usage, they provide the information necessary for NPAFC member states to arrest violators and prevent further illegal fishing in international waters. In essence, this enables land-based authorities lacking available long-range seagoing assets to deny certain users the ability to use the seas hundreds of kilometres away from land; this illustrates the diverse ways in which Canada can conduct maritime security missions without using agencies traditionally associated with that role, such as the CCG and RCN.

However, the long distances between the main Canadian airbases in the south of the country and the Central Arctic poses a significant logistical challenge for such aerial-centric enforcement of the Arctic moratorium. This favours the use of assets capable of remaining on station for longer periods, such as CCG icebreakers and the *DeWolf* class. While they may not have the same capability to quickly surveil vast areas of the ocean as fixed-wing aircraft, they have the benefit of being able to more directly and immediately affect actor behaviour on the ocean surface. Fishery officers can board and inspect vessels, halting illegal fishing before the violator returns to shore and thereby reduce potential damage to the fish stocks.

The rising number of users in the Arctic will require greater presence by Canadian authorities, but there will be challenges to meeting such demand. While the RCN is developing a fairly robust Arctic capability for the summer navigational months, the agency traditionally responsible for Canadian Arctic maritime security is facing decreased fortunes in its ability to maintain a reliable northern presence: the CCG's icebreaker fleet is nearing the end of its lifespan. Despite the recent decision by the Trudeau government to purchase and convert three second-hand commercial medium icebreakers,[64] plans to recapitalize the heavy icebreakers capable of operations in the Central Arctic throughout most of the year remain in a state of uncertainty. Although one new ship is currently planned and has already been named—*John G. Diefenbaker*—the ship it replaces, CCGS *Louis St. Laurent*, will likely be over a half-century old by the time it is replaced. Meanwhile, plans to replace the remainder of the CCG ice-capable fleet have yet to be elucidated.[65]

---

[64] Public Services and Procurement Canada, "Canada to Acquire Three Interim Icebreakers," *Government of Canada*, June 22, 2018, https://www.canada.ca/en/public-services-procurement/news/2018/06/canada-to-acquire-three-interim-icebreakers.html.

[65] Public Services and Procurement Canada, "Shipbuilding Projects to Equip the Royal Canadian Navy and the Canadian Coast Guard," *Government of Canada*, September 27, 2018, https://www.tpsgc-pwgsc.gc.ca/app-acq/amd-dp/mer-sea/sncn-nss/projets-projects-eng.html.

While the light icebreakers are still fairly young by government vessel standards (the six *Martha Black* class have been in service for around thirty-one years), the medium icebreakers are approximately 30–40 years old.[66] In addition to their lesser icebreaking capabilities that are more suited for the Gulf of St. Lawrence and the eastern coast of Canada than the Arctic, their collective age creates a block obsolescence problem when the time comes for their replacement. This will be exacerbated if the government of Canada wishes to maintain the current schedule of its National Shipbuilding Strategy, which will not be able to deliver the *Diefenbaker* until well into the mid-2020s due to Seaspan Vancouver Shipyard's limited building capacity.[67] The follow-on effects will be such that the remaining legacy icebreakers will likely reach their fiftieth anniversaries before permanent replacements are received—with attendant reliability problems.[68] While the three commercial interim purchases alleviate this issue to an extent, the overlaps between their availability and the existing four medium icebreakers' will be minimal as the interim vessels are partly meant to stand in for the older ships as they enter refit.[69] As a result, it is unlikely that the CCG will be able to increase the number of icebreakers despite the increasingly busy Arctic, and much of the rising demand for monitoring and enforcement capacity will have to be met by the new *DeWolf* class patrol ships. Consequently, Arctic maritime security—and its attendant sea control activities—will fall increasingly under the purview of the RCN rather than the CCG.

[66] Stephen Saunders, *Jane's Fighting Ships 2011–2012* (Coulsdon: IHS Jane's, 2010), 106–107; Canadian Coast Guard, "Appendices—Icebreaker Requirements," *Government of Canada*, February 9, 2018, http://www.ccg-gcc.gc.ca/Icebreaking/Icebreaker-Requirements/Appendices.

[67] The Canadian Press, "Arctic Icebreaker Delayed as Tories Prioritize Supply Ships," *CBC News*, October 11, 2013, https://www.cbc.ca/news/politics/arctic-icebreaker-delayed-as-tories-prioritize-supply-ships-1.1991522.

[68] The 30-year-old CCGS *Terry Fox*, already one of the fleet's youngest, experienced mechanical failure that prevented it from assisting a trapped ferry in early 2018. "Cold Snap Raises Concerns About Coast Guard's Aging Icebreakers in the St. Lawrence," *CBC News*, January 7, 2018, https://www.cbc.ca/news/canada/montreal/quebec-icebreakers-coast-guard-aging-fleet-1.4476465.

[69] Public Services and Procurement Canada, "Canada to Acquire Three Interim Icebreakers."

Conclusion

This chapter aimed to demonstrate how a broadened concept of sea control can be used to analyse how different governmental agencies contribute to a state's peacetime sea power. Particularly, the focus on fisheries control highlights one way sea control can be exercised in peacetime with corresponding contestation elements. By emphasizing the fisheries control origins of Canada's maritime forces, this chapter complements discussions elsewhere in this volume on how larger powers have gradually took on greater interests in such peacetime management issues. At the same time, it illustrates how even as a navy grows in size and capability to take on higher intensity warfare missions, it remains key to securing domestic interests alongside dedicated civilian institutions. Such actions rarely involve the actual use of force, but rather, latent threats of escalatory actions that can suffice to effect desired political change. The nature of this threat comes from having the capability to contest sea control at some level, and even if actual contestation does not occur, the end result can nonetheless be the successful exercise of "untested" sea control.

Recognizing the relationship between sea control and peacetime maritime security requirements will become increasingly crucial in the coming decades. In addition to climate change's effect on increased Arctic access mentioned above, recent maritime violence elsewhere in the world and described in this volume suggest an end to Canada's mostly unchallenged control over the resources on its other two coasts. However, with RCN platforms seeming to take on more peacetime law enforcement roles, Canada appears to be materially prepared to address this potentially more aggressive world where the force required for securing maritime resources may move further right on the sea control spectrum's contestation axis. But materiel is not enough—a country must have the will to use that force. Here, too, Canada has demonstrated through repeated historical instances that it has been willing to employ armed force to ensure its ability to use the sea's resources. From the CGS *Petrel* firing on American garbage tugs to HMCS *Thiepval* inspecting foreign fishing licences and the *Cape Roger* bringing the *Estai* into St. John's Harbour, Canada has proved time and time again that it is ready to secure its use of the seas from the Pacific to the Atlantic. Time will tell whether this resolve extends to the country's third ocean, the Arctic.

CHAPTER 13

The Navy-Coast Guard Nexus in Argentina: Lost in Democratization?

Nicole Jenne and María Lourdes Puente Olivera

Argentina's Navy (ARA, Armada Argentina) and its coast guard, the Naval Prefecture (Prefectura Naval Argentina [PNA]), have their origins in the Spanish colonial administration. Except for a short interlude in the 1950s, the Prefecture depended on the Navy until 1983. With the end of Argentina's military dictatorship (1976–1983), the PNA was transferred to different entities until it was placed under a newly created Ministry of Security. The organizational dissociation was motivated by the desire to strictly separate defence and homeland security, limiting the role of the armed forces to defence matters except under exceptional circumstances. Therefore, by definition, "maritime security" has been placed under the legal orbit of the Prefecture.

N. Jenne (✉)
Institute of Political Science, Pontificia Universidad Católica de Chile,
Santiago, Chile
e-mail: njenne@uc.cl

M. L. Puente Olivera
School of Politics and Government, Pontificia Universidad Católica de
Argentina, Ciudad de Buenos Aires, Argentina
e-mail: lourdes_puente@uca.edu.ar

© The Author(s) 2019
I. Bowers and S. L. C. Koh (eds.), *Grey and White Hulls*,
https://doi.org/10.1007/978-981-13-9242-9_13

However, given the difficulty of clearly separating security and defence, the laws and regulations that govern Argentina's maritime areas leave room for interpretation about the responsibilities of the Prefecture and the Navy in a number of areas. Since Argentina's return to democracy, in all areas of common competence policy-makers have emphasized the concept of security over the concept of defence, thus giving preference to the Prefecture (as a security force) rather than the armed forces. The Argentine public and, although to different degrees, the civilian leadership still distrust the Navy, the institution that thirty-five years ago was engaged in what became known as the "Dirty War" against the population it was supposed to protect. Thus, the tainted reputation of the armed forces left the navy with no political lobby. In addition, there has been a sense of growing public insecurity that has further aided the empowerment of the Prefecture in that it provided a justification for growing expenditures on security. Only recently, in 2018, the administration of Mauricio Macri (2015–) adopted several regulations that broaden the role of the armed forces in internal security. To what extent the new competencies will actually be used and whether they will alter the relation between the Prefecture and the Navy, however, remains to be seen.

In practice, Argentina's maritime security does not present major deficiencies because of any clash over competences. Neither is there a significant duplication of tasks or infrastructure to the extent that it could be considered a serious lack of efficiency. Short of these two extremes, however, competition for responsibilities and resources exists in several areas. Greater synergies could be achieved through cooperation in the areas of common competence where there has been hardly any communication and cooperation. As we shall argue in this chapter, the link between the two services was lost in democratization due to the politicization of resource allocation, which ended up determining the division of labour between the Prefecture and the Navy. Having said so, the question mark in the title indicates that democratization is not the whole story. The relation between the Navy and the Naval Prefecture has long been an uneasy one, which explains why today none of the two services looks favourably at cooperating with each other. Unless the political leadership decides to maximize the country's resources to safeguard Argentina's maritime interests, therefore, the status quo is likely to remain.

The remainder of this chapter is divided into six parts. First, we describe the historical development of the Navy–Prefecture nexus since Argentina's independence in 1810. Next, we explain how the separation of the PNA from the Navy at a critical juncture in Argentina's history, the return to democracy in 1983, determined the assignation of competences to each of the two services. The third part describes the growing relevance of the Prefecture relative to the ARA's role in maritime security. The few, largely unsuccessful attempts undertaken to develop inter-agency cooperation are dealt with in the fourth part. Fifth, we discuss the role of each institution in seven areas of common competence and highlight how the freedom of regulatory design has been interpreted in each of them. The concluding part summarizes the problems of the current status quo, looks at the reforms from 2018 and offers some reflections on possible scenarios for the future.

HISTORICAL DEVELOPMENT

With 4989 kilometres of coastline in the South Atlantic, Argentina is number 26 among the longest coastlines in the world.[1] In addition, it claims territorial rights in the Antarctic and the corresponding maritime zones, including an Exclusive Economic Zone (EEZ) of 200 nm. Due to an immense plain of sediment off the Argentine coast, the extension of economically profitable waters reaches well beyond its EEZ and continental shelf, which extends to 350 nm beyond the territorial sea, the maximum possible envisaged under the United National Convention on the Law of the Sea (UNCLOS) provisions.

During the Spanish empire, the port of today's capital of Buenos Aires had a special status in the colonial administration. From its very creation in 1756 on, the Port Captaincy (*Capitanía de Puertos*) fulfilled the functions of its successor organization, the Naval Prefecture. According to the General Regulations dictated by Spain's King Carlos IV (Article 7, 1793), its responsibilities included the following tasks: pilot authorization and certification; inspection of safety conditions on board; summary procedures for offences in navigation, crimes and contraventions;

---

[1] World by Map, Coastline length. Online at http://world.bymap.org/Coastlines.html.

the dispatching of ships; control of navigators and passengers; ensuring compliance with the prohibition of discharging garbage and debris into waters; and oversight over the Board of Health.[2] The Port Captaincy survived the collapse of the Spanish empire until it was renamed the Naval Prefecture in 1896. In a major modernization process driven by the so-called Generation of '80, Argentina's elites looked to Europe as a successful example of development. While the model for the Army was Germany and for the Navy Spain and later Britain, it was France's *Préfet Maritime* that gave the Prefecture its name. A new law (Ley 3.445) codified the Prefecture's role as a police force with competence over the seas, rivers, waterways and ports under national jurisdiction, thus maintaining the same tasks previously carried out by the Port Captaincy.[3]

The Prefecture, like the merchant navy, was an integral part of Argentina's emerging geostrategic thinking towards developing the country's maritime interest.[4] Therefore, the head of the Prefecture was a Navy officer. This changed briefly only under President Juan Domingo Perón who, following a rebellion by the armed forces in 1951, sought to increase control over the security forces by placing both the Prefecture (then under the Ministry of Maritime Affairs) and the Gendarmerie (then under the Ministry of the Army) under the responsibility of the Ministry of Interior. This period, when the Prefecture was led by a Prefect for the first time in its history, was of short duration. In 1955, Perón was ousted by a military coup and the Prefecture came under the Navy again.

The growing, global interest in maritime resources was reflected in increasing legal activity in Argentina. Among others, Law 3.445 was replaced, in 1969, by Law 18.398, which remains the basic regulatory framework for the Prefecture today. Shortly after, a new Law on Navigation (Ley 20.094) was passed integrating the previously

---

[2] Prefectura Naval Argentina, Notas sobre una tradición funcional [Notes on a Functional Tradition]. https://www.prefecturanaval.gob.ar/cs/Satellite?d=&c=Page&pagename=Institucional_Publico%2FPage%2FPaginaInterna%2FVista1&cid=1436818007188.

[3] All laws and executive decrees referred to in this chapter can be found online at http://servicios.infoleg.gob.ar/infolegInternet/, accessed January 22, 2019.

[4] The most influential promoter of Argentina's maritime awareness at the time was Admiral Storni. Storni's seminal lectures delivered in 1916 carried a strong Mahanian imprint. See Guillermo Montenegro, *An Argentina Naval Buildup in the Disarmament Era: The Naval Procurement Act of 1926* (Buenos Aires: Universidad del CEMA).

existing provisions into a comprehensive framework. Driving these regulatory activities was above all the Navy. The Argentine military had involved itself in politics through successive coups d'états since 1930, culminating in the last, infamous dictatorship that lasted from 1976 to 1983. The last dictatorial regime was the country's most radical in terms of its ideological ambitions and the scope of violent repression. One of the most vividly remembered symbols from this period is the Navy Mechanics School known as ESMA, a notorious site of torture and murder. Having left a deep scar on Argentina's national psyche, the Navy's Dirty War is crucial to understanding the restricted role it would come to play in the country's maritime security framework under democracy.

In addition to democratization, in order to fully comprehend the Prefecture's role vis-à-vis the Navy and the (missing) relationship between the two, it is necessary to consider a second factor, namely the differences that have historically shaped two distinct organizational cultures and have given rise to an unequal relation between the Navy and the Prefecture. The example that best illustrates this is that the two institutions have created different foundational narratives even though they have been organizationally united more often than not. The Prefecture traces its origins to the Port Captaincy and thus, like the Argentine Army, to the creation of *la patria* in 1810 at the beginning of the independence struggle. Given that it was part of the Navy until 1984, however, it is the ARA Argentine history books refer to. The Navy takes pride in its long-standing tradition, which it dates to the 1814 Battle of Montevideo, a crucial milestone in the country's path to independence. Nevertheless, the Prefecture has historically been a force closer to the people through its responsibility to save lives and because it was less exclusive than the Navy, accepting the less educated, lower social strata into its ranks.[5]

The class differences gave rise to an unequal relation in which the Navy was seen as superior to the Prefecture. The existing hierarchy was further reinforced by the separation of their respective tasks. While war, the ambit of "high politics", belonged to the Navy, crime was seen as

---

[5] Interview with Eugenio Luis Facchin, retired ARA officer and PhD in political science, Buenos Aires, November 15, 2017.

a rather ordinary issue of domestic politics.[6] Therefore, once the two institutions were organizationally separated in 1984, there was no push for cooperation on either side. The Prefecture has sought to assert itself independently while the Navy, on the other hand, was too proud to extend a request to coordinate efforts in the areas of common competence. Likewise, and as the next section will explain, the political leadership failed to forge cooperation as the missing Navy–Prefecture link was perceived not as problematic but indeed as necessary to check the power of the armed forces.

DEMOCRATIZATION: THE CRITICAL JUNCTURE

The fact that Argentina is the only Latin American country with a coast guard independent from the Navy is explained by the way it democratized. In contrast to its neighbours, which were also ruled by military dictatorships, Argentina's armed forces suffered a triple defeat on the economic, humanitarian and the military front. Years of corruption and mismanagement, state terror and eventually the defeat in the war against Great Britain over the Malvinas returned Argentina to free and fair elections in 1983.[7] Raúl Alfonsín, the head of the new democratic government, moved swiftly to implement civilian control over the armed forces.[8] Key among the institutional reforms was the creation of functional bureaucratic rivalries by relocating the Naval Prefecture and the Gendarmerie from the orbit of the armed forces to the Ministry of Defence. From there, between 1992 and 1996, the Prefecture was gradually moved to the Secretary of Internal Security under the Ministry of Interior until in 2010 when the role of the Secretary was enlarged to become the Ministry of Internal Security.

---

[6] Interview with Jorge Battaglino, Senior research fellow at Argentina's National Science and Technology Research Council (CONICET) and Professor in the Department of Political Science and International Studies at the University Torcuato Di Tella, Buenos Aires, November 14, 2017.

[7] We use the official Argentine term of Islas Malvinas. The inhabitants of the islands refer to them as the Falkland Islands.

[8] See Raúl Alfonsín, *Memoria política: transición a la democracia y derechos humanos* [A Political Memory: Transition to Democracy and Human Rights] (Buenos Aires: Fondo de Cultura Económica de Argentina, 2004).

The organizational restructuring was followed by wide-ranging legal reforms. For the division of labour between the Navy and the Prefecture, three laws are of special relevance. The first is the National Defence Law of 1988 (No. 23.554), which is the main referent defining the responsibilities of the armed forces as those of national defence. According to its Article 2,

> national defence is the integration and coordinated action of all of the country's forces for the resolution of those conflicts that require the use of the Armed Forces, in a dissuasive or effective way, to confront aggressions of external origin.[9]

Three years later, the Law of Internal Security (No. 24.059/1991) delineated the role of the Prefecture as a security and police force. The military was excluded from this competence unless the President considers the existing system of governance as insufficient to restore internal security (Article 31).

The separation between security and defence has been taken extremely seriously and is reflected also in the third law, the 2011 Law on Intelligence (No. 25.520), which defines the roles and competences of the Navy and the Prefecture, respectively. This law stipulates that strategic intelligence is organizationally separated from criminal intelligence, leaving the Navy with the responsibility to gather and process information regarding external enemies only. In case it acquires information about criminal offences such as drug trafficking, it is obliged to pass on the data to the intelligence services' Criminal Directorate without analysing it. Criminal intelligence, like strategic intelligence, is directed by civilians.

The Argentine position remained unchanged until 2018, even as the 9/11 attacks on the USA further blurred the thin line separating security and defence. The US' attempts to combat terrorism emphasized the dangers coming from so-called new threats, an umbrella term used to describe transnational challenges putting citizens' security at risk including organized crime, migration and environmental degradation. From the USA's point of view, these challenges created fertile conditions for radical ideologies to spread and facilitated the

---

[9]Argentina, *Ley de Defensa Nacional* [National Defense Law]. Ley 24/554/88. Available at http://servicios.infoleg.gob.ar/infolegInternet/anexos/20000-24999/20988/texact.htm.

global reach of terrorist networks. Countries around the world echoed the "new security agenda", and in Latin America, the USA stepped up efforts to persuade governments to adopt a hard line against the "new" threats. Mexico, Colombia and some Central American countries were among the first that expanded the internal role of the armed forces, deploying the military on the streets mainly to combat drugs. Argentina, then under the rule of the US-critical, Peronist *Partido Justicialista*, took a different position. Based on the existing legal framework, the government pointed out, internal security was beyond the competence of the military.

Strictly speaking, Argentine laws only become applicable through an executive decree that regulates a law's individual provisions. In the case of the National Defence Law, no such decree was issued for almost three decades. Only in 2006 were the limitations on the military's role solidified as it was specified that the armed forces could be used internally to counter aggressions of external origin, where this meant "the use of armed force by a *state* against the sovereignty, territorial integrity or political independence of our country" (Decreto 727/2006, Article 1, emphasis added). Narrowing the Navy's role in maritime security, the decree left no doubt that "new threats" did not justify the use of the military internally.[10] Instead, following the regulatory decrees of National Defence (No. 727/2006, Article 24) and the Armed Forces (No. 1691/2006), it was "exclusively dedicated to enlist, train and sustain the means put at their disposal, in order to guarantee their effective use in the framework of military planning". This included, based on the same decree of the Armed Forces and National Defence plans (see Decreto 1729/2007), that the ARA undertook activities of surveillance and control so long as these activities were directed to strategic alert, but exclude criminal offences such as contraband.

The organizational separation of the Prefecture was smooth. Although the Navy resented the loss of organizational power and competence, the sharp break with society at the end of the dictatorship left the military

---

[10] This was modified by Decree No. 683/2018, which no longer limits external threats to states. The new decree was issued by Mauricio Macri (2015–), who made the fight against drug trafficking a priority of his presidency, allowing him to use the armed forces for logistical support in the anti-narcotics campaign.

with no political clout. Moreover, the prosecution of human rights violations absorbed much of the military's attention, and it was thus in no position to offer resistance.[11]

For the Prefecture, its independence from the Navy was a triumph. Apart from the uniform of its director and the insignia at the Prefecture's office building, however, not much changed in the day-to-day of the institution given that the relevant legal framework defining its tasks was largely already in place. Yet, it was now able to prove itself as an independent actor vis-à-vis the Navy, which had long looked at the Prefecture as a necessary, though subordinate organization that required lower entry standards and was paid less. The political conditions were favourable for the Prefecture's new, protagonist stance to bear tangible results. As Argentina's political elites sought to subordinate the military to civilian leadership and limit its role to national defence it turned to the security forces and mainly the Prefecture and the Gendarmerie, providing both with the necessary organizational and financial resources to establish themselves as independent actors.

In sum, the end of the military dictatorship and Argentina's democratization in the 1980s delineated the position of each, the Navy and the Prefecture, within the country's maritime security framework. Previously as part of the ARA, the Prefecture had been equally implicated in the horrors of Argentina's Dirty War. Subsequently, however, it is possible to say that it managed to create the image of an efficient (read: less corrupt) institution at the service of society rather than against it.[12]

---

[11] Jorge Battaglino, "Fuerzas Intermedias y Lucha Contra El Tráfico de Drogas: El Caso de La Gendarmería En Argentina" [Intermediate Forces and the Fight Against Drug Trade: The Case of the Gendarmerie in Argentina]. *URVIO, Revista Latinoamericana de Estudios de Seguridad* 18 (2016): 76–89.

[12] This claim has been made also for the Gendarmerie, which is in a similar position as an intermediate force between the Army and the police (Battaglino, "Fuerzas Intermedias y Lucha Contra El Tráfico de Drogas: El Caso de La Gendarmería En Argentina").

THE ESTABLISHMENT OF A NEW EQUILIBRIUM

The Prefecture has expanded organizationally and in terms of manpower. Comprising eleven directorates in 2004, it is now made up of 14 directorates plus an additional one for its activities in the northern, central and southern region. In 2007, the Prefecture's first institute for higher education, the University Institute of Maritime Security, was created. In terms of personnel, between 1980 and 1990, the number of active service members in the Prefecture increased from 11,000 to 13,000.[13] During the same decade, the Navy was reduced from 35,000 to 20,000 personnel. Since Argentina abolished conscription in 1995, the size of both the ARA and the PNA has largely remained stable. In 2018, there were 18,500 active service members in the ARA and 13,250 in the Prefecture.

The growing importance of the security forces relative to the military is reflected in the development of salary and pension allocations as well as in the overall budget for security and defence. While historically payment rates in the security forces were lower than in the military, in 2017 salaries in the Armed Forces were on average only 43% of the salaries for the corresponding ranks in the security forces.[14] Today, defence expenditures are about 20% less than those dedicated to security, creating a de facto situation in which the Prefecture is better positioned than the Navy to claim resources and take on tasks.[15]

The Prefecture is well inserted into the decision-making process, with a permanent representation in the Foreign Ministry and in Congress. The representation of the three armed forces in Congress (*enlace*, literally meaning "link") was temporarily substituted by a civilian representative from the Defence Ministry but returned under Macri's presidency. Nevertheless, according to the Prefecture's own account, its lobby was hardly necessary to ensure it was provided the necessary resources to grow.

---

[13] IISS, *The Military Balance 2018* (London: IISS, 2018).

[14] Sputnik, "Brecha salarial entre FFAA y de seguridad de Argentina se redujo a 43% [Wage Gap Between the Armed Forces and Security Forces of Argentina Down to 43%]," *Sputnik*, March 17, 2017, https://mundo.sputniknews.com/defensa/201703171067657508-fuerzas-armadas-argentina/.

[15] Ministerio de Hacienda, "Presidencia de la Nación, *Presupuesto 2018* [Budget 2018]," *Composición del gasto por Finalidad-Función y por Jurisdicción - Nº 3 Anexa al Art.1º*.

A strong perception of deteriorating public security obliged the authorities to invest in combatting organized and petty crime. Although the rates of both crime and violent crime are lower in Argentina than in most other Latin American countries, the perception of insecurity is comparatively stronger and has largely increased over the past decades.[16]

From 1995 to 2001, the opinion survey Latinobarómetro reported that between 68 and 95% of all Argentines felt that crime "had increased a lot", while another 5–27% said it had remained the same or increased slightly.[17] Presented with the choice of how to react, the civilian leadership preferred the intermediate forces, the Prefecture and the Gendarmerie, over the military and the police.

The Prefecture's political clout was illustrated in the controversial decision over who would exercise jurisdiction in Buenos Aires' showcase district Puerto Madero. After the city of Buenos Aires became an independent jurisdiction in 1992, the corporation of Puerto Madero was established as a conglomerate of private, national and local investors. Instead of the Federal Police, the Prefecture was given jurisdiction over policing duties in the port district including managing the police stations.

Building on the favourable conditions which allowed the Prefecture to establish itself as an independent, respected actor, the institution has taken a pro-active stance to expand the range of its tasks. Among others, this is reflected in its regulatory activity. The Prefecture has the authority to publish ordinances (*Ordenanzas*) that regulate the specific provisions relevant to its competences as defined in the national legislation and international law. Since 1983, it passed 133 such ordinances.[18] Since the Prefecture has no obligation to translate international agreements into Argentine

---

[16] Battaglino, "Fuerzas Intermedias y Lucha Contra El Tráfico de Drogas: El Caso de La Gendarmería En Argentina," 80; Lucía Dammert. *Perspectivas y dilemas de la seguridad ciudadana en América Latina* [Perspectives and Dilemmas of Citizen Security in Latin America] (Quito: Flacso-Sede Ecuador, 2007), 284–298.

[17] "Time Series Analysis: Democracia, Confianza En Las Instituciones Nacionales [Democracy, Trust in National Institutions]," *Latinobarómetro*, http://www.latinobarometro.org/latOnline.jsp.

[18] "Ordenanzas," *Prefectura Naval Argentina*, http://www.prefecturanaval.gov.ar/web/es/html/dpla_ordenanzaslistadover.php?&Pagina=10&Pagina=9&Pagina=1&Pagina=5&Pagina=7&Pagina=8&Pagina=9&Pagina=10&Pagina=9&Pagina=10&Pagina=1.

ordinances, their promulgation shows an eagerness to prove the institution's relevance. This is especially true given that the majority of ordinances are based on the legal instruments of the International Maritime Organization (IMO). The IMO is an important source of legitimation for the Naval Prefecture given that the national legislation based on the IMO's legal regime recognizes it as Argentina's maritime authority.

At the IMO, the Prefecture tends to have a stronger presence than the Navy. Both have a permanent technical advisor that assists the Argentine representative at the organization, usually a career diplomat who attends the biannual Assembly. The IMO's five main committees and the technical subcommittees are integrated by representatives of the member states' maritime institutions. While these may be either PNA or ARA officers, during the past decades it was mostly a Prefect representing Argentina. The Prefecture's comparatively stronger presence is justified by the expertise and educational record of its members, which reflects the growing professionalization of the Prefecture as a whole. Building on its long-term relations at the IMO, the PNA was thus able to exert greater influence in negotiations behind closed doors.

In 1988, the PNA established an International Affairs Secretariat to coordinate its international activities. Other than the IMO, the Prefecture participates in the International Mobile Satellite Organization (IMSO); IALA, a non-profit, technical association active in the area of maritime aids; and the Operative Network of regional Cooperation among Maritime Authorities of the Americas (ROCRAM). At the request of the Foreign Ministry, it also takes part in regional cooperation schemes such as the Common Market of the South (MERCOSUR), the Administration Commissions of the Río de la Plata (CARP) and Río Uruguay as well as the bilateral border committees with Paraguay and Chile. Since 2000, Prefects are present as delegates at Argentine embassies in the USA and in several Latin American countries. Lastly, international cooperation also takes place based on bilateral agreements, through which the Prefecture's training and education institutions receive foreign students.

Attempts to Foster Inter-agency Cooperation

The establishment of a new equilibrium between the Navy and the Prefecture triggered some attempts to coordinate efforts between the two forces. The political leadership has shown little interest in getting the two sides to work together due to a mix of what has been called an "attention-deficit" regarding defence matters and the view that inter-agency competition was not necessarily a bad thing as it provided an additional check on the navy.[19] Indeed, the latter could hardly be expected to reach out to the newly empowered institution that had escaped its tutelage and thus failed to push for cooperation. The Prefecture, on the other hand, remains wary and guards its newfound prerogatives against the ARA's potential interference.

The first attempt to foster inter-agency cooperation dates from 1989. The two institutions committed to cooperate in 13 areas but none of the 13 points was ever taken up. In 2011, another initiative was launched at the ministerial level. The Agreement on Cooperation and Complementation on Matters Related to the ARA and the Prefecture aimed at increasing efficiency in two areas, ocean control and information. With respect to the former, the agreement called for the coordination of patrols and the inclusion of members of one force on board of the other. Until today, however, there has been no coordination of patrols between the two organizations. The embarkation of personnel with the respective other was practised with some frequency in the 1990s but has become increasingly rare in the past decade or two. Only when the Prefecture lacks its own equipment to carry out complex search and rescue operations do Prefects embark on ARA vessels.

With regard to information sharing, the 2011 agreement calls for coordination between the Navy and the Prefecture at the IMO and for the purpose of national integrated information systems. The agreement makes specific references to the integration of the international long-range identification and tracking (LRIT) system, in particular for search and rescue, and the automatic identification system (AIS) for activities in the Antarctic. LRIT and AIS feed into the independently operating information and tracking systems of the Navy and the Prefecture, with the latter being given control as administrator. This has caused resentment in the ARA, which is the legally designated authority for search and rescue (SAR, see below) and looks at the Antarctic as a strategic issue of fundamental relevance to national defence.

---

[19] David Pion-Berlin and Harold A. Trinkunas, "Attention Deficits: Why Politicians Ignore Defense Policy in Latin America," *Latin American Research Review* 42, no. 3 (October 30, 2007): 76–100.

In order to improve cooperation in the two areas, the agreement provides for the establishment of specific programmes under an executive committee integrated by both forces. According to information from the ARA, the members of the committee were appointed but never met.[20]

In sum, it is fair to conclude that the political leadership failed to come forth with a decisive initiative to foster inter-agency cooperation. At the same time, neither the disempowered Navy nor the Prefecture can be expected to take the initiative given the historically unequal relationship explained above, even if this would improve their performance and legitimacy. The Navy tends to see the Prefecture as ever further encroaching upon its turf. Complaints of a missing cooperative spirit like the following are thus frequent:

> The PNA asks marine pilots and captains to present a series of nautical and signalization reports upon their arrival at the port. This information, which should then be quickly transferred to the Naval Hydrography Service [under the Navy] for its processing and dissemination, usually suffers excessive and unjustified delays, which affect the task of the NAVAREA VI Coordinator –Armada Argentina– Naval Hydrography Service.[21]

The Prefecture, on the other hand, tends to see the ARA as a past evil. A senior Prefect summarized the general perception within the organization as follows: "We look at the Navy as the institution responsible to defend us in the case of war. Having said that, the risk of war for Argentina is really rather low".[22] Notwithstanding the fact that the PNA is well established as the main actor in maritime security, mistrust remains whether the Navy would accept working with the Prefecture on equal terms.

---

[20] Interview, Buenos Aires, November 13, 2017.

[21] Fernando Horacio Rial, *La Seguridad Naútica y Las Relaciones Institucionales Entre La Armada Argentina y La Prefectura Naval Argentina* [Safety of Navigation and Institutional Relations Between the Argentine Navy and the Naval Prefecture] (Buenos Aires: Instituto Universitario Naval, Escuela de Guerra Naval, 2003), 60.

[22] Interview, Buenos Aires, November 14, 2017.

Policy Areas of Common Competence and Competition

Room for interpretation regarding the roles of the ARA and the PNA, respectively, arises from the fact that the applicable laws and regulations define their competences in functional as well as in geographic terms. With respect to the geographic criterion, moreover, there is a blind spot in Argentine law regarding zones of jurisdiction that are not fully sovereign, such as the EEZ and Antarctica.

Take the laws of the Prefecture (No. 18.398), security forces (No. 18.711, 1970) and internal security (No. 24.059), which define the extent of the Prefecture's competence as the seas, rivers, waterways and ports under national jurisdiction. According to the UNCLOS provisions that became part of Argentine law when UNCLOS entered into force in 1995 (Ley No. 24.543), the waters of national jurisdiction that are under the responsibility of the Prefecture extend 200 nm from the country's baselines, including Argentina's EEZ. As a policing force, the PNA is also assigned the functional competence to control fishing in the EEZ, but it may be the case the ARA, while on exercise in the EEZ, will detain a fishing vessel operating illegally. This is consistent also with the ARA's legally delineated ambit of action outside the realm of internal security, since the limit of Argentine sovereignty is the territorial sea boundary at 12 nm. While in this case the Navy is required to hand over any seized vessel to the PNA, both institutions can legitimately claim competence for the act of detaining the fishing vessel based on the functional as well as the geographic criterion.

The Prefecture can do so because it is the organization responsible for fisheries control and generally for the security and safety in waters under Argentine jurisdiction. The Navy, on the other, can rightly base its claim on its responsibility to drill and exercise sovereignty beyond the country's territorial sea. The same legal ambiguity occurs with respect to acts of piracy, contraband and drug trafficking within the EEZ and the contiguous zone. In consequence, in some policy areas the lack of a clear regulatory framework leaves room for privileging either the functional or the spatial criterion to allocate responsibilities to the Prefecture or the Navy with no clear guiding principle other than political preferences.

It is worth noting that both the Navy and the Prefecture use the geographic and the functional arguments in an inconsistent manner depending on the circumstances that favour their own position, respectively.

This section discusses seven areas of common competences. The analysis shows that there is little overlap in practice and a limited amount of evidence for a harmful duplication of tasks. In almost all areas, the question of why overlap, duplication and collisions in carrying out certain tasks have been largely avoided can be answered by reference to budget allocations reflecting the political preference for the Prefecture.

Surveillance and Control

The Law of the Prefecture (No. 18.398) stipulates that the PNA's competence in Argentine seas and rivers has exclusive character (*exclusivo y excluyente*). The geographic criterion has been weakened by the additional use of a functional criterion to ascribe competences, such as surveillance and control. Since the publication of Argentina's 2010 Defence White Paper surveillance and control has been defined as the Navy's primary peacetime task, it was reemphasized again in the new National Defence Policy (Decree 683/2018). As such, it has been part of the Navy Command's Recruitment and Training Plan. From the ARA's perspective, surveillance is indispensable for the collection of information necessary for strategic warning as well as the country's bilateral and multilateral foreign policy.

Although the two institutions' tasks overlap in the EEZ, in practice, the PNA and the Navy have hardly gotten into the way of each other. In case an ARA patrol detects an infringement with Argentina's maritime regulatory framework, the laws described above provide for the handover of the case to the Prefecture (or another competent institution). In any case, such situations have rarely occurred. Given the PNA's institutional expansion, it is the institution that effectively carries out surveillance and control in Argentine jurisdictional waters. While the Prefecture lacks the means to adequately patrol the EEZ, so does the Navy, which has repeatedly expressed the need "to improve its maritime patrol, surveillance, and control capabilities".[23] The lack of attention to this peacetime task

---

[23] Admiral Marcelo Eduardo Hipólito Srur, "The Commanders Respond: Argentina," *Proceedings Magazine* 143/3/1,369 (March 2017): 24–37, 37. In November 2018, based on the new security and defence policy of President Macri, the government approved the purchase of four new patrol vessels to improve the Navy's surveillance and maritime control capabilities.

specifically, relative to peacekeeping and the safeguarding of Argentine interests in the Antarctic, is reflected in the failure to establish a Maritime Surveillance Command under the Joint Operations Command as envisaged in the Decree of National Defence Planning (1729/2006) over a decade ago. According to Argentine law, the planning and carrying out of strategic surveillance and control is the responsibility of the Maritime Surveillance Command. While the equivalent Command for Aerial Surveillance was established, however, the Navy's patrol activities are still under the Naval Command for Recruitment and Training instead of the planned, joint Maritime Surveillance Command.

Organized Crime, Contraband, Terrorism and Piracy

Criminal activities and terrorism within Argentina's maritime areas are the primary responsibility of the Prefecture according to its territorially defined responsibility over the country's jurisdictional waters. As stated above, the arrangement in place until 2018 contrasted with the tendency especially since 9/11 to deploy the armed forces against terrorism and illicit activities alleged to facilitate terrorist activity. The 2010 Defence White Paper stated unequivocally that

> [p]henomena such as drug trafficking, organized crime, economic crimes and money laundering or transnational terrorism do not correspond in the Argentine legal and organizational framework to the responsibilities, competences and instruments of the Defence System. Dealing with these criminal phenomena is the responsibility of the Internal Security System.[24]

Accordingly, the Prefecture has been put in charge of the IMO's International Ship and Port Facility Security Code (ISPS), a set of measures to enhance the security of ships and port facilities developed in response to the 9/11 attacks on the USA.

The 2018 reforms increased the possibilities for greater involvement of the armed forces to respond to criminal activities internally as long as these constitute a threat emanating from outside the country and especially if these fall under the jurisdiction of international law (Decree 683/2018). In addition, the new regulations emphasize the

---

[24] Ministry of Defense of Argentina, *Libro Blanco de La Defensa* [Defense White Paper] (Buenos Aires: Ministry of Defense of Argentina, 2010), 92–93.

logistical support role of the military to complement the security forces in what is sought to become a more integrated approach to security. The reforms legitimize the potential involvement of the Navy alongside the Prefecture in combatting organized criminal activities, terrorism and piracy, although it is worth mentioning that Argentina does not actually face problems of piracy and terrorism. Contraband is a significant problem but occurs almost exclusively in fluvial and riverine areas.

Search and Rescue

Law No. 22.445 of 1981 incorporated the International Convention on Search and Rescue adopted in Hamburg in 1979 into Argentine national law. Article 2 defines as its authority the Navy "through its competent organisms". The Prefecture was then an organism of the Navy, but since it no longer depends on the ARA, it still remains the main agency to carry out SAR operations. It is the ARA though, through its Training and Recruitment Command, that issues the National SAR Plan implementing Law 22.445. The National Plan of 2015 and its predecessor of 1989 list both the PNA and the Navy as responsible agencies. In practice, however, the distribution of capacities renders the Prefecture the relatively more active agency in SAR.

Up to 90% of all registered cases occur either within Argentina's fluvial and riverine areas or within the 12 nm of territorial waters. These areas are undisputedly under the competence of the Prefecture. Beyond the 12 nm line, it is the PNA that also detects or is called to deal with SAR cases. The Prefecture reports that it carried out a total of 454 SAR operations in 2016, roughly about the same number as in the preceding years.[25] More than half of these incidents occurred in Argentina's maritime areas, with the remaining 30–40% in rivers and lakes. It is worth noting that there does not appear to have been an increase in incidents taken care of by the Prefecture: the number of SAR operations has been largely comparable and even slightly higher in 1990 (564 cases), 1995 (629 cases) and 2000 (664 cases).

---

[25] Information provided by the Servicio de Tráfico Marítimo [Service for Marine Traffic], PNA, November 27, 2017.

The Prefecture's predominant profile in SAR is justified also by budgetary considerations. It is more cost-efficient and in most cases sufficient to use the smaller and technologically more advanced PNA ships. Only in rare, complex and far-offshore cases is it necessary to revert to the Navy. The ARA lacks suitable equipment, however, and its capacity shortage is compounded by the size of the so-called Search and Rescue Region, the international ocean regime the IMO assigns to Argentina. Argentina is one of five countries responsible for maritime SAR in the Southern Ocean and the only one together with Chile that maintains dedicated assets in the Antarctic portion of its SAR region.[26] Although the regions largely correspond to states' maritime zones, they are technically not connected. Nevertheless, the Navy (as well as the Ministry of Foreign Affairs) has paid special attention to SAR activities surrounding the Falkland Islands and Antarctica linking those to its role in national defence. In the Antarctic region, the Navy carries out combined patrols together with Chile. The so-called Naval Antarctic Patrol, which takes place between November and March every year, was established in 1998 and covers the area between the 10-degree and 130-degree lines south of the 60th parallel.

Fisheries Control

A glance at Global Fishing Watch's digital map suffices to show the importance of regulating fishing in Argentina's jurisdictional waters.[27] The lights indicating commercial fishing activity illuminate the country's entire coast and outshine those in most other parts of Latin America. Argentina's Fisheries Law (No. 24.922) assigns authority in this area to the Federal Fisheries Council, which is responsible for the development of the National Plan to Prevent, Discourage and Eradicate Illegal, Undeclared and Unregulated Fishing. The Law and the Plan state that the Prefecture, being the country's maritime authority, is responsible for controlling fishing activities and maritime traffic as well as to prevent

---

[26] Natalie Klein, Joanna Mossop, and Donald R. Rothwell, *Maritime Security: International Law and Policy Perspectives from Australia and New Zealand* (Oxon: Routledge, 2009), 130.

[27] "Global Fishing Watch Map," *Global Fishing Watch*, http://globalfishingwatch.org/map/.

illicit activities.[28] Further, the plan reads: "In its competence as auxiliary fishing police, [the PNA] initiates the proceedings for infractions committed against the fishing regulations of the country, both by vessels sailing under national and foreign flag".

The Navy is not mentioned in the Fisheries Law but, together with the Air Force, it is tasked to "assist [...] in the control of fishing through the deployment of their respective equipment".[29] Apart from control, the Navy also "participates in the conservation and protection of the resources of the sea through the use of ships and aircraft deployed in waters of national and international jurisdiction, obtaining an effective deterrent effect on possible offenders to the rules of administration and conservation of fishery resources".[30]

Based on the designated tasks, both the Prefecture and the Navy have the responsibility to protect Argentina's fishery resources in the ocean. The role of the latter, although secondary, has been strengthened by the fact that Argentina's defence policy directives have assigned greater importance to natural resources in recent years. The strategic relevance of natural resources globally and those corresponding to Argentina's disputed areas in the South Atlantic is recognized in the Defense White Papers and the first Political Directive of National Defense (Decreto 1714/2009), which is issued every four years. The second Directive of 2014, however, was already more specific when it defined natural resources as a "central aspect in the formulation of the strategic attitude regarding its defensive character". Given the careful use of the term defence in Argentine policy circles, the mentioning of the "defensive character" is significant as is suggests the armed forces play a role when it comes to natural resources, including fish (see also the new Decree 703/2018). In practice, however, the ARA's activity is limited due to budgetary constraints.

For the Navy, the primary concern related to fishing activities and, in consequence, trans-shipping are those carried out along or just outside Argentina's disputed EEZ. The problem of regulating fishing activity

---

[28] Consejo Federal Pesquero, *Plan de Acción Nacional Para Prevenir, Desalentar y Eliminar La Pesca Ilegal, No Declarada y No Reglamentada* [National Action Plan to Prevent, Discourage and End Non-declared and Non-regulated Illegal Fishing], 14.

[29] Ibid., 9.

[30] Ibid., 15.

at the 200 nm EEZ boundary is dealt with under the United Nations Agreement on the Conservation and Management of Straddling Fish Stocks and Highly Migratory Fish Stocks, which Argentina has ratified but not legally deposited due to its disputed claims over the islands of Malvinas, Georgia del Sur and Sandwich del Sur. The Agreement calls upon the riparian state and the state under whose flag the fishing boats sail to accord criteria for fishing along the EEZ boundary. However, the fact that some of the areas are disputed makes the conclusion of formal agreements for Argentina extremely difficult, thus compounding the problem of lacking the capacity to control the 200 nm offshore.

To oversee fishing activities, the applicable legislation provides for an integrated information system (SICAP) managed by the Ministry of Agroindustry. Among other agencies, both the Prefecture and the Navy are party to SICAP and are required to cooperate based on a specific agreement within the framework of the 2011 inter-ministerial cooperation agreement (see above). While both comply with their responsibilities to supply SICAP with the relevant information, however, officials acknowledge that "if we had a harmonious relation, this could further benefit the system".

Activities in the Antarctic

According to the Law of the Prefecture's Article 4.b, the Prefecture has exclusive competence in the Argentine-claimed territories of the Antarctic. At the same time, the Navy claims responsibility there as it is a disputed area that is not under national sovereign jurisdiction. Consequently, several functions carried out on the Antarctic continent overlap.

The competence to define Argentina's policies in the area lies with the Ministry of Foreign Affairs, acting mainly through the Argentine Antarctic Institute and its National Antarctic Directorate, which operates six permanent and seven temporal research bases in the territory. The Navy, as part of the armed forces, supports the national scientific programme in accordance with both the strategic value of the territory and its special legal status as defined by the Antarctic Treaty. Article IV of the treaty interdicts activities that "constitute a basis for asserting, supporting or denying a claim to territorial sovereignty". This means the Prefecture can act as a national police force in the Antarctic as long as it exercises competence over Argentine citizens and objects, but not over territory. In addition, the Prefecture also carries out scientific research, which is justified by its responsibility to control contamination.

While the Navy has maintained its presence with one permanent base (Orcadas, 1951) and five temporary bases during the summer months (Ellsworth, Petrel, Melchior, Decepción, Corbeta Uruguay) largely unchanged since the 1960s, like in other areas, the Prefecture has gradually expanded its activities in the Antarctic. Previously, it participated in the annual Summer Antarctic Campaigns on a voluntary basis until in 2012 when it began operating its own vessels in support of the mission to resupply the National Antarctic Directorate's research bases. Since the 1990s, Prefects are also present at the Directorate-operated base of Carlini (formerly Jubany).

The missing coordination between the research programmes undertaken by the Navy and the Prefecture may come to the detriment of science, although from a state point of view, the duplication of scientific efforts is not necessarily problematic. Notwithstanding the Antarctic Treaty provisions, an enhanced range of activities by a larger number of agencies may favour an Argentine future bargaining position over Antarctic territory.

Scientific Studies

The National Council for Scientific and Technical Research (CONICET) is responsible for Argentina's state scientific programme. Besides CONICET, the Navy and since 2001 also the Prefecture carry out their own marine scientific programmes. From the armed forces' view, science and research is part of their responsibility to acquire strategic intelligence. For the Prefecture, on the other hand, research activities are justified by its role as a marine police mainly in the area of environmental protection as regulated under the IMO's International Convention for the Prevention of Pollution from Ships (MARPOL). Joint competence in this area has led to competition for resources and the duplication of capacities on a minor scale. Overall, the Prefecture has been able to gradually strengthen its profile and—counting with better equipment and more resources than the ARA—establish itself as a permanent partner for the responsible state agencies in carrying out scientific studies.

Based on an agreement with the Ministry of Defence, CONICET has traditionally relied on equipment and personnel of the Navy's Hydrographical Office, which operates two oceanographic vessels, the *ARA Puerto Deseado* and the *ARA Austral* in high seas and the *ARA Comodoro Rivadavia* within 50 nm offshore. CONICET's last acquisition, the *Azara I*, is to be manned by the Prefecture. Similarly, the National Institute for Fisheries Research and Development (INIDEP) decided to have its new ship *Victor Angelescu* operated by the PNA. In line with the 2015 Pampa Azul Project, a national plan aimed at sustainable maritime development, there have been proposals to unify marine research under a single agency located within the Ministry for Science, Technology and Innovation. Until such a proposal materializes, however, activities in the area will be carried out relying on the Navy and the Prefecture according to political preferences and the development of relevant capacities of each.

Defence

The military is the primary instrument of external defence, but also the PNA is part of the national defence system. As such, according to Article 31 of the Defence Law, it develops the necessary capacities for the permanent control and surveillance of Argentina's borders and maritime areas. In times of war, the relationship between the armed forces and the security forces changes from coordination to the latter's subordination under the Military Operations Command. In this case, the Prefecture is required to follow the orders of the ARA and provide complete information about any of its operations. The missing link between the two organizations raises the question of whether they can effectively operate together given both the absence of joint plans on recruitment and training during wartime, as well as the lack of practical experience through joint exercises. Although this is a question worthwhile considering given the current state of affairs, however, in practical terms the potential lack of interoperability is less of a problem given that the current risk of war is minimal for Argentina.

Since its return to democracy, the official Argentine position has been that the prospect of an external armed conflict is negligible if not inexistent. The Defence White Papers published in 1998, 2010 and 2015 all state that Argentina has no conflict plans with any neighbouring country.[31] Nevertheless, the formally ascribed defence mission renders the question of interoperability at least theoretically relevant especially considering the conflicting territorial claims with Great Britain over the Malvinas/Falkland Islands, South Georgia, the South Sandwich Islands, the South Orkney Islands and large areas of the Antarctic, though the latter are frozen under the Antarctic Treaty of 1959. The competing territorial claims gave rise to overlapping claims over vast maritime areas in the South Atlantic and Southern Oceans. From Argentina's perspective, any activity in these areas amounts to a matter of national defence.

Conclusion

If strictly interpreted, Argentina's maritime security has been the sole responsibility of its Naval Prefecture after it was separated from the Navy in 1984. Since the country's return to democracy in 1983, there has been a strong emphasis on the distinction between internal security, the ambit of action of the security forces such as the police, the Gendarmerie and the Prefecture, on the one hand, and external defence, under the responsibility of the armed forces, on the other. The new regulations from 2018 blur the formerly strict separation to some extent, but it remains to be seen whether future government policies will make use of the new possibilities to use the military internally in support of the security forces. In any case, given the broad understanding of the term maritime security, as outlined in the introduction to this volume, it is apparent that the ARA plays a role in Argentina's maritime security.

In this chapter, we argued that the navy-coastguard nexus in Argentina is one of a missing relationship. The end of the military dictatorship and the path to democracy the country has taken explain why the Prefecture has acquired greater importance relative to the Navy since 1983. Both, politicians and the public still distrust the armed forces. In addition, the Prefecture has acquired greater importance due to a growing demand for

---

[31] Argentina, *Libro Blanco de La República Argentina* [Defence White Paper of the Republic of Argentina], 1998, 2–19; Ministry of Defense of Argentina, *Libro Blanco de La Defensa*, 2010, 29, 192, 217; Ministry of Defense of Argentina, *Libro Blanco de La Defensa* (Buenos Aires: Ministry of Defense of Argentina, 2015), 32, 35, 116.

public security. While the Prefecture has successfully distanced itself from the infamous image of the Navy still tied to its role in the dictatorship, the roots of the missing link between the two institutions goes back further. Although the Prefecture had for the longest time stood under the Navy's command, both developed their own institutional cultures. Mainly due to class differences, the Prefecture was not seen as an equal partner and has therefore shown little enthusiasm to cooperate with the Navy.

Although the missing link raises questions about the successful management of Argentina's maritime security, this chapter has shown that there are few areas where clashes of competence occur. We argued that this is due to political preferences that tilted the small margin of regulatory freedom and potential legal ambiguity in favour of the Prefecture. Nevertheless, the situation falls far short of ideal. The navy-coast guard nexus is about more than inter-agency competition but raises bigger questions about the role of the armed forces. The country's maritime security will benefit from a more profound engagement with defence matters and a clear definition of the Navy's role in those areas where the spatial and functional criteria of competence allocation overlap with those of the Prefecture. In addition to greater clarity, there is no doubt on either side that coordination and cooperation between the two forces can achieve synergies that have so far been lost.

The new security and defence policy of president Macri (2015–) may be the beginning of a changing equilibrium between the ARA and the Prefecture, given that it places greater emphasis on inter-agency cooperation for internal security, including the armed forces (see Decrees 174/2018 and 350/2018 and Resolution 47/2018 of the Cabinet Central Office). The military has now an explicit role to play in providing logistical support to counter any type of external threats inside Argentina and unlike before, it can be used to guard strategic objects as defined by the government (Decree 683/2018). Although the new competences could alter the relationship between the Navy and the Prefecture, it remains to be seen to what extent they will be used. At least in the short term, the prevailing attitude in society is such that major changes in the distribution of tasks between the two forces are unlikely.

Acknowledgements We thank the various Navy officers, Prefects and state officials who shared their views and information with us while writing this chapter. Nicole Jenne gratefully acknowledges financial support to this project from the Chilean National Commission for Scientific and Technological Research (CONICYT), Programa Fondecyt de Iniciación [Project No. 11170387].

CHAPTER 14

Conclusion

Swee Lean Collin Koh and Ian Bowers

There is little reason to believe that the sources of instability on the world's oceans will be alleviated in the coming decades. Instead, the global maritime security landscape is likely to become increasingly complex. New, unforeseen threats will arise and traditional threats will evolve, thereby continuously challenging the maritime security architectures of seafaring states around the world.

Collectively, the case studies in this volume have shown that within the navy-coastguard nexus there has been an increasing level of operational interaction and between navies and their maritime law enforcement agencies (MLEA) counterparts. This does not necessarily translate into bureaucratic or operational efficiencies. For states where navies and MLEA exist as separate institutions, there will always be a competition for scarce resources, including much-needed funding, skilled and talented manpower, and other forms of capital investment.

S. L. C. Koh (✉)
S. Rajaratnam School of International Studies,
Nanyang Technological University, Singapore
e-mail: iscollinkoh@ntu.edu.sg

I. Bowers
Royal Danish Defence College, Copenhagen, Denmark
e-mail: iabo@fak.dk

© The Author(s) 2019
I. Bowers and S. L. C. Koh (eds.), *Grey and White Hulls*,
https://doi.org/10.1007/978-981-13-9242-9_14

The navy-coastguard nexus will change not only in response to alterations in the maritime security environment, but also as a result of the internal political, bureaucratic and economic circumstances of each individual state. Given the strategic environment, it is evident that states believe that both types of actor remain relevant and that cooperation between them is increasingly strategically salient. Navies and MLEA increasingly will operate in the same strategic space and the nexus between them will only grow in strategic importance.

Due to this importance, the goal of this volume was to better understand the positive and negative, internal and external determinants of the navy-coastguard nexus and what implications would a shifting navy-coastguard nexus have on stability at sea. We have drawn the following salient observations from the preceding chapters.

The Blurring of the Lines Between Civilian and Military Actors Will Persist

A recurring theme throughout the chapters in this volume concerns how actors within their respective national maritime security architectures respond to the evolving maritime security landscape. A consistent argument is that there is an ongoing blurring of the operational lines between navies and their MLEA counterparts. This blurring is largely driven by changes in the strategic landscape; however, it does not always occur efficiently and can result in significant duplications in capabilities, unclear lines of command and heightened inter-agency competition.

In some cases, by initial design some MLEA are already subordinate to a parent defence or military organization. In this type set-up, it is typically the navy that stands out as the leading actor while the MLEA will operate under the same overarching ministry or defence organization. Although their roles at sea may be quite distinct, this structure has the potential to, but does not always succeed in facilitating better coordination. It may also alleviate the problem of inter-service competition for resources. In other cases, navies and MLEAs will operate under separate organizations or commands but will be forced to respond collectively and may undergo ad hoc organizational restructuring in response to the operational landscape they face.

Vietnam is a good example of how a state is attempting to formalize the operational roles of their maritime organizations and the difficulties it faces in doing so. Truong-Minh Vu and Nguyen The Phuong demonstrate in Chapter 5 how greater operational integration between the Vietnamese People's Navy (VPN) and the Vietnam Coast Guard (VCG) remains a work in progress. This is despite the fact that both organizations fall under the control of the Ministry of National Defence. Both organizations have their own command and control structures, and there is no comprehensive cooperative framework between the VPN and VCG. This impacts efficient operations when contingencies arise that require immediate coordination. The Coast Guard Law promulgated in 2018 could go a long way in clarifying the exact roles of the VCG relative to the VPN. That said, however, by design clearly this will also enhance the further integration of the two services in a more efficacious manner, thus blurring the civilian-military line.

Similarly, China is amalgamating its maritime organizations with a similar blurring of the civil-military divide. The China Coast Guard (CCG) was hitherto separate from the People's Liberation Army Navy (PLAN); the former previously being an amalgamation of diverse MLEAs. Zheng Anguang in Chapter 2 outlines in detail how China has consolidated its array of maritime law enforcement agencies and how they are used alongside the PLAN to promote China's maritime interests across East Asia and beyond. The CCG's recent placement under effective military administration is in large part motivated by the evolving security environment and persistent calls internally to consolidate the actors and streamline the national maritime security architecture. In so doing, the lines between civilian and military actors are blurred. As Zheng also pointed out, the nexus between the navy and MLEAs will become more prominent, especially when the PLAN partakes in joint maritime law enforcement with the CCG.

Russia is another interesting example where the lines are also blurred due to the exigency of an evolving maritime security environment much like the case encountered by China and Vietnam. Ingvill Elgsaas and Liv Parmo in Chapter 10 explore the nexus between the Russian Navy and the Federal Security Service (FSB) coast guard. They argue that the division of responsibilities is diffuse, largely owing to the wide scope of the FSB's mandate, even though there are unclear lines of responsibility which allow for flexibility in terms of operational mandates but also for inadequate management of Russia's maritime security. The broadening portfolio of the coast guard reflects growth and diversification of activities in the Arctic. While the navy retains a clear principal role, the explicit inclusion of the FSB in military activities in the maritime domain, the authors pointed out, underscores the hard security component in the coast guard's broad and diverse portfolio. Although they speculate that this opens for a return to the Soviet precedent with the coast guard functioning as a "Navy reserve", which is also in line with the broad threat perception of the current Russian regime, law-enforcement and other civilian tasks remain the coast guard's main functions and its new status as an important military-maritime actor is secondary.

Neighbouring Canada appears to be motivated by the same external factors, although the shift takes place in the navy instead of the coast guard. In Chapter 12, Timothy Choi expounds on the relationship between sea control and peacetime maritime security requirements. These will become increasingly crucial in the coming decades and set in the backdrop of an evolving and dynamic Arctic security environment, the Royal Canadian Navy seems to be taking on more peacetime law enforcement roles, something that traditionally has been under the purview of the Canadian Coast Guard.

In the case of Italy, Alessandra Dibenedetto highlights in Chapter 9 how the pressures of the refugee crisis in Mediterranean exposed faultlines between various MLEA and the Italian Navy. Italian structures administering the work of the various agencies operating in that region are very broad and lack specific details on reciprocal duties. The current division of labour between the agencies had been determined by primarily external but also internal drivers including domestic politics and intra-agency dynamics which shaped the functions and tasks assigned to each maritime body. Amongst Italian maritime agencies, Dibenedetto argues, reciprocity and duplications of duties prevail over efficacy and efficiency when tailor-made dispositions are not provided. In this case, the navy-coast guard nexus was blurred not only because of external factors but also internal, pre-existing inefficiencies.

Strained Bedfellows?

Whereas in some countries, navies and coast guards fight to the bitter end over scarce resources that have to be shared by multiple agencies, in others these actors engage in rivalries despite having little or no need to tussle for resources.

Sukjoon Yoon in Chapter 4 highlights how structural, bureaucratic and operational differences between the navy and coast guard of the Republic of Korea have hindered closer inter-agency cooperation. The common maritime security challenges both institutions face, and the fact that both agencies enjoy their own fair share of resources, do not prevent the two agencies from viewing each other more as competitors than partners. As Yoon points out, each of these actors would prefer to take the credit, independently, for any non-military maritime security missions achieved, which stems from a fundamental culture clash between the military-influenced attitudes of the ROKN and the law-enforcement force mentality of the KCG.

Japan's two primary actors within its national maritime security architecture, the JMSDF and JCG are each in their own rights sizeable and well-funded agencies. But as Shimodaira Takuya in Chapter 3 highlights, while both the JMSDF and JCG are operating in an increasingly close manner as necessitated by the evolving security environment, further integration is still required. As Takuya points out, prior to recent years JMSDF and JCG had not had the habit of close cooperation. They lacked compatibility in terms of the systems and equipment they use, and they basically fulfilled different roles as mandated in no small part by the Pacifist Constitution, which imposes restrictions on the JSDF, not least its maritime arm JMSDF. This division however will continue to evolve as the exigencies of the security environment require, which thereby could lead to better nexus between JMSDF and JCG.

Japan and the ROK might be one of the few examples in the world where countries maintain sizeable, separate navies and coast guards that enjoy a degree of comfort in drawing necessary resources—though of course, there is never enough resources to go around and the actors will always crave for more. Still, it is clear that resources alone may not necessarily be the main cause of problems encountered in promoting the nexus between navies and coast guards. Habits of cooperation between MLEA and navies could have been non-existent or never considered a possibility thereby creating a very low expectations for efficient operational coordination. Even if the exigencies of an evolving security environment necessitate closer cooperation between both sides, the lack of willingness to do so may lead to further frictions and inefficiencies within the navy-coast guard nexus.

No One-Size-Fits-All Model

It is pertinent to emphasize here that there is no one-size-fits-all model when it comes to creating a national maritime security architecture. It can take the form of a sole agency, dual-agency or multiple-agency approach. This depends on the country's national context and character, the nature of domestic politics and the bureaucracy and other key determinants such as perceptions of the security environment, as highlighted in the introductory chapter.

This leads to a review of what one should refer to as national maritime interests. As noted earlier, so-called national maritime interests transcend direct threats and how best to address them, and may emanate from not only national sovereign and jurisdictional maritime zones but also further afield. Broadly defined, "national maritime interests" may mean more than just threats and solutions, but also how policy actors within the said maritime security architecture perceive their respective positions and how the country's political leadership balance those internal interests—which may not always be harmonious and could be at times conflictual—in order to attain an equilibrium. This equilibrium may not always be optimal, it can even be suboptimal. The end effect could be therefore a flawed prioritisation of strategic focus and a misallocation of limited resources. One may not find the maritime security architecture necessarily optimized to cope with the obvious security challenges, not because policy elites are ignorant of those issues and the urgency of addressing them, but because they are held back by the extant domestic circumstances.

As Muhammad Arif expounds at length and in good detail in Chapter 7, Indonesia as a vast archipelagic nation has a large number of maritime security interests, yet despite efforts to bolster the Maritime Security Agency (BAKAMLA), significant problems exist in a creating a coordinated approach with the Indonesian Navy. As he points out, Indonesia has never been familiar with the concept of a coast guard as a dedicated civilian maritime law enforcement institution with a clear delineation of responsibilities vis-à-vis other agencies. To compound the problem, the geographical nature of the country makes it challenging to delineate the roles and responsibilities as well as to divide the areas of operation of the various maritime security agencies. Further to that, Arif also sheds light on the long-standing, blurred distinction in Indonesia between "defence" and "security" that makes it almost impossible to force the military to focus solely on defence roles and relinquish internal security or law enforcement tasks.

Indonesia's diverse array of agencies within its national maritime security architecture is probably not too unique and would count as one of those countries which possess such onerous set-up of actors. Can one say that it is ineffective? Perhaps this can be better addressed if one looks beyond purely from the perspective of identifying maritime security challenges and defining solutions. The answer is more nuanced. Given Indonesia's circumstances, some of which are deeply entrenched within the national strategic culture and psyche, the current arrangement could well be the optimum that can be best attained in order to maintain the equilibrium—at least for now. National maritime interests are not just about addressing extant threats at sea, but also balancing intra-national interests.

Though of course, what works for Indonesia needs not necessarily apply to others. Neighbouring Singapore may have less actors within its national maritime security architecture but as Collin Koh in Chapter 6 elaborates: the country may have benefitted from the fact that it is a relatively young nation state with less of the strategic cultural baggage that might roll forward to influence or shape the architecture. The tiny island city-state could essentially start from a "clean slate", coupling political will with a decisive manner in which actors' roles and responsibilities are determined from the start. Amongst the six agencies responsible some way or another for maritime security, the navy can be described as "first amongst equals"—taking on the mantle of lead actor in Singapore's maritime security architecture, yet not overpowering the civilian policy strata and being able to serve as also a team player to other agencies in this whole-of-government approach. Having a small sovereign and jurisdictional maritime zone to police, Singapore can benefit from the relative "ease" of managing security at sea. Though of course, it is not to say that the maritime security threats it faces are not complex or pertinent. Just that managing security at sea becomes easier when resources can still be considered adequate and more than proportionate to the maritime responsibilities. There is consequently less incentives or reason to fight with each other for relevance and resources.

In fact, small states like Singapore tend to face similar circumstances in building and shaping their national maritime security architecture. The small Nordic maritime states Denmark, Norway and Iceland, which Andreas Østhagen describes in Chapter 8, chose dissimilar coast guard models. Yet, by going through each model and set-up in the coast guard/navy balance, it becomes apparent that the models are not that different after all. On paper, they are of different characters, but their mandates, tasks, and structures are surprisingly similar, determined by geography, the resource situation at a national level, and overarching security considerations.

Whole-of-Nation, Whole-of-Government the Way Forward?

Successful examples do exist where the navy and coast guard can cooperate effectively, even for countries with extensive national maritime interests. The case of the US Navy and Coast Guard being one such instance. As Jonathan G. Odom points out in Chapter 11, the question is how the governments of individual nations can reduce gaps and seams, bridge stove piping and share rice bowls amongst the actors within their national maritime security architecture. Success requires concerted direction from the political levels of a nation's government, both through legislation and policy directives. But success also requires the individual maritime security agencies within each government to innovate ways that counter maritime security threats in a cooperative and collective manner, through a fusion of those agencies' authorities, capabilities and capacities. Furthermore, as Nicole Jenne and María Lourdes Puente Olivera also argued in Chapter 13 for the case of Argentina, a clear definition of the respective roles of the navy and coast guard in those areas where the spatial and functional criteria of competence allocation overlap is required. Eventually, what matters is whether a nation's maritime agencies can form a nexus to respond to maritime threats effectively.

Throughout the volume, authors have converged on the need for the "national fleet" concept—not a unified entity amalgamating navies and coast guards per se, but a central organizing principle that sets a vision, directions and guidelines on how distinct actors within a national maritime security architecture can function alongside one another in a coherent, effective and efficient manner that can best overcome the problem of duplicities and overlaps in competences and roles. Such an overarching concept can also allow each actor to maximize their strengths without being unduly embroiled in cultural, operational and cultural differences. It is clear that throughout the case studies examined in this volume, only a handful of these states have such a concept in place, or at least a resemblance of such.

As maritime security challenges continue to evolve and become more complex, the demands on the national maritime security architectures will correspondingly increase. Actors existing within these structures will continue to face pressing needs to do more with less. Not every country can possess both a powerful navy and a powerful coast guard simultaneously. As such, the trends ahead could be:

- Navies define and redefine their roles, if only to stay relevant and draw funding, which compels them—whether they do want it or otherwise—to dip their hands into maritime law enforcement.
- Because coast guards or other MLEAs are more likely to receive foreign capacity-building assistance, they will continue to hold an existential value within the national maritime security architectures of countries that lack the wherewithal to expand their navies through self-help.
- Navies and coast guards will continue to share not only the same realm within the architecture, but on the ground, share the same maritime strategic space as well. They will continue to operate alongside each other to tackle extant maritime security threats. But in geopolitical flashpoints such as those seen in the Asia-Pacific region, such nexus can become a cause for concern.

Increasingly more governments are beginning to wake up to the realities of having to cope with resource constraints and the need to strike that equilibrium amongst diverse, distinct and often competitive actors within their national maritime security architectures against the backdrop of evolving security challenges. This has led to more governments also recognizing the need for a national plan or policy that harmonizes or synergizes these inter-agency efforts. Indonesia is an example where the government came to understand how an overarching national ocean policy can provide the essential visions and directions for not only proper management of national marine resources but also broader maritime interests at large, including how best to harmonize and synergize efforts between the actors of the national maritime security architecture through coordination and collaboration.

INDEX

0-9
9/11 attacks
  and South American security, 251, 261
  and US maritime security, 252
1871 Treaty of Washington, 228
1999 suspicious boat incursion, 45
2018 Illulisat declaration, 241

A
Abe, Shinzo, 54
Aircraft
  CASA C-212, 78
  CP-140 *Aurora*, 241
  Dash-8, 146
  Harbin Y-12, 28
  MA-60H, 29
  P-1, 67
  P-8 Poseidon, 156
Air Defense Identification Zone (ADIZ), 46
Alfonsín, Raúl, 250
Antarctic, 194, 247, 257, 261, 263, 265, 266, 268
Anti-Smuggling Bureau (ASB), China, 18, 24
Arab Spring, 160
Arctic
  increase in maritime traffic, 139, 155, 162
  moratorium on commercial fishing, 240
  strategic importance, 182
Arctic Coast Guard Forum (ACGF), 52, 155
Arctic Command (Denmark), 145
Arctic Council, 155
Arctic Offshore Patrol Vessel (AOPV), 239
Arctic Response Force (Denmark), 145
Argentina
  after 9/11, 251, 261
  and the Antarctic, 247, 261, 263, 265
  and the Falkland Islands, 250, 263, 268
  democratisation, 13, 246, 249, 253
  Dirty War, 246, 249, 253

© The Editor(s) (if applicable) and The Author(s), under exclusive license to Springer Nature Singapore Pte Ltd. 2019
I. Bowers and S. L. C. Koh (eds.), *Grey and White Hulls*,
https://doi.org/10.1007/978-981-13-9242-9

281

domestic politics, 250
Fisheries Law, 263
maritime interests, 246, 248
maritime territory, 247, 261, 262, 268
National Council for Scientific and Technical Research (CONICET), 266, 267
navy-coastguard nexus, 13, 268
Argentina Navy
after democratisation, 13
cooperation with the PNA, 260, 262
establishment, 253, 256, 258, 261
operations, 257, 262
personnel, 254, 257, 267
role in the Antarctic, 257, 265, 266
Armada Argentina. See Argentina Navy
Automatic Identification System (AIS), 257

B

Badan Keamanan Laut (BAKAMLA)
capabilities, 112, 129, 130
establishment, 110, 113–115, 129, 130
interagency tension, 113, 114
leadership, 115, 126
operations, 114, 129
responsibilities, 112–114, 276
Badan Koordinasi Keamanan Laut (BAKORKAMLA)
establishment, 129
organisation, 123, 129
reliance on the navy, 123
responsibilities, 126
transformation to BAKAMLA, 126
Bill of Rights (US), 204
Border Defense Coast Guard, 23, 24, 33

C

Cable, James, 228
Canada
and the Arctic, 239
Coastal Fisheries Protection Act, 236
fisheries, 223, 228, 235
marine police, 228
maritime interests, 232
National Shipbuilding Strategy, 243
Naval Service Act, 232
navy-coastguard nexus, 13
Nose and Tail, 236
UNCLOS, 235
Canadian Coast Guard (CCG)
and the Arctic, 239, 241–243
loss of capabilities, 243
responsibilities, 223, 239
Canadian Coast Guard (CCG) ships
Cape Roger, 237
John Cabot, 235
John G. Diefenbaker, 242
Labrador, 239
Louis St. Laurent, 242
Wilfred Grenfell, 237
Canadian Government Ships (CGS)
Canada, 233
Neptune, 231
Petrel, 229, 244
Vigilant, 231
Canadian Navy. See Royal Canadian Navy (RCN)
Caribbean Sea, 207, 209
Central Military Commission (CMC), 24, 25, 30, 40, 91, 94
Changi Command and Control Centre (CC2C), 100, 101, 103
China
and the Arctic, 240
The Diversified Employment of China's Armed Forces, 31

exclusive economic zone (EEZ), 9,
    17, 18, 33
First Island Chain, 85, 87, 90
five dragons, 18
Five Year Plan (FYP), 32
maritime claims, 18
Maritime Great Power (MGP), 19,
    20, 32, 35
maritime Silk Road, 30
navy-coastguard nexus, 9, 11
operations in the East China Sea, 31
operations in the South China Sea,
    40
relations with Japan, 50
strategic interests, 9, 53
China Coast Guard (CCG)
    capabilities, 22, 28, 35, 40
    cooperation with the PLAN, 31–35
    education and training, 34
    establishment, 30
    gray Zone, 41, 87
    militarization of, 23
    operations, 28, 33, 34
    responsibilities, 34
    restructuring, 17, 30
    structure, 23
    under Central Military Commission
        (CMC), 24
China Coast Guard (CCG) ships, 33,
    34, 49, 87
Haijing 3901, 43
China Maritime Police Bureau
    (CMPB). *See* China Coast Guard
    (CCG)
China Maritime Surveillance (CMS),
    18, 21, 22, 29
Chinese Navy. *See* People's Liberation
    Army Navy (PLAN)
Climate change, 240, 241, 244
Coastal Command (COSCOM), 97,
    98
Code for Unplanned Encounters at
    Sea (CUES), 52

Cole, Bernard D., 4, 40
Combined Operations Manual, 52
Common Market of the South
    (MERCOSUR), 256
Communist Party of China (CPC),
    19, 40
    18th Party Congress, 19
Comprehensive Maritime Awareness
    Group (CMAG), 98, 101
Crisis Management Group (CMG),
    99, 100, 102

D

Danish Navy. *See* Royal Danish Navy
Denmark
    and the Arctic, 12, 135, 136,
        143–145, 156, 157
    Defense Agreement 1995–1999,
        143
    Defense Agreement 2000–2004,
        143
    maritime interests, 12, 136, 152,
        155
    maritime territory, 153
    navy-coastguard nexus, 12
    relationship with Greenland, 136,
        149, 157
Department of Homeland Security
    (DHS), 213, 214, 220
DeWolf class, 239, 241–243
Diaoyu Islands. *See* Senkaku Islands
DN-2000 offshore patrol vessel, 78
DN-4000 offshore patrol vessel, 78
Dokdo, 57, 60
Donghai Collaboration-2012 exercise,
    31

E

East China Sea, 26, 28, 31, 32, 38,
    49, 50, 66, 87
Elektron incident, 154

Erickson, Andrew S., 40, 41
Estai, 237, 238, 244
EU Border and Coast Guard, 173, 174
  maritime operations, 174
EU Frontex, 165, 172–176, 178, 179
EUNAVFOR, 172, 176, 179
European Coast Guard Cooperation Network, 174, 178
European Union (EU), 13, 170, 172–180, 235, 236, 240
EU Satellite Centre (SatCen), 155
Excess Defense Articles (EDA), 79
Exclusive Economic Zone (EEZ), 4, 10, 48, 56, 58, 59, 75, 112, 122, 124, 128, 131, 149, 150, 185, 190, 194, 196, 210, 212, 235, 240, 241, 247, 259, 260, 264, 265
Exercise Apex, 96, 103
Exercise Blue Dolphin, 103
Exercise Highcrest, 97, 102, 103
Exercise Northstar, 96, 102

F
Falkland Islands, 250, 263, 268
Faroe Islands, 138, 143, 149, 155, 157
Federal Security Service (FSB), Russia, 13, 183, 185, 188, 191–193, 196, 198, 200, 273, 274
  responsibilities, 12, 183, 273
  role in the Arctic, 13, 183, 185, 191, 192, 196–200, 273
Finance Guard (Italy)
  operations with Italian coastguard, 173
  operations with Italian navy, 165, 173, 180
  responsibilities, 164, 175
  role in JO Triton, 173, 175
  role in *Mare Nostrum*, 175

Fisheries Law Enforcement Command (FLEC), China, 18, 21, 22, 29
Fisheries Protection Service (FPS), Canada, 189, 190, 229, 231, 232
Fishery Protection Zone (FPZ), Norway, 150–152
Five Dragons, 17, 18, 21

G
G7 Foreign Ministers, 39
Gepard class, 82, 89
Girardelli, Valter (Admiral), 180
Global Maritime Fulcrum (GMF), 12, 111, 127
Grand Banks, 236, 237
Gray zone, 38, 51, 52, 54, 90
  and China, 41
  Vietnam anti-gray zone strategy, 81
Greenland, Iceland, UK (GIUK)-gap, 152
Greenland, 136–140, 143, 144, 146, 147, 149, 152, 153, 155–157
Greenland Police Authority, 144
  cooperation with Royal Danish Navy, 143, 147
  responsibilities, 143
Guantanamo Bay Naval Base, 217
Guardia Costiera. *See* Italian Coast Guard
Gulf of Mexico, 207, 209

H
Haijing 3901, 43
Hamilton class cutter, 79
HD-981 stand-off, 88
Heads of Asian Coast Guard Agencies Meeting (HACGAM), 66
Homefront Crisis Executive Group (HCEG) Maritime Security, 99
Hong Ik-tae, 62

INDEX   285

Huangyan Island. *See* Scarborough Shoal
Hybrid Warfare, 49

I
Iceland
  cruise ship tourism, 138
  fishing industry, 138
  maritime territory, 152
  navy-coastguard nexus, 6
Icelandic Coast Guard (ICG)
  budget, 145
  capabilities, 147, 149, 152, 240
  helicopters, 145
  operations, 6
  responsibilities, 6, 145
  size, 149
Ieodo, 60
Illegal, Unreported and Unregulated (IUU) fishing, 1, 2, 57, 58, 60, 65, 210, 212, 220
Immigration and Checkpoints Authority (ICA), 97, 98, 101
Indian Ocean, 53, 127
Indonesia
  2015-2019 National Midterm Development Plan, 127
  fishing industry, 128
  Global Maritime Fulcrum (GMF), 12, 111, 127
  maritime interests, 279
  maritime territory, 112, 114, 116, 120, 122, 125, 127–129, 131
  military doctrine, 120
  navy-coastguard nexus, 12
  Orde Baru, 116, 120, 124
  post *Orde Baru*, 116, 130
  pre *Orde Baru*, 116, 120
  vessel sinking policy, 128

Indonesia Navy. *See* Tentara Nasional Indonesia Angkatan Laut (TNI-AL)
Information Fusion Centre (IFC), 101
Inter-Agency Coordination Group, 98
International Maritime Organisation (IMO), 256, 257, 261, 263, 266
Ishigaki Island, 51
Italian Coast Guard
  capabilities, 161
  cooperation with Italian Navy, 162, 167, 175
  establishment, 172
  operations, 169, 170, 173
  role in *Mare Nostrum*, 159, 160, 166–169
  role in *Mare Sicuro*, 169, 170, 178
  structure, 7, 172, 173, 179
Italian Navy
  capabilities, 161
  cooperation with Italian Coastguard, 160, 162, 166, 167, 169, 173, 175
  fleet renewal, 161, 162
  operations, 160, 163, 165–167, 169, 172, 175, 178–180
  responsibilities, 160, 163, 175
  role in international operations, 163
  role in *Mare Nostrum*, 160, 166–169
  role in *Mare Sicuro*, 169, 170, 178
Italian Navy Ships
  Luigi Rizzo, 178
Italy
  maritime interests, 159, 160, 169
  maritime territory, 161, 165, 166, 169, 173, 175
  navy-coastguard nexus, 13
  refugee crisis, 13, 274
  relationship with the Mediterranean, 13, 159, 160, 164–167, 169, 170, 172, 178–180

J

Japan
  international capacity building, 37
  maritime interests, 37, 38, 40
  maritime territory, 38, 41, 43–45, 49, 51
  National Defense Program Guidelines, 38, 43, 44
  navy-coastguard nexus, 9, 275
  Proactive Contributor to Peace, 39
  relationship with China, 37, 50
  relationship with the US, 9
  and the South China Sea, 50
Japan Coast Guard (JCG)
  1999 suspicious boat incident, 45
  capabilities, 18, 39, 50–52, 240
  cooperation with the JMSDF, 11, 37–39, 43–46, 48, 51, 52, 54
  fleet renewal, 43, 51, 52
  international cooperations, 39, 52
  operations, 37, 38, 42, 44, 45, 47, 51, 53
  responsibilities, 45, 54
  structure, 43
Japan Coast Guard (JCG) Ships, 42–44, 48, 49, 51, 79
  Amami, 48
  Inasa, 48
  Mizuki, 48
Japan Defense Agency (JDA), 45–47, 49
Japan Ground Self-Defense Forces (JGSDF)
  coast surveillance units, 44
Japan Maritime Self-Defense Forces (JMSDF)
  capabilities, 37, 46
  cooperation with the Japan Coast Guard, 11, 38, 39, 45–47, 51
  counter-piracy, 53
  operations, 37, 47, 48, 51, 67
  structure, 44

Japan Ministry of National Defense (JMOD), 38, 43, 45
Japan Self-Defense Forces (JSDF), 37, 38, 43, 46, 49, 51, 275
Jiangkai II class, 33
JMSDF ships
  Abukama, 45
  Haruna, 45
  Kirishima, 48
  Miyako, 45
Joint Interagency Taskforce (JIATF), 214, 219
Joint Interagency Taskforce (JIATF)-South, 214, 215, 219
Joint Operation (JO) Triton, 165, 172, 173, 175, 176, 179
Joint Rescue Coordination Centre (JRCC), 142, 144
Joint Task Force (JTF), 64, 219
Jokowi, 120, 127, 128, 130, 131
Joko Widodo. *See* Jokowi
Jung Ho-sub (Admiral), 61, 62

K

Keflavik Naval Air Station, 145, 156
Kim Young-sam, 59
Kola Bay, 198
Konstantinov, Igor (Mayor General), 191
Korea-China Provisional Waters Zone, 63
Korean Coast Guard (KCG)
  after the sinking of the MV *Sewol*, 61
  capabilities, 58, 60, 64–66, 68
  fleet renewal, 61, 64, 65, 69
  operations, 56–65, 68
  relationship with Korean police, 57
Korean Coast Guard (KCG) ships
  Lee Chang-ho, 66
  Sambong, 65

Korean Maritime Police (KMP), 57
Kraska, James, 49
Kulishov, Vladimir, 192

L
Lake Erie, 229
Libyan Coast Guard, 170
Liu Cigui, 24, 29
Long Range Identification and
 Tracking System (LRIT), 257

M
Macri, Mauricio, 246, 252, 254, 269
Magnuson-Stevens Fisheries
 Conservation and Management
 Act, 211, 220
Malvina Islands. *See* Falkland Islands
Mare Nostrum
 area of operations, 166–168
 cost, 166
 division of labour, 160, 168
 participants, 175
 success, 167
Mare Sicuro
 area of operations, 169, 170
 division of labour, 179
 participants, 179
 success, 168
Marina Militare. *See* Italian Navy
Maritime and Port Authority of
 Singapore (MPA), 98, 101, 103,
 105, 106
Maritime geography, 8, 10
Maritime Guard (Russia), 189, 190
 dissolution, 189
Maritime law enforcement agencies
 (MLEA), 1–4, 6, 7, 9–11, 13, 19,
 32, 37, 129, 271–275
Maritime militia (China), 9, 41, 76,
 87–89

Maritime Operational Threat Response
 (MOTR) Plan, 216–218
Maritime Police Bureau. *See* China
 Coast Guard (CCG)
Maritime Police Command Centre, 22
Maritime Safety Administration
 (MSA), China, 6, 18
Maritime Safety Agency (MSA), Japan,
 18, 41, 44
Maritime Security Task Force (MSTF),
 65, 97–99, 101, 105, 115
Maritime Surveillance Command
 (Argentina), 261
Martha Black class, 243
Matteo Renzi, 163
Mazarr, Michael J., 86
Mediterranean Sea—migration crises,
 165
MENA area, 159, 171, 179
Meng Hongwei, 21
Metal Shark patrol boats, 79
Ministry of Defence (MINDEF),
 Singapore, 97–99, 101, 102, 105,
 107, 112
Ministry of Home Affairs (MHA),
 Singapore, 97–99, 105, 112
Ministry of National Defense
 (MoND), Vietnam, 75, 91, 93,
 273
Ministry of National Safety and Public
 Affairs (NSPA), 64
Ministry of Ocean and Fishery Affairs
 (MOFA), 64
Ministry of Public Security (China),
 18, 21, 22
Ministry of Transport (China), 18
Missile systems
 Bal-E, 82
 EXTRA missile system, 82
 K-300P Bastion, 82
 Kh-35 Ural-E, 82
 P-5 Shaddock, 82

Mitchell, Peter, 228
Molniya class fast attack craft (FAC), 83
Moon Jae-in, 67
Murmansk, 138, 191, 192, 198
MV *Limburg*, 97
MV *Sewol*, sinking of, 61

N
Nansha Islands. *See* Spratly Islands
National Maritime Common Operating Picture (NMCOP), 101
National Maritime Operations Group (NMOG), 101
National Maritime Security Strategy (NMSS), 58, 94, 96, 99, 100, 102
National Maritime Sense-making Group (NMSG), 101
National Oceanic Administration (NOA), 21, 22
National Security Presidential Directive (NSPD) 41, 216
Naval Prefecture Argentina (PNA)
  capabilities, 260
  cooperation with the Argentina navy, 256, 262
  establishment, 256, 258, 263
  independence from navy, 253
  international affairs secretariat, 256
  operations, 259
  personnel, 254
  responsibilities, 258, 259, 262, 263
Navy-coastguard nexus, 7, 11, 13, 96, 104, 268, 271, 272, 274
  determinants, 8, 272
  organizational typologies, 5
Navy Mechanics School (ESMA), 249
Nikolsky, Aleksey, 189, 190
NORDFECO, 156

North Atlantic Treaty Organization (NATO), 145, 150, 152, 161, 174, 187, 194, 238
Northern Clover, 185
Northern Limit Line (NLL), 56, 58, 63, 65
Northern Sea Route, 182, 191, 192, 194, 195, 197
North Korea, 46, 48, 56, 57, 59, 65, 66, 68
North Pacific Anadromous Fish Commission (NPAFC), 241, 242
North Pacific Coast Guard Agencies Forum, 30
Northwest Atlantic Fisheries Organization (NAFO), 236, 241
Norway
  arrest of Russian vessels, 152
  Fisheries Protection Zone, 149, 150
  maritime interests, 157, 191
  maritime territory, 149, 153
  navy-coastguard nexus, 12
Norwegian Coast Guard
  establishment, 146, 154
  operations, 152
  relationship with Royal Norwegian Navy, headquarters, 146
  responsibilities, 147
  structure, 148
Norwegian Navy. *See* Royal Norwegian Navy

O
Oceania Maritime Security Initiative (OMSI), 212, 220
Offshore Multipurpose Patrol Ship (PPA), Italy, 161, 162
Okean class patrol vessel (ice), 192
Operation Driftnet, 241
Operations Group, 98

Operation Sophia
  mandate, 177, 178
  participants, 177
  phases, 177
Operation Themis, 172, 175, 176
Operative Network of Regional Cooperation among Maritime Authorities of the Americas (ROCRAM), 256

P
Pajon, Céline, 50, 51
Paracel Islands, 84
People's Armed Police (PAP), 23–25, 30, 34, 35, 39, 40
People's Liberation Army Navy (PLAN)
  capabilities, 31
  cooperation with CCG, 32
  education and training, 33, 34
  modernisation, 32
  operations, 33, 34
  responsibilities, 26, 31, 33
People's Liberation Army Navy (PLAN) ships, 33
  Shaoguan, 33
Perón, Juan Domingo, 248
Persian Gulf War, 213
Phalanx close-in weapon system (CIWS), 79
Police Coast Guard (PCG), 96–98, 101, 103, 104, 106
Posse Comitatus Act (US), 205
Pudjiastuti, Susi, 128

R
Regional Humanitarian Assistance and Disaster Relief Coordination Centre (RHCC), 101
Republic of Korea (ROK)
  illegal fishing, 67
  joint military strategy, 60
  maritime geography, 56
  National Security Strategy, 67
  navy-coastguard nexus, 55
  One National Fleet (ONF), 55, 61–65, 69
Republic of Korea Navy (ROKN)
  capabilities, 68
  deterrence, 59
  operations, 58
  relationship with JMSDF, 67
  relationship with Korean Coast Guard, 56, 59, 60, 63, 64, 67, 68
Republic of Korea Navy Ships (ROKS)
  Cheonan, 61
  Kwanggyeto the Great, 65, 67
Republic of Singapore Air Force (RSAF), 98, 101
Republic of Singapore Navy (RSN), 12, 96–98, 101, 103–107
Royal Canadian Navy (RCN)
  and the Arctic, 274
  cooperation with Canadian Coast Guard, 223, 242
  establishment, 232
  fleet, 232
  ice breaker capacity, 242
  operations, 235, 239, 242
Royal Canadian Navy (RCN) ships
  Gatineau, 238
  Harry DeWolf, 239
  Niobe, 232
  Nipigon, 238
  Rainbow, 233
Royal Danish Navy
  Arctic Command, 143, 144
  area of responsibility, 143
  capabilities, 155
  capacity gap, 146
  ice breaker capacity, 143
  operations, 143, 146
  structure, 143

Royal Norwegian Navy
  area of responsibility, 147
  capabilities, 153
  cooperation with the Norwegian Coast Guard, 146, 150
  operations, 157
Rubin class patrol vessel, 192
Rush-Bagot Agreement, 230
Russia
  Arctic interests, 186, 194
  Foundations of the Russian Federation's State Policy for Military-Maritime Activities until 2013, 195
  Maritime Doctrine for the Period until 2020, 193
  maritime interests, 11, 186, 190, 196
  maritime territory, 185, 191, 196
  military districts, 185
  navy-coastguard nexus, 182
  State Armament Programme towards 2020, 186
  threat perceptions, 182, 200, 274
Russian Coast Guard
  capabilities, 182
  cooperation with Russian navy, 183, 193
  exercises, 183, 197, 199
  operations, 192
  organisation, 183, 199
  as part of FSB, 183
  reform, 183, 184
  responsibilities, 183
  structure, 150
Russian Coast Guard Ships
  Polyarnaya Zvezda, 192
  Predanny, 192
Russian Navy
  capabilties, 187
  cooperation with Russian Coastguard, 182, 183, 190, 193, 196, 197, 199
  decay, 184
  modernisation, 187
  operations, 184
  responsibilities, 13, 182
  structure, 188
Russian Navy Northern Fleet
  Arctic, 141, 182–186, 194, 198–200
  area of responsibility, 185
  fleet, 184, 185, 194
  prioritization, 194

S
SAF Act, 104
Scarborough Shoal, 25
Sea and Coast Guard Indonesia (SCGI), 114, 115
Sea control, 13, 61, 67, 85, 223–235, 237–241, 243, 244, 274
Sea denial, 224
Sea lines of communication (SLOC), 63, 83, 95, 109, 117, 169, 172
Search and rescue (SAR), 3, 6, 25, 26, 38, 41, 44, 57, 58, 61, 65–67, 113, 114, 140, 142, 143, 145–147, 162, 166–170, 173–176, 185, 198, 200, 257, 262, 263
  difficulties in arctic, 141
Second Thomas Shoal, 32, 87
Self-Defense Forces Law (Japan), 44, 47
Senkaku Islands, 25, 37, 49–51
Senkaku Islands—Chinese operationsaround, 38
Serdyukov, Anatoly, 186
Serzhanin, Vyacheslav (Vice Admiral), 190, 191
Shikishima class, 29
Shiprider agreements, 211
Silver Spray, 229
Sim Seung-seob (Admiral), 68
Singapore Armed Forces (SAF), 98, 103–105

Singapore Civil Defence Force, 103
Singapore Customs (SC), 98, 101
Singapore Maritime Crisis Centre (SMCC), 100–103
Singapore Straits, 97, 99
South China Sea, 4, 9, 12, 19, 26, 29, 32, 34, 35, 39–41, 49, 53, 73, 74, 76, 80, 81, 83, 84, 87, 88, 90, 92, 94
South Georgia, 268
South Korea. *See* Republic of Korea (ROK)
South Orkney Islands, 268
South Pacific, 210, 211, 220
South Sandwich Islands, 268
Spanish Navy, 238
Spratly Islands, 84
Standing Committee of the National People's Congress (China), 26
State Oceanic Administration (SOA), China, 18, 21, 22, 29, 30
Straits of Malacca and Singapore (SOMS), 95, 97, 99
Strategic culture, 8, 10, 277
Suharto, 116, 120, 122
Svalbard Island, 139
   fisheries, 139
   Treaty of Svalbard, 147

T
Tarantul class fast attack craft (FAC), 83
Task Force 115, 128, 130
Tentara Nasional Indonesia Angkatan Laut (TNI-AL)
   capabilities, 130
   dominance of, 110, 130
   operations, 123
   responsibilities, 125
Thayer, Carl, 83
Thule Airbase, 152, 156
Turbot War, 236–238

Type 054A Frigate. *See Jiangkai* II class
Type 218 Patrol Craft (China), 27
Type 728 Cutter (China), 33
Type 818 Patrol Ship (China), 33

U
United National Convention on the Law of the Sea (UNCLOS), 3, 4, 56, 57, 88, 91, 123, 131, 177, 235, 247, 259
United Nations Command (UNC), 56
United States (US)
   anti-narcotics operations, 252
   capacity building, 209, 217
   maritime interests, 8, 212, 227, 278
   maritime territory, 152
   navy-coast guard nexus, 5, 8, 9, 11, 13
   terrorism, 251
United States Coast Guard (USCG)
   after 9/11, 251, 261
   capabilities, 18, 40, 58, 66
   cooperation with international partners, 63, 215
   cooperation with US Navy, 62
   District 14, 211
   drug enforcement, 53, 57, 58, 66, 69, 73
   illegal Immigration, 217
   law enforcement detachments, 53, 209
   legal restrictions, 205
   limitations, 209
   operations, 8, 40, 53, 58, 62, 174, 208, 209, 211–215, 220
   responsibilities, 205, 211, 216, 218
   structure, 9, 203, 216, 218–220
   Title 14, 206, 208
   transfer to the Department of Homeland Security, 213

United States Coast Guard (USCG)
  ships
    Bertholf, 66
United States Maritime Strategy, 62
United States Navy (USN)
  capabilities, 206, 209, 221
  cooperation with US Coast Guard,
    9, 13, 53, 62, 203
  operations, 204, 209, 211, 213,
    218–220
  Pacific Fleet, 211, 212
United States Office of Naval
  Intelligence, 41, 42
U.S. Department of Defense (DoD),
  205, 206, 208, 209, 212–216,
  219, 220
USS *Cole*, 97
USS *John S. McCain*, 105

V
Vietnam
  asymmetrical wartime doctrine, 81,
    83
  Coast Guard Law, 79, 80, 273
  cooperation with outside powers, 75
  defense budget, 91
  maritime interests, 12
  maritime territory, 84
  relations with China, 88, 273
  *Resolution on Vietnam Maritime
    Strategy to 2020*, 77
  *Resolution on Vietnam Maritime
    Strategy to 2030, with the Vision
    to 2045*, 77
Vietnam Coast Guard (VCG)
  capabilities, 73, 78, 81, 84, 93, 94
  challenges, 12, 74, 80, 90, 91, 93
  cooperation with the navy, 12, 84,
    89, 93

establishment, 74
future procurement, 91
operations, 12, 75, 84, 85, 93, 94,
  272
responsibilities, 74, 79, 80, 83
wartime role, 74, 81, 84, 85, 93, 94
Vietnam Marine Police, 78
Vietnam People's Navy (VPN)
  capabilities, 84, 90, 93, 94
  cooperation with Vietnam Coast
    Guard, 12, 81, 90, 91, 273
  modernisation, 81, 83, 85, 92, 94
  operations, 80, 85, 93, 94, 273
  responsibilities, 83
  structure, 90, 93, 273

W
Wen Jiabao, 19
Western Pacific Coast Guard Forum
  (WGCGF), 52
Western Pacific Naval Symposium
  (WPNS), 66
Whole-of-Government (WoG), 32, 58,
  99, 101–104, 107, 239, 277
Whole-of-Nation, 278

X
Xi Jinping, 19, 20, 31, 32
Xisha Islands. *See* Paracel Islands

Y
Yeonpyeong Island, shelling of, 61
Yevmenov, Nikolay (Admiral), 186